Prince Harry

Prince Harry
Brother|Soldier|Son

Penny Junor

GRAND CENTRAL
PUBLISHING

NEW YORK   BOSTON

First published in Great Britain in 2014 by Hodder & Stoughton
An Hachette UK company

Grand Central Publishing
Hachette Book Group
237 Park Avenue
New York, NY 10017

www.HachetteBookGroup.com

Printed in the United States of America

RRD–C

First Grand Central Publishing Edition: September 2014
10 9 8 7 6 5 4 3 2 1

Grand Central Publishing is a division of Hachette Book Group, Inc.
The Grand Central Publishing name and logo is a trademark of Hachette Book Group, Inc.

The Hachette Speakers Bureau provides a wide range of authors for speaking events. To find out more, go to www.hachettespeakersbureau.com or call (866) 376-6591.

The publisher is not responsible for websites (or their content) that are not owned by the publisher.

Library of Congress Control Number: 2014946243
978-1-4555-4983-2

To Marlene, Max, Oscar, Emilia, and Jonah Leith

CONTENTS

CONTENTS

CONNECTION

It was May 2013 and Prince Harry was in Harlem, holding a baseball bat in his hand. He had never played the game before. The New York Yankees first base star, Mark Teixeira, was about to pitch. The world's media were watching from the sidelines. And a little girl, dressed in body armor and face grille, was standing stoically behind the plate ready to catch. Harry ignored the flashing cameras, he ignored Mark Teixeira, and he put his own nerves to one side. He squatted down beside the little girl and peered through her grille and said, "Are you all right in there?"

Harry has many strengths—and his fair share of weaknesses—but his passion for children's welfare and his empathy with those who have suffered during their childhood is what ultimately defines the man. Perhaps because he too suffered as a child.

Prince Harry is never going to be King. Unless the unthinkable happens, the Queen will be succeeded by his father, the Prince of Wales, who in turn will be succeeded by Prince William, and in another half century or so, Prince George. And it is generally agreed, by those who know Harry, that this is a good thing. If it were the other way round, if he was in line for the top job and not his brother, then we would all be in big trouble. It is always said with an affectionate laugh, because people love Harry, but Diana's younger son, who turned thirty in September 2014, has always had a wild, unpredictable streak to him, even as a little boy, but a future King can't afford to be caught playing strip billiards in a Las Vegas hotel bedroom, no matter what the circumstances.

But he's not going to be King and, as fourth in line, and arguably the most charming and down-to-earth member of the entire family, he can afford a little slack. At least while he is young and single. Indeed, it is his Las Vegas moments as much as anything—his knack of getting into trouble—that appear to endear him to the public. They make him seem a little more like the rest of us.

His detractors say they just prove he's not very bright. His detractors need to think again. Anyone who thinks Harry is not bright seriously underestimates the man. He may not be academic, but he has emotional intelligence coming out of every pore. He was also one of the best Apache attack helicopter co-pilot gunners in the British Army Air Corps, and that is no mean feat. His ability to think on his feet, to think laterally, and make life-or-death decisions under the most stressful circumstances would leave most academics in the shade.

There was a time, granted, when it did look as though Harry wasn't too bright. A time when he behaved like a mindless Hooray Henry with too much money, too much privilege and no self-control. A time when one wondered whether his mother's death and the chaos of his childhood had set him on a dangerous downward spiral. There's no doubt he was an angry adolescent, who drank a great deal more than was good for him. Even as an adult he does like to party, and there's no pretending that when Harry goes on a bender he does it in short measures. But the flip side of Harry that has emerged in the last few years is very different. And that flip side could be life changing for thousands of forgotten and disadvantaged people, not just in Britain, but across the world.

He is the Queen's grandson, a senior member of the most important family in the land; he lives in palaces, plays expensive sports, drinks in exclusive clubs and holidays in exotic locations. He has a private fortune, beautiful girlfriends and wants for nothing. On the face of it, everything about him should repel the tough inner-city kid with a knife in his pocket and no qualms about using it. Yet he has taken a close interest in the escalation of knife crime in Britain's cities and through the Royal Foundation of The

Duke and Duchess of Cambridge and Prince Harry has funded youth projects, and those kids like him. Because they can see that if you strip away Harry's titles and the privilege, underneath it all he's someone like them, who had a rotten childhood and a broken home—and a dad who was often absent. Like them, he gets into trouble and he knows how to fight; he understands violence. The difference between them is that Harry had people in his life who were there for him, so his fighting has been in Afghanistan and it's been internationally condoned. These kids with knives at the ready weren't so lucky. They had no one to pick up the pieces, so they gravitated towards gangs and the streets and a very different sort of violence. But fundamentally, there's a connection. And Harry has that connection with all sorts of disparate groups. He wears the right clothes for the occasion and, with a witty remark or a gentle tease, he immediately connects with people of every age, every class, every gender and from every walk of life. Like his mother, he is tactile, he's relaxed, he's fun and he's not afraid to show his humanity. It's a rare gift.

He hates special treatment, hates the cameras that follow him and hates much of what goes with being a member of the Royal Family. He is fiercely and rightly jealous of his privacy. But he accepts who he is and the responsibility that goes with it. His future is not as easily defined as his brother's, but after years of observing his parents and grandparents, he is inculcated with a sense of duty and service to others that most of us—let alone most thirty-year-olds—could not begin to comprehend.

"When we're doing public engagements, I often have to check myself and remind myself who he is," says Edward Parker, who co-founded Walking With The Wounded (WWTW). "I have to start off with 'Your Royal Highness'—and it's what his position deserves and expects—but it's great when the door closes and the people on the outside can't see in anymore and you can go back to being normal people. And I think that's what he is; a normal person in an abnormal position."

Anyone whose heart was broken by the sight of Harry as a little boy, walking so bravely behind his mother's cortège, alongside his father, grandfather, brother and uncle, will agree with that. And in many ways it's a miracle that he came through the abnormality and trauma of his childhood with such equilibrium. His relationship with his brother was a vital part of that. They are as close as it is possible for two brothers to be. Though two very different people, with very different approaches to life, they have shared experiences and memories that no one else can imagine; and that is maybe where their extraordinary empathy for others comes from. Harry's relationship with his father is more complicated. There have been difficulties and frustrations between them over the years but, beneath it all, there has been deep love.

It is William and Harry's differences, according to the man who worked as their Private Secretary for eight years, that make them such a good team. He likens them to the historical figures, John of Gaunt and Edward, Prince of Wales, known as the Black Prince. "A lot of people would grind their teeth at the name of John of Gaunt," says Jamie Lowther-Pinkerton, "but he was the Black Prince's younger brother, a man in his own right who took a lot of the weight off, and shared the burden at a strategic level. You've got a really trusted sibling who is incredibly complementary to you in character as well as in outlook and belief and ideals and values and that sort of thing, which Prince Harry undoubtedly is with Prince William. He can apply different skills and talents to some of the issues that William as monarch may not have the time for, or which might not be quite appropriate for the top man to do but which the man one down can do."

What both can do, he believes, is provide moral and community leadership that is badly lacking in Britain today. "I always think at times when the political credibility is low, you ask the man in the street what do you think of the leadership of this country and the really intelligent, instinctive *Sun* reader, of which there are millions out there, common sense coming out of every pore, will say, 'What bloody leadership, mate?' And then you say, 'What about the Queen?' And he'll say, 'She's great.' There's a disconnect because he immediately thinks you're talking about political leadership and it doesn't have to be, and that to me is the role. These guys have got it and that's what can't be wasted."

This is the story of how Harry—the spare, the ginger one, the wild child—came so spectacularly good.

MY LITTLE SPENCER

Harry looks more like the Prince of Wales with every day that passes. They have the same-shaped faces, the same mannerisms, the same build and the same eyes, just like Harry's grandfather, the Duke of Edinburgh. His height and the red hair comes from his mother's side of the family, which is perhaps why Diana called him, among other things, "My little Spencer." He is not, by any stretch of the imagination, the son of James Hewitt, the good-looking, not-too-clever, red-headed Lifeguards officer, who became Diana's lover in the mid-1980s.

Rumors about Harry's paternity have persisted ever since their five-year affair became public in 1991, when Harry was seven. That was the year it came to an end; and the facts have been known for almost as long. Yet if I'd had a penny for every time I have been asked—even today—whether Hewitt is Harry's father, I would be very rich. The fact is, Diana did not know James Hewitt until after Harry was born, and they didn't begin their affair until 1986, by which time Harry was nearly two years old. And for those who refuse to believe it, it may come as no surprise to know that the *News of the World*, the Sunday tabloid that closed down in the wake of the phone-hacking scandal, had strands of Harry's hair DNA-tested in February 2003. If Harry had been shown to be James Hewitt's son, you can be sure we'd have known.

Harry was born in the private Lindo Wing of St. Mary's, Paddington, at 4:20 p.m. on Saturday 15 September 1984. It was the hospital where his brother, William, had been born two years earlier, and where the Duchess of Cambridge gave birth to William's son, Prince George, in 2013. Harry weighed a healthy six pounds fourteen ounces. There was huge excitement from the crowds that had waited patiently in the street outside. When Charles appeared, having been by Diana's side throughout the nine-hour labor, he declared himself delighted. He said the birth had been "much quicker than last time" and that the baby had "pale blue eyes and hair of an intermediate color." The next morning he brought William to meet his brother, along with his nanny, Barbara Barnes, and at 2:30 in the afternoon, the crowd was finally rewarded with a first glimpse of mother and baby, although Harry was so well wrapped in a lacy blanket that his face was invisible. Diana held him in her arms, looking a little fragile but as beautiful as ever. She stood on the steps of the hospital alongside Charles for a moment, while the crowds cheered and the cameras flashed, then the family climbed into the waiting cars and they were off.

It is well known that Charles and Diana's marriage was not a happy one, which was immensely sad for both of them, but it would be quite, quite wrong to assume that there had never been love or happiness in the relationship. At the time of Harry's birth, it was as good as it had ever been. Diana's view of her marriage was jaundiced by the end, and the accounts she gave of it to both Andrew Morton, author of *Diana: Her True Story*, and Martin Bashir for the TV program, *Panorama*, were unreliable. But even she admitted that they had been happy in the lead-up to Harry's birth.

A lot has been written about the marriage and why it failed, but the facts need to be reiterated, not least because it affected Harry deeply, and the man he is today is a product of that broken home, and of all that he heard and felt during his childhood.

The marriage did not fail because of Camilla Parker Bowles, the woman Diana famously called the "third person" in her marriage. It failed principally because it was a tragic mismatch. They were wrong for each other in almost every way possible, but they rushed into marriage before they knew each other well enough to realize that. And they rushed into it because the media were harassing Diana and, at thirty-two, Charles was under huge pressure from both the media and his father to find a wife.

On the face of it, Lady Diana Spencer could not have been a better match for the Prince of Wales. She came from the very top drawer of British society. Her father, the 8th Earl Spencer, had been an Equerry to the Queen and, before that, King George VI. Her maternal grandmother was a friend and Lady-in-Waiting to Queen Elizabeth, the Queen Mother. She grew up in a house on the Sandringham estate in Norfolk, where the Royal Family go every year for Christmas and New Year. She knew the family, she understood the protocol, she enjoyed a similar lifestyle, and she was young enough to be not yet set in her ways or to have a "past" for the media to trawl through, which had been the downfall of several previous girlfriends.

But Diana had had a difficult start in life. When she was just six years old, her parents divorced and her mother left home, leaving her and her siblings with their father. Frances Althorp, as she then was, had endured an unhappy marriage until she had given Johnny the heir he so badly wanted. They had two girls, Jane and Sarah, then a boy, John, who died after ten days. Diana came next, and finally Charles, who is now the 9th Earl Spencer. Frances left Johnny to be with Peter Shand Kydd, a man with whom she thought she could be happy, with every expectation that the children would follow. But in the custody proceedings, Ruth, Lady Fermoy, gave evidence against her own daughter, so all four of her children stayed with their father. It must have been unbearably painful for her.

It was painful for her children as well. The elder two were already at boarding school. Diana was the one who seemed most affected by her mother's disappearance. She knew nothing about the goings-on in court; all she surmised was that her mother didn't love her enough to want to be with her. She had the further insecurity of thinking she had not been wanted. In tape recordings she made for Andrew Morton, for his book *Diana: Her True Story*, she said, "The child who died before me was a son and both [parents] were crazy to have a son and heir and there comes a third daughter. What a bore we're going to have to try again. I've recognized that now. I've been aware of it and now I recognize it and that's fine. I accept it.

"In my bed I'd have twenty stuffed bed animals and there would be a midget's space for me, and they would have to be in my bed every night. That was my family. I hated the dark and had an obsession about the dark, always had to have a light outside my door until I was at least ten. I used to hear my brother crying in his bed down at the other end of the house, crying for my mother and he was unhappy too.

"I remember Mummy crying an awful lot and every Saturday when we went up [to London] for weekends, every Saturday night, standard procedure, she would start crying. 'What's the matter, Mummy?' 'Oh, I don't want you to leave tomorrow,' which for a nine-year-old was devastating, you know."

Rightly or wrongly, Diana felt rejected, worthless and unwanted. Those were the feelings that she nursed throughout her childhood and teenage years and, three weeks after her twentieth birthday, on 29 July 1981, took with her into her marriage to Charles.

Their romance had begun in 1980, almost a year after the murder of Charles's great uncle, Lord Mountbatten of Burma, who was blown up by an IRA bomb on a fishing trip with his family off the coast of Ireland. The Prince had adored the man he called his "honorary grandfather" and was devastated by his sudden and violent death; and when Diana poignantly said how sad and lonely Charles had looked at the old man's funeral, he was touched.

Charles hadn't felt especially valued while he was growing up. There had been nannies and long periods of separation from his parents. Friends remember his mother sitting him on her knee at teatime and playing games with him when he was small, but say she didn't often visit the nursery because she felt intimidated by the nanny—and as an older child there were no overt signs of affection. He treated her, they say, more as a Queen than a mother; and his father was rough with him. Charles was a sensitive and emotional child who grew into a sensitive and emotional adult, and the Duke, perhaps hoping for a son in his own image, made him feel that he was a disappointment. They share many interests and enthusiasms, yet even into middle age Charles was searching for his father's approval; never feeling he was quite good enough. And praise was thin on the ground from both parents. Yet, in the way that so often happens in families, William and Harry have a much easier relationship with their grandparents than Charles ever had with the Queen and the Duke. Theirs is a very close and warm and supportive relationship.

Charles had first met Diana as a fourteen-year-old, when he was briefly dating her sister, Sarah. Now she was a bubbly nineteen-year-old with a dirty laugh, very pretty, good fun and utterly charming. He began to see more of her and invited her to Balmoral with a few of his friends during the traditional family summer holiday there. Everyone was entranced by her; she seemed to be almost too good to be true.

Friends say his excitement at finding her was touching. He was brought up to hide his emotions in public and, until very recently, the mask he presented to the outside world was impenetrable, but in private, Charles has always been deeply emotional. His friends cautioned him to slow down.

But Charles thought he had finally found a soul mate; a girl who seemed to love him, who didn't seem put off by the limelight, and who seemed perfect in every way. And, as Harry is finding today, there were not many young women prepared to sacrifice their freedom for life in a goldfish bowl, or a lifetime being followed and photographed. And so, knowing nothing of Diana's complex nature, Charles asked her to marry him.

His childhood experiences had been quite different from Diana's, but he had the same crippling lack of confidence and self-esteem. Apart from that, they had little else in common. Diana was twelve years younger and loved the bright lights of the city and all that it offered. At nineteen, she was interested in pop concerts, films and shopping. She read women's magazines and romantic fiction. Charles, old for his years, was a country-lover, never happier than riding his horses, painting the landscape or digging the garden; his bedtime reading was philosophy or history. But Diana wanted so desperately to be loved, and was so skilled at keeping her feelings deep inside her, that no one who saw her in the lead-up to the engagement—not Charles, not friends, not family—had any idea that she was anything other than a happy, funny girl who would fit into his life like a hand into a glove.

THE ROOT OF THE PROBLEM

Once the ring was on her finger, Diana's life turned upside down. To protect her from the media, she was moved from a friendly, giggly, gossipy all-girl flat in Fulham to a suite of rooms at Buckingham Palace, where she felt very isolated. It must have brought back memories of the painful move from Norfolk to Northamptonshire at the age of thirteen, after her grandfather died and her father inherited the title and the family home, Althorp. This move was every bit as extreme. While everyone did their best to make her feel at home in the Palace, courtiers were no substitute for her chatty young flatmates.

The move, the stress, the attention of the press, the uncertainty, the loneliness, the overwhelming sense of being out of control, were the triggers for the eating disorder that went on to dog her for most of the rest of her life, and destroyed any chance of happiness that she and Charles might have had. She told Andrew Morton in 1991 that the bulimia had begun during the first week of her engagement. She became moody and willful, angry and suspicious, and Charles couldn't understand it. One minute she was happy and laughing and the next she was screaming at him. She displayed a temper that he had never seen before; it came from nowhere, along with hysterical tears, and it could be gone as quickly as it came. She turned against people she had appeared to like and said they were out to get her, to undermine her, or spy on her. He didn't know what had happened. Could it be nerves, or the stress of being in the public eye, or even the prospect of being married to him? He said nothing to anyone, but just hoped that it would right itself once they were married and the pressure was off.

Bulimia is not well understood, but one of its possible causes may be major trauma or upset in early childhood. It most commonly—but not exclusively—affects teenage girls, and sufferers often return to it as a coping mechanism in later years. Bulimia usually involves binge eating followed by self-induced vomiting. Secrecy is key, also denial. It can result in dangerous weight loss and a host of related medical problems. It can even be fatal.

Who knows how Diana had imagined life with the Prince of Wales might be. Kate Middleton had eight years to take a long, hard look at royal life before marrying Prince William, and she was nearly ten years older than Diana had been on her marriage day. Charles was heavily engaged in royal duties. When he wasn't working, he was playing: fox hunting and shooting in the winter, polo and fishing in the summer; and spending weekends, as often as not, in the country houses of good and established friends. He already had his own country house in Gloucestershire—Highgrove—and, having reached the age of thirty-two on his own, looked after by servants who took care of his every need, he was set in his ways and quite content with life as it was. All that was missing was a family of his own—the warmth and companionship of a wife and the pleasure and excitement of children.

He fondly imagined Diana would fit into his life without the need for any radical change, but he didn't realize what a determined woman he had taken on.

To those celebrating on the day they married, it seemed like the culmination of a fairy tale, but in reality it was the beginning of one of the saddest stories of modern times; even as they walked down the aisle of St. Paul's Cathedral, they both knew in their heart of hearts they were making a mistake.

Charles found it difficult to cope with Diana's demands and her mood swings, and his own moods became increasingly unpredictable and volatile; if she was disappointed by her first taste of marriage, so was he. Both their expectations of marriage were unrealistic; neither could gain from the other even a fraction of what they needed.

The arrival of Prince William on 21 June 1982 brought brief respite, but it didn't last long. Although delighted to be pregnant, Diana had suffered from morning sickness for most of the pregnancy and, according to her "was as sick as a parrot the whole way through the labor...Anyway the boy arrived, great excitement. Thrilled, everyone absolutely high as a kite—we had found a date where Charles could get off his polo pony for me to give birth. That was very nice, felt very grateful about that!" She went home to Kensington Palace the next day, where a nursery nurse was waiting to help take care of William, but she plunged almost immediately into severe postnatal depression.

But to family, friends and the country at large (with the exception of some vociferous republicans), Diana's baby brought nothing but elation. He was the first direct heir to the throne to be born in a hospital, and he could not have been born at a more auspicious time. Just the day before, Margaret Thatcher, the Prime Minister, had announced that hostilities between Britain and Argentina over the Falkland Islands had finally ceased. Victory restored national pride and brought huge relief to families whose loved ones had been fighting in the South Atlantic, not least the Royal Family. Prince Andrew had served as a Royal Navy helicopter pilot, insistent, despite protests from Cabinet members, who wanted him transferred to a desk job, that he should be allowed to do the job he had trained for. The Queen and the Duke of Edinburgh supported him, just as they did nearly thirty years later when Prince Harry wanted to serve on the front line in Iraq and Afghanistan.

Prince Harry's birth, two years later, on 15 September 1984, was also a cause for national jubilation, and despite Diana's rather bitter memory of her husband's reaction to his birth, those who knew them at the time say Charles was every bit as excited as he was the first time around, and if he was disappointed that Harry was either a boy or red-haired, he showed no sign of it.

Harry was christened Henry Charles Albert David (to be known as Harry) and was given a younger and less daunting selection of godparents than his brother, including more of Diana's friends. They were her old flatmate, Carolyn Bartholomew, Princess Margaret's daughter, Lady Sarah Armstrong-Jones, Gerald Ward, a businessman and landowning friend of Charles, the artist, Bryan Organ, who had painted Diana in 1981, Lord Vestey's second wife, Cece, and Charles's younger brother, Prince Andrew.

The christening, held four days before Christmas at St. George's Chapel, Windsor, was shown on the Queen's traditional Christmas television broadcast. It was memorable for William, well into "the terrible twos," misbehaving. He tried to grab the antique christening robe his brother was swathed in (it was already on its last legs having been worn by every royal baby since 1840); he complained that he wasn't allowed to hold the baby, and chased his cousin, Zara Phillips, round the legs of the Archbishop of Canterbury, which everyone including the Queen and the Queen Mother seemed to find funny. The two Queens had brought up their own children with iron discipline from an early age but, for now, William got away with it. It was not until he was a pageboy at Prince Andrew's wedding to Sarah Ferguson, two years later, when he fidgeted throughout, rolled his order of service into a trumpet, scratched his head, covered his face with his fingers, poked his tongue out at his cousin Laura Fellowes, and left Westminster Abbey with his sailor hat wildly askew, that the Queen let it be known his behavior was not acceptable.

Looking at the Princes today, it seems hard to believe that William was the naughty one and Harry a shy little boy who was overshadowed and bossed about by his big brother. But all of that was to change.

OUT WITH THE OLD

Diana stopped seeing her psychiatrist after Harry's birth. She felt she was better and no longer needed professional help, but although she put on a brave face in public, as she always did, behind closed doors she and the Prince continued to have volcanic exchanges. She seemed convinced that his friends were conspiring against her. She didn't want anything that was associated with his old life to be around them, not even his old Labrador. And so desperate was he to make her happy, so desperate to make her well, that he did everything she asked. Though it distressed him greatly, everyone she wanted to be rid of went.

Out of a mixture of embarrassment and loyalty to his wife, Charles took the easy way out and said nothing to his friends by way of explanation. They only realized they had been dropped when the phone stopped ringing, the letters stopped coming and the invitations to Highgrove and Balmoral stopped arriving; unsurprisingly they were hurt. As for Harvey, the dog, he was sent off to see out his days with the Prince's Comptroller at his house in Kent.

Her demands spilled into his working life too. Diana wanted him at home with the children and after Harry's birth, sent Edward Adeane, the Prince's Private Secretary, a note to the effect that the Prince would no longer be available for meetings at either end of the day because he would be upstairs in the nursery. Adeane couldn't believe it. He was an old-school courtier, a barrister and a bachelor, eleven years older than the Prince. He had no understanding of what it was like to change a nappy, bathe a baby, or read a little boy a bedtime story. New man he certainly was not, and he was not happy for his boss to become one either. His best times of day with the Prince were first thing in the morning and last thing at night. They were the two moments in a normally very busy day when there was some peace in which to talk and to go through vital briefings for the day ahead. But to appease Diana, Charles cut down on his official engagements and on time spent with his Private Secretary. "He loved the nursery life and couldn't wait to get back and do the bottle and everything," Diana told Morton. "He was very good, he always came back and fed the baby. I [breast]fed William for three weeks and Harry for eleven weeks."

The press soon noticed that he was doing less and called him workshy and lazy. He became alarmingly depressed. While his contemporaries were all heading for the peak of their careers, he felt he served no useful purpose. He was facing possibly decades of opening buildings and visiting foreign lands, meeting only those people who had been carefully selected to shake his hand. Everywhere he turned there were people in need. Often the solutions seemed simple but nobody seemed to be addressing them, and he was being told he must not get involved. He knew well enough that the sovereign and heir should remain above politics, and that social deprivation was as political as it gets, but he couldn't just sit on his hands and do nothing. He knew there was a social revolution going on outside the palace gates and felt compelled to help in some way, but how? This was not a question previous Princes of Wales had asked: there was no blueprint.

In 1972, he had given away, anonymously, his naval allowance of £3,000 a year, to help disadvantaged young people get small business enterprises off the ground. It was the beginning of the Prince's Trust, which was formally launched in 1976, the year he left the Navy. What started as a few ideas scribbled on the back of an envelope has grown into the UK's leading youth charity, with a multimillion pound income. It is as mainstream as it is possible to be. It has given a leg-up in life to well over half a million eighteen- to thirty-year-olds, and spawned many other extraordinarily successful initiatives.

It took courage to keep addressing the ills of society when news-paper headlines, his father and his most senior advisors were all telling him he should keep out of it. But in his working life the Prince of Wales has never been short of courage, and he continued to say what he believed, and to stick his head recklessly above the parapet when he felt passionately that something was amiss. In the year of Harry's birth he took almost the bravest risk of all. Against the backdrop of terrifying race riots, he accepted an invitation from Stephen O'Brien, who ran a catalyst organization called Business in the Community, to convene a conference at Windsor for busi-ness community and black community leaders to meet. It was one of the most significant advances in race relations ever made, but it could have gone terribly wrong.

His son has inherited a lot of his determination.

THE MIDDLE PERIOD

Parenthood had affected Charles dramatically. It had focused his mind on the future and on the world that his children would inherit; made him re-evaluate his philosophy and his life; given him a whole new perspective. Looking at alternative ways of doing things—in medicine, architecture, farming and everything else— was a natural follow-on to his conviction that the established ways were inadequate; that the greatest profit was not always the best motive, that people's quality of life was important for the peaceful future of mankind; that everyone, no matter what their color, creed or disadvantage, has a valuable role to play in the grand scheme of things. He entered what he said Carl Jung would have described as "the middle period." The press interpreted it as encroaching lunacy.

These were difficult years for Charles; he was being pulled in too many different directions. There were Diana's demands and his anxieties about her; there was Adeane wanting him to confine his activities to safe, traditional areas, and there was Michael Colborne, a trusted friend and aide, telling him to forget what previous Princes of Wales had done—and to look about him. There was a whole generation of young people out there who needed his leadership and he should stop feeling sorry for himself and go out and do something about it. Colborne had followed the Prince from the Navy—he had been a Chief Petty Officer—and he was one of the few people who told the Prince of Wales what he needed to hear.

There was no denying Charles did feel sorry for himself. Meanwhile, the media's obsession with Diana, which had begun before they were even engaged, had continued remorselessly. Day after day, trivial stories made the headlines. If she accompanied him to an engagement, it was her the newspapers wrote about: her clothes, her hairstyle, her weight, her body language, accompanied by endless speculation about what this or that look or gesture might imply. Prince Charles might not have been there for all the notice the press took of him or his speeches. The frustration was unbearable. He was being eclipsed by his wife.

She read the newspapers obsessively: she reveled in her fame and superstardom; she basked in the adulation, but the slightest criticism hurt her to the quick. Charles was not the only one who was worried about the effect it was having on her. He tried inviting the editors to Kensington Palace to meet him and Diana for lunch so they could try to reason with them, but to no avail. Diana sold newspapers.

He began to lose heart, and it was a very unhappy household in those early years after Harry's birth. Charles was demanding and quick to lose his temper over nothing. His staff tiptoed around him and, one by one, they left. First Colborne then Adeane. Adeane's successor was Sir John Riddell, an investment banker in his early fifties, who had a young family and a delightful attitude to life. As one of his staff said of him, "I cannot count the number of times I have been into John's office with a disastrous problem to solve, to come out again with the problem still unsolved but feeling that the world was a much nicer place." He was one of the Prince's best appointments; he gave him a new lease of life. His humor did wonders for the office, which was not the happiest of places; and over the next five years the Prince's public life began to flourish. Having been tortured and uncertain of where he was going or what his role should be, he began to see a way forward.

The irony was that, in the mid-1980s, the Prince and Princess of Wales were an unbeatable double-act. Abroad, they were a sensation, and on every trip—to Australia, America, the Gulf States, Italy, Japan, Canada—the reception was rapturous. At home he was saying all the uncomfortable things that needed to be said and making a serious contribution. She, meanwhile, was sprinkling fairy dust, not just in the most likely and convenient places, but also in more challenging areas, which the world would rather have forgotten—like drug addiction, leprosy, AIDS and homelessness. She was proving quite unparalleled in her ability to charm, communicate and empathize with ordinary people. She was beautiful; she wore glamorous clothes, sparkling jewels; the cameras loved her, the public loved her, and the happy, smiling face that she presented so professionally to the outside world never faltered.

At home it was a different story.

Charles was not the person best suited to deal with Diana, but he had done all he could to make her happy. It was never the case that he didn't care—he was simply at a loss. As the months and the years rolled by with no let-up in her behavior, he became hardened and at times downright callous in his attitude towards her. When she became hysterical, there was nothing he could do or say to calm her down; so when she made dramatic gestures, he walked away. When she self-harmed, he walked away. Not because he didn't care but because he knew he couldn't help.

As anyone with experience of an eating disorder will know, it is an incredibly destructive illness and can break up even the most secure and normal of families; and this family was not normal. One of the Prince's former Private Secretaries once said to me, "I've never succeeded in describing to anybody who wasn't in the middle of it, the pressures of that life and that relationship, and looking as she looked and being who she was. Almost any human being would have found it absolutely intolerable. Wherever you happened to be, every look, every gaze, every smile, every scowl, every hand you held or touched, under the microscope every time, front-page news in the tabloids day after day, sometimes of your own volition, I know, but everybody after you. It was the most extraordinary pressure. I did the same sort of work for politicians. It was utterly different. There was a clear-ish divide between public and private life and I didn't need to cross any of these dividing lines.

"Here the whole thing was a great big ball of wax: the job, the public life, the private life; it was all indistinguishable—not just for them, but for us too. The phone calls would come at any time of the day or night, wherever you were in the world; your involvement with them was twenty-four hours a day and you couldn't distinguish because they didn't distinguish. How could they distinguish between what was public and private, what was work and what was play? It was all part of the same thing. There wasn't much respite and that clearly took its toll on her. It takes its toll on him, too, but he's been brought up to it and developed his own defense mechanisms, his own thick skin."

THE NURSERY

Given what an extrovert Harry is today, and how very measured his brother is by comparison, it is hard to believe that for the first two or three years of his life, the roles were reversed and Harry was the quiet one. William was exuberant and cheeky—some would say, completely out of control—like many a firstborn, and Harry was entirely overshadowed, sweet and well behaved. Charles said of him that he was "extraordinarily good, sleeps marvelously and eats well." He was "the one with the gentle nature." Charles adored him; he adored them both—and with two boys he was well on the way to a full polo team. What could be better?

William was a handful; he had been the center of attention and indulged by everyone, and his parents were not consistent in their discipline. According to William's godfather, King Constantine, Charles always treated both boys like young adults. He didn't force them to do anything but would explain and reason with them; William, who was bright, exhausting and extremely willful, would have stretched the patience of a saint at times. If he refused to put his gloves on and then started crying because his hands were cold, Charles would tell him to stop whining. But at other times he allowed William to run rings around him. Diana would either burst out laughing at William's antics or angrily smack him on the bottom; however, the nanny, who was the most consistent and effective with the children, was forbidden to raise her voice to them, far less raise a hand. At his nursery school he was so boisterous they called him "Basher Wills" or "Billy the Basher." Diana simply called him "Your Royal Naughtiness." And Harry, who was a slighter build than William, was too small to fight back when his big brother bowled him over or snatched his toys. The Queen's intervention—after William had disgraced himself at Prince Andrew's wedding—came not a moment too soon, but that same year William's behavior underwent a radical change without any need for harsh discipline.

Nannies played a very significant role in the Wales household—and it was lucky for the emotional well-being of the boys that they did. There was a self-contained nursery on the top floor of both their London and country homes, and that was where William and Harry ate, slept and lived for much of their childhood years. They did not eat meals with their parents and they did not have the run of the house. Patrick Jephson, who was Diana's Equerry and then Private Secretary for nearly ten years, wrote in his book *Shadow of a Princess*: "They and their organization were collectively known as 'the nursery.' It was almost a court in its own right. There were bedrooms, playrooms, a kitchen and a dining room snug under the eaves of KP [Kensington Palace]. There were full-time and part-time nannies, policemen, a shared driver and a separate routine of school runs, parties, shopping and trips to the cinema. Every Friday morning almost the whole apparatus would transport itself a hundred miles to the west, to spend the weekend at Highgrove in Gloucestershire. There a duplicate set of rooms awaited, together with all the attractions and diversions of life on a small, picture-postcard country estate."

The principal nanny that Diana chose to run this operation was Barbara Barnes, a forester's daughter, who took up her position within weeks of William's birth, taking over from a specialist in newborn babies. William became very attached to her, as children invariably do to the person who cares for them round the clock. She was in her early forties and came highly recommended. She was just the sort of nanny Diana was after: she didn't want someone who would take over. She wanted to be involved in the care of her children herself and, although she may not have been able to articulate it in quite this way, she wanted to be the one they loved best of all.

But small children can't differentiate. The person with whom they tend to bond the closest is the person they see most, and in William and Harry's early years, that person was Barbara Barnes, or Baba as they called her. It was not surprising. Baba was the one into whose bed William would climb for a cuddle when he got up in the morning. He might sometimes go down the stairs and climb into his mother's bed for a second cuddle afterwards, but Baba was the first person he turned to for all his wants and needs.

Sadly, with all her insecurities coming to the fore, Diana saw the nanny as a threat. She loved her boys with a complete passion that no one ever doubted; she was warm, expressive and tactile with them; she loved them more than anyone else on earth. She "loved them to death," she would say, but she wanted them to love her better than anyone else too. She wanted 100 percent of them, in the same way that she had wanted 100 percent of Charles, to the exclusion of all others.

The relationship between the two women deteriorated—as Diana's relationships often did—until finally, without a thought for the children's psychological well-being, she peremptorily relieved Barbara Barnes of her post. Had she only been able to take a step back, she would have realized that what she was doing to William and Harry was precisely what had happened to her when she was six years old. She had felt the pain of loss and grief and bewilderment in exactly the same way that William, and to a lesser extent Harry, felt it. Diana's mother had gone with no explanation that she could understand as a child. Barbara Barnes had gone with no explanation either.

The safe little world that William had lorded over was no longer so safe. Her loss triggered a fundamental change in him. He became less outgoing, less trusting, less inclined to make himself vulnerable. Harry, two years younger, was less visibly affected; and with William no longer stealing all the limelight, there was room for Harry to come slowly out from under his shell.

Two other nannies followed, Ruth Wallace and Jessie Webb, but neither stayed for more than two or three years. Jessie Webb (who came out of retirement to help William and Kate with Prince George) vanished from the household when Harry went to boarding school at the age of seven. She had looked after him for two years when he'd been alone at home, after William had already started boarding, at a time when things were particularly difficult there. She was another one who was frozen out by the Princess. Finally, Olga Powell, who had been deputy to all three nannies, stepped seamlessly into the role. She was fifty-two when she arrived, a widow with no children of her own, and, as Diana's mother remarked, "Was more granny than nanny." She built up a very close bond with both boys and was their rock of security in the emotional maelstrom that was to come. Hugely loving but consistently firm, she remained with the boys until their mother's death in 1997. After her retirement, both boys kept in touch with her, and when she died two years ago, William was at her funeral. Had he not been in Afghanistan, Harry would have been there too.

Charles and Diana had been united in their desire to allow William and Harry to have as normal and informal an upbringing as was possible. And while a fleet of nannies and domestic staff may not be normal to most families, they were normal to most aristocratic households. Charles and Diana had both been brought up with nannies and staff, and neither of them would have considered life without them. They were also essential to have in place if the Prince and Princess were to be able to do their charitable and royal duties. All that was abnormal was the close protection, which both boys have had throughout their lives.

Their Police Protection Officers (PPOs) are members of the Royalty and Diplomatic Protection Department of the Metropolitan Police. In the case of William and Harry, they were specially chosen to get along with growing boys. Most of William and Harry's PPOs have been with them for years and they have built up a very valuable relationship with them. They've been part of the nursery, they've eaten their meals with them, had pillow fights with them, watched movies together; they've been to their schools, to their friends' houses, to birthday parties and to restaurants and amusement parks; they've been with them on car journeys, planes and trains; they've been with them on the royal yacht, *Britannia*, before she was scrapped; they've been to Balmoral, Sandringham and Windsor, and on every holiday they've ever taken at home and abroad. Wherever the boys have been, so have their PPOs; sometimes at a discreet distance, at other times providing company, and—just occasionally, when the need has arisen—protection. They are with each other week in and week out and are, inevitably, very close, but like members of the Household, they have never allowed themselves to think they are friends of the Princes. They instinctively know when to provide company and when to keep their distance. It is a professional relationship, yet no one was expected to address either boy as "Sir" or "Your Royal Highness" or give them any special treatment. As Patrick Jephson wrote: "I will not forget in a hurry the distinguished, but perhaps overpunctilious cavalry Colonel who bowed low in front of Prince Harry and greeted him with a ringing military 'Sir!' The look of bemused delight on the three-year-old Prince's face almost made him fall off his tricycle."

KP VERSUS HIGHGROVE

In London the family lived at Kensington Palace, or KP, as it is known to all who live and work there, which is not as grand as the name or the familiar façade in the photographs might suggest. It no doubt once was, in the seventeenth and eighteenth centuries when it was the primary London residence of successive sovereigns. It sits at one end of Hyde Park, surrounded on three sides by park and on the fourth by the smart houses in "Millionaires' Row." The State Apartments on the northeast side where Mary II lived have been beautifully preserved, but by the time the young Wales family was living there, the rest was a warren of courtyards and gardens and smaller apartments housing a remarkable concentration of royalty. Among their neighbors were the Queen's sister, Princess Margaret, Princess Alice, Duchess of Gloucester, the Duke and Duchess of Gloucester, and Prince and Princess Michael of Kent. Members of the Royal Household also lived within the warren, including Robert Fellowes, then Deputy Private Secretary to the Queen, who was married to Diana's sister, Jane. Their three children are much the same age as William and Harry, but Diana's relationship with her sister—as with the rest of her family and friends—waxed and waned.

Apartments 8 and 9 were tucked into the heart of the complex, and rather dark and viewless as a result. They had not been lived in for over forty years, so were entirely refurbished for Charles and Diana before they moved in in 1981. The accommodation comprised three reception rooms, a dining room, three bedrooms including a master suite, and a nursery suite on the top floor, which included rooms for the staff. There was also a roof terrace where Diana liked to sunbathe. On her mother's recommendation, Diana had chosen Dudley Poplak, a South African to help with the interior décor. The result was an elegant but comfortable mixture of antique and modern furniture, and pretty fabrics and wallpapers. Paintings from the Royal Collection hung on the walls, also prints and original cartoons depicting the Prince of Wales. The carpet in the hall and stairway was lime green and pink, with a Prince of Wales feather design woven through it.

The Princess's sitting room was the sunniest room in the house. Its tall windows looked out over a pretty walled garden where the children played and where she sometimes relaxed on summer evenings. By one of them was the writing desk, from which she wrote her many, many notes and thank-you letters in her big, rounded hand. According to Patrick Jephson, "It was cheerful, girlish and very cluttered. It smelt good too. There were always flowers—lilies were a favorite—as well as potpourri and scented candles."

The Prince, also famous for his long, handwritten letters and "black spider memos," crafted his in his study, a small, dark, masculine room on the first floor, which was cluttered with books, papers, paintings and sketch pads, some of it in piles on the floor.

It was a house for the family first and foremost (a family that needed butlers, valets, chefs, dressers and housekeepers, nannies and chauffeurs), but it was also an office. So all the people needed to keep the royal show on the road came and went, such as Private Secretaries and their assistants, Press Secretaries, Ladies-in-Waiting and Equerries, not to mention the individual PPOs for every member of the family, for whom a police room was provided in the basement. It was a small house for so many people and the walls were badly soundproofed. There was little privacy, and it was no secret within those four walls that Charles and Diana's marriage was in trouble.

KP was also a place where business was enacted, although visitors to the house in an official capacity might find themselves getting embroiled in family life as well. When Roger Singleton, who was then Director of Barnardo's, one of Diana's charities, arrived for lunch one day, William and Harry came bounding down the stairs to greet him. He was carrying a large green plaster frog, a gift from a group of disabled children at a school in Taunton that Diana had visited the previous week. As he was ushered through the front door, the boys instantly began clamoring for the frog. It was too heavy for either of them to carry alone, so William went racing off up the stairs, excitedly yelling to his mother that a frog was coming, while Harry, who refused to be parted from the creature, staggered up the stairs with one small hand resolutely on the frog's bottom and the other tightly clutching Singleton's free hand.

Highgrove, which sits in 410 acres not far from the pretty Cotswold town of Tetbury, was also dual purpose—a further indication of how blurred was the distinction in their lives between private and public, work and play. The Duchy of Cornwall had bought the house for the Prince of Wales in August 1980; when he becomes King, the house—along with the Duchy and all that it owns—will go to William, who will automatically become Prince of Wales. With nine bedrooms, six bathrooms, four reception rooms, a nursery and staff accommodation, stables, barns, cottages and outbuildings, it is neither as large nor palatial a country house as one might expect the heir to the throne to be living in, but Charles fell in love with it. It became his sanctuary: the place he could relax and be himself, where he could wind down, take himself off for walks, clear his head, be alone, think. It has remained one of the greatest pleasures in his life, especially the land that surrounds it. To Harry it is simply home and he knows every nook and cranny. He has played in every corner of the garden, ridden over every field, shot in every hedgerow.

In his book about the estate, written many years after he bought the property, the Prince said that one of the most crucial and persuasive factors in buying it was the presence of Paddy Whiteland, whom he inherited from the previous owners. Paddy was groom and general factotum; also peddler of all the local gossip. Paddy, he wrote, was "one of the most inimitable Irishmen I have ever come across...A former prisoner of war of the Japanese, he can only be described as one of 'Nature's Gentlemen.' Meeting him for the first time, you invariably came away (a considerable time later!) feeling infinitely better. Once met he is never forgotten. His rugged features and twinkling eyes are one of the most welcoming features of Highgrove and his Irish stories are famous."

Paddy became a permanent fixture in all of their lives, someone the boys sought out when they arrived from London and whose side they rarely left. He was a grandfatherly figure, who had a way with horses, and he captivated William and Harry with his tales of country lore. They loved him. He died of cancer at the age of eighty-five, in 1997, the year Diana died, and he was much mourned; but he had worked until he could work no longer. The Prince looked after him and paid for his care to the end.

Strangely for such a substantial house, there was no garden at Highgrove when the Duchy bought the property, and although he had no experience of gardening or farming and had only ever planted official trees in holes already dug, Charles knew, "I wanted to take care of the place in a very personal way and to leave it, one day, in a far better condition than I found it."

At Highgrove, Charles has five full-time and four part-time gardeners, but he knows every square meter of the ground intimately and he planted most of the trees and plants himself. He has a cottage garden, a rose garden, a bog garden, a stumpery (a strange collection of tree stumps arranged to extraordinary effect), a sculpture garden, a woodland garden, a thyme walk, a rose walk, an avenue of pleached hornbeams; he has giant Ali Baba pots filled with scented geraniums, and ponds and fountains, an Italian garden and an Islamic garden. And the walled kitchen garden, which is a mixture of flowers, fruits, vegetables and clipped box hedges, is as beautiful as it is functional. The sewage garden is perhaps marginally less beautiful, but certainly functional.

To two small, noisy, energetic and inquisitive little boys, Highgrove and its tapestry of gardens was a giant playground; after the confines of Kensington, they couldn't wait to get to the freedom it offered on a Friday. They were not automatically allowed the run of the house, but there was plenty of space in the nursery on the second floor, and they went in and out of the kitchen freely, where they had a tropical fish tank, and where they used to chop up carrots and apples for their pets. They also had the run of the garden and the outbuildings. There was more than enough to do outside, games to play, bikes to ride, people to see and places to go. There were hay-lofts and barns, where they found eggs that the hens had laid, which they would deliver to the kitchen; there were ducks and moorhens on the pond, tawny owls in the barn, sheep and black Aberdeen Angus cows in the fields. There was a heated outdoor swimming pool, which was enclosed in an inflatable plastic bubble in the winter, a climbing frame and a swing on the lawn; and, in the woodland garden, Charles had commissioned the Bath architect, Willie Bertram, to build them an elaborate tree house that sits twenty feet above the ground in a holly tree. It is still there. It has a thatched roof, a green holly leaf for a front door and red windows, and inside are handmade chairs and cupboards. It was wittily known as Holly-rood-house, reflecting the pronunciation of the Queen's official residence in Edinburgh. Both boys and their friends spent many happy hours in it. Charles also gave each boy a little patch of ground in the walled garden where they could grow whatever they chose.

But their activities weren't all rustic. Aston Martin had presented the Prince of Wales with a miniature replica of his own car for the young Princes, and this became their pride and joy. They would squabble over who drove. William, being the eldest, invariably won, but the pair of them were a familiar sight on the drives between the various cottages and other buildings on the estate. Later they moved on to go-karts and then trail bikes.

In the early days, when Charles was starting work on the garden, Diana had taken photographs of his progress and produced a wonderful record of the transformation, season by season, which she painstakingly pasted into leather-bound albums. By the time Charles was working on a book about the estate ten years later, and wanted to reproduce the photos, he asked her if he might have them, but the relationship between them was so hostile by then that she never gave them to him and, sadly, that record is lost.

COUNTRY PURSUITS

The Prince of Wales is a country person through and through—he felt suffocated in London—and his master plan had been to use Highgrove in Gloucestershire as the family's home and Kensington Palace as a city base. He had given Diana a free rein with the interior, and once again she used Dudley Poplak, whose design was contemporary, colorful and comfortable. Highgrove is a neoclassical Georgian house, built at the end of the eighteenth century, and is everything that Kensington Palace is not. There are big rooms with high ceilings, large windows and polished wooden floors with rugs; but, as in London, there were fresh flowers in every room and also large potted plants. All over the surfaces stood silver photo-frames and Herend porcelain, as well as the Wemyss Ware pottery that the Prince liked.

There was a large open fireplace in the sitting room, and a television set, in front of which the Prince and Princess used to eat their supper off a card table in the evenings. The children loved Highgrove as much as their father did, and would no doubt have been very happy living there and going to local nursery schools, as did the Princess Royal's children, Peter and Zara Phillips, who lived six miles away at Gatcombe Park. But Diana didn't wholeheartedly enjoy the countryside. She loved swimming, which she could do in the garden, but she didn't ride horses, having been put off them as a child by a fall; she didn't like dogs, had no interest in any other country pursuits, and gardening left her cold. London was where she wanted to be, where she could shop, see her friends, go to the gym, go to the cinema, go to smart restaurants and concerts and generally have fun. Despite having lived in the country as a child, it held limited appeal as an adult, and as the years went by she made fewer and fewer visits to Highgrove. Later she professed to "hate the place."

So the master plan never worked as the Prince had hoped. And once the decision had been made to send William to Mrs. Jane Mynors,' a nursery school in Notting Hill, the die was cast. They were committed to spending the week in London. Harry followed William to Mrs. Mynors' two years later, and from there to Wetherby, a private day prep school also in Notting Hill, and then to Ludgrove, a boarding prep school in Berkshire, at the age of eight. As time passed, Charles based himself more and more at Highgrove, arriving—as often as not—in a big noisy, red Wessex helicopter. The Wessex landed in the field at the front of the house, where sheep grazed, and when the boys were little, as soon as they heard it approaching they would rush out excitedly to see their father. Once the blades had stopped turning, they would hurtle across the field and jump into his arms, as often as not covering his smart suits with sheep droppings.

William and Harry's two lives—urban and rural—could not have been more contrasting. With their mother they went to the cinema, shopping, or to the zoo or the London Dungeon; they ate McDonald's hamburgers, listened to music and watched videos. With their father, they romped around with the dogs, they rode ponies, they went for country walks, they looked after their pets—William had a guinea pig and Harry a gray, lop-eared rabbit, which lived in a hutch in a corner of the stable yard that they cleaned out themselves. At Highgrove they learned about the natural world and traditional country pursuits. They loved both parents and, therefore, both lives, but they always felt that Highgrove was home. Among the pleasures for Harry were the horses. William at first shared some of his mother's nervousness, although that didn't last, but Harry immediately took to riding and was competent enough to be off the leading rein by the age of four. They each had a Shetland pony—Smokey and Trigger—and most mornings

Marion Cox, a local woman, would take them out for a riding lesson over the fields. Come the summer, the ponies traveled up to Balmoral with them for the holidays. As they grew more confident, they went to the occasional gymkhana and other events organized by the Beaufort Pony Club, where they met and mixed with local children from horsey families. Harry became so impressive on horseback that his aunt, Princess Anne, a former Three-Day Event champion, remarked that he had a "good seat" and that he had the talent to compete and reach an international standard.

In time, he moved on to polo. The Beaufort Polo Club was about half a mile from Highgrove—it is where Charles regularly used to play and the Prince of Wales became good friends with its founders, Simon and Claire Tomlinson. It is a small, friendly club, now run by Claire alone following the couple's divorce. Claire once captained the England Women's team; she was one of the highest-rated women players in the world. She also coached the England team, and although Harry didn't start until his mid-teens, his polo skills, like his brother's, are down to Claire's expert tuition.

Claire is unmoved by titles, and prepared to push the Princes as hard as anyone else to get them to play well; she admires the way they have both combined their position with their sporting talent. Polo is all about being a good horseman, good hand—eye coordination and being a team player. Robert ffrench Blake, who was his father's polo manager, said of Harry when he was still in his teens, "He is naturally very talented, well co-ordinated and he's a natural sportsman. How good he becomes depends entirely on how much effort and time he gives to the game. But he has the ability to become a four- or five-goal player." The higher the handicap, the better the player. Sadly, Harry didn't have the time to practice and is now, like his brother, a one-goal player, but he is potentially the better of the two. Claire also admires their attitude to their horses. So many men tend to treat their horses like machines, riding them to the point of exhaustion, but both William and Harry are sympathetic riders. They respect their animals, understand them and care about them and therefore get the best out of them.

Charles had often said that if he hadn't been a Prince he would have liked to be a farmer, and his passion for conservation is well known, so when Broadfield, a farm with a further 710 acres, came up for sale on the other side of Tetbury in 1984, the Duchy bought it and appointed David Wilson, a young farmer with a wife and two young sons to manage it. The Prince had become involved in the organic movement a couple of years earlier and, being a firm believer in the importance of leading by example, had felt that if he was ever to persuade farmers to abandon chemicals, then he must first do so himself and prove to others that it was viable. Most weekends, he would visit the farm and take William and Harry and his Jack Russells, Tigger and Roo, with him. They would all jump into the Land Rover for the short drive to the other side of Tetbury, eager to romp around the fields and hedgerows alongside their father, to go and see the animals or clamber on the tractors and other huge bits of machinery.

The sheep grazed at Highgrove; at lambing time, usually in the Easter holidays, the boys would go into the lambing pen near the house with Fred Hartles, the shepherd. Harry loved it. He would spend hours filling water buckets, bringing in hay and picking up the lambs. Charles was delighted to see how much both boys loved the countryside. It was important to him that his children should see nature at work and understand and respect the natural order; and important for them to see how food is produced, how animals are reared and to learn the value of good husbandry of both land and livestock. It is something he feels very strongly about and it goes to the heart of the man.

In David Wilson, Charles had found a kindred spirit, in total agreement with him about the environment and future sustainability of the planet. Convincing the men in suits who ran the Duchy of Cornwall at that time, whose statutory obligation was to safeguard its capital assets, was another matter, but the Prince was adamant. "If the Duchy of Cornwall can't afford to try organic farming," he stormed, "then who the hell can?" So gradually they converted the land and started experimenting in organic production. They planted copses and mixed hedges to enhance the landscape and to encourage birds; slowly skylarks began to sing again above, and wild poppies to grow through the wheat. They planted barley and oats too, and clover to regenerate the soil, and they bought livestock: a dairy herd of 110 Ayrshires and 400 Mule sheep, which lambed for the first time in the spring of 1987, when Harry was two. To those they added Aberdeen Angus beef cattle, Gloucester heifers, Gloucestershire Old Spot pigs and a few other rare breeds to provide a gene base for the future. And because they don't use chemical sprays, the hedgerows are bristling with wild-life, including partridge.

Shooting has long been a royal enthusiasm, which Harry took to with gusto. Diana was falsely accused of turning Charles against it when he gave it up in the mid-1980s. It had nothing to do with Diana; he had given up because he was bored by it and the ease with which thousands of birds were bagged in a day. She was no opponent of the sport—far from it. She didn't care to do it herself, but her father and brother always had and there had been regular pheasant shoots at Althorp. It was what happened on big country estates from October to February. So she was just as keen as Charles for William and Harry to start learning how to handle a gun when they were not yet in their teens.

They were taught to shoot by Willie Potts, the gillie at Balmoral, and they practiced their newfound skills anywhere and everywhere, sometimes at Highgrove or—for a change of scene—over at the farm, always telephoning beforehand. Their PPOs would drive them over and they would spend a happy few hours shooting rabbits and pigeons, always taking what they shot home to the Highgrove kitchen. They had been taught that this was an important part of it all. Willie Potts also taught them to cast for salmon, and to track, kill, gralloch (disembowel) and skin a deer. "Contrary to a lot of people's beliefs," says David, "shooting and dealing with wildlife and eating it helps build respect and the balanced view for all conservation matters. All the Royal Family totally get the whole nature, conservation, food, farming balance."

Harry was a good shot. He'd sometimes bring over a clay pigeon trap, which was good for getting his eye in; and sometimes he and a friend or two would go out at night with a powerful torch. At other times, he would get someone to drive him around the fields in a Land Rover while he shot out of the window. David was only too pleased to see him with his gun. As far as he was concerned it was vermin control—rabbits and pigeons both eat young crops.

As soon as they were big enough to ride trail bikes, they each had one, long before the age at which they could legally ride on the roads. They roared across the fields on them both at Highgrove and the farm. One of the estate workers would bring the bikes over in a trailer and, again, they would always phone before turning up. "Harry was always well mannered," recalls David (although no better mannered than his brother). "I remember a member of the Household staff pulling him up over something when he was very young. He was very, very polite. He hadn't done anything in my opinion but they corrected him."

In summer, Prince Charles played polo fanatically, but in winter it was fox hunting that consumed his spare time and he enthused both boys from an early age. They would go to meets on foot and follow the hunt with Paddy until they were old enough to go out on horseback themselves. Even then, what Harry particularly enjoyed was riding on the back of a quad bike with the terrier man, whose job was to send terriers below ground to flush the fox out if it went to earth. On those days, Harry always had rather superior sandwiches from the Highgrove kitchen. It is a very cohesive community, and both Princes made close friends through hunting and the social activities that go with it. It's a dangerous sport, but it was the danger and the exhilaration that they loved, and they and their father were very sad to have to give it up when it was banned in 2004. Their friends continued to ride to hounds, ostensibly following a scent dragged across the countryside, but there was always the possibility that the dogs would pick up the scent of a fox instead. While their friends could take that risk, they were different.

PLAYING AWAY

It is impossible to overestimate just how difficult William and Harry's home life was—and how lucky we as a nation are that they both came out of it so apparently unscathed. They will both, of course, have demons. And there is a lot of anger in Harry, and a lot of hurt, but it is a measure of what a loving start he had in life that he has not allowed that anger to destroy him. Expensive rehab clinics are filled with the children of broken homes and bitter divorces, who end up throwing their lives away, some of whose experiences pale beside Harry's. What almost certainly saved him and his brother was the army of people employed to look after them: the nannies, the PPOs, the school teachers and others who were there for them while they were growing up and who were able to provide the continuity, support and consistency that wasn't always there from their warring parents.

Diana's *Panorama* interview in November 1995, when Harry was just eleven, was hugely damaging. Looking vulnerable but brave, sitting alone in the middle of a room, explaining to the millions glued to their television sets that her marriage had never stood a chance because, to use her words, "there were three of us in the marriage, so it was a bit crowded," convinced the viewing public that Charles was the villain. His obsession with Camilla Parker Bowles—his infidelity—had destroyed their marriage and made Diana bitterly unhappy.

Charles has never defended himself, but Charles takes a very long view of life—in his inimitable, philosophical way. He is content for history to be the judge of what happened in that marriage, when he is long dead and all the papers and the diaries and the facts are known. He feels a crushing sense of guilt that he was unable to help Diana, but he knows in his heart that he did everything he could to make their marriage work, and Camilla played no significant part in its failure.

They were both desperately lonely within their marriage, both desperately wanting to be loved and both desperately in need of support. So it was not surprising that Diana should have sought out the comfort of other men; or that Charles should have turned back to Camilla Parker Bowles. Under other circumstances, it could have worked. Members of the aristocracy have been having extra-marital affairs for generations. If their marriages didn't work out, they discreetly (and occasionally not so discreetly) took lovers, but stayed together for the sake of their children and their estates. But they had no paparazzi to worry about. This was the most high-profile couple in the country, and the media watched their every twitch.

For five years Diana found happiness with James Hewitt who, like so many men, was instantly smitten by her. They had met at a party. He was a talented horseman; she told him she had lost her nerve as a child but would like to learn to ride again; he offered to teach her. Twice a week she would go to Knightsbridge Barracks, where the mounted division of the Household Cavalry was based, and they would ride round Hyde Park together. They fell in love. He was not the first, but this was the most enduring of her love affairs and he was the lover that William and Harry, particularly Harry, knew best. Hewitt became a frequent visitor to Kensington Palace when they were there and he also went to Highgrove on occasions when the Prince was away. She took carefully selected employees into her confidence, people like Paul Burrell, the butler at Highgrove (and, after the divorce, her butler at Kensington Palace), to help. Sometimes he would be one of several friends staying for the weekend and would always be given a room across the corridor from the Princess's, but everyone in the house knew precisely where he was for most of the night.

She made no attempt to keep him a secret from her children; and by all accounts positively encouraged a relationship between them. He insisted afterwards that he never tried to be their father, saying, "They had a perfectly good father of their own," but he inevitably slipped into a similar role and obviously felt sufficiently at home to take his Labrador, Jester, with him to Highgrove. He would sit and watch television with them, play ball games on the lawn with them, have violent pillow fights with them at bedtime (along with their PPOs), read them their favorite stories, give them riding lessons on their ponies, and he sometimes took them to visit the barracks at Windsor, where his regiment was based. "They climbed all over the tanks and other armored vehicles," he recalled, "and appeared to have the times of their lives." He even had little military uniforms specially made for them by the regimental tailor. And sometimes she and the children went with Hewitt to stay with his mother for the weekend in Devon. He appeared to adore William and Harry and they certainly seemed very comfortable with him. Perhaps what they liked about him was the fact that he made their mother happy.

Meanwhile, another face was becoming a familiar sight at the Prince's otherwise solitary lunch table. Charles had first fallen in love with Camilla, then Camilla Shand, in the autumn of 1972 when he was nearly twenty-four and she a year older. He was in the Navy. She had an on-off boyfriend, Andrew Parker Bowles, who played polo with Charles, and had been a one-time boyfriend of Princess Anne. He was a charming, good-looking Cavalry officer who had swept Camilla off her feet when she was eighteen— she had been mad about him ever since. But when she met Charles, Andrew was stationed in Germany and their relationship was going through a rocky patch. She and Charles had an immediate rapport; they made each other laugh and he thought he might have found someone he could share his life with, but he was young and he was about to set sail for eight months in the Caribbean, and was too reticent to dare talk about the future. By the time he came back, she had married Andrew. When Charles heard he was heartbroken. As he wrote to a friend, it seemed particularly cruel that after "such a blissful, peaceful and mutually happy relationship," fate had decreed that it should last no more than six months. "I suppose the feeling of emptiness will pass eventually."

Despite the disappointment, he and the Parker Bowleses all remained good friends. Charles became a frequent weekend visitor to their house in Wiltshire, and godfather to their first child, Tom, born in 1974. Princess Anne became godmother to their daughter, Laura, born four years later. For many years their friendship was entirely platonic but, because of that earlier attachment, it was a particularly close and trusting friendship. And so it would possibly have remained. But things were not right in her marriage and, after Laura's birth, Camilla increasingly found herself sitting at home alone. By the late 1970s, she and Charles had begun an affair, both knowing that it was never going to lead anywhere. Camilla didn't want to leave Andrew and break up the family; even if she had done, Charles could never have married a divorcée.

As Charles's romantic interest in Diana developed, the physical side of his relationship with Camilla came to an end, as he assured Diana. What he failed to realize was that an insecure nineteen-year-old would be jealous of past relationships and that verbal reassurances would not be enough. She remained suspicious, but after their engagement he and Camilla scarcely saw or spoke to each other. He was sincere about wanting his marriage to work. He'd been lonely; he'd longed to find someone to share his work and his future with; he wanted to have children and the sort of cozy home life that his friends had. But by the mid-1980s, Charles had given up all hope of ever being able to change things. He was once again seeing some of the friends Diana had disliked, while she was separately seeing her own friends. They did fewer public engagements together and spent more and more time apart.

Two of the friends he saw were Charlie and Patti Palmer-Tomkinson, neighbors in Wiltshire, with whom he used to go skiing each year in Klosters. They were not alone in being worried about how dramatically he had changed. Charles hadn't spoken about his marital problems to any of his friends and they were shocked by the difference in him. He had always been prone to melancholy, but all the humor and sparkle had gone, all the fun. He was not in a good way. They rightly guessed that if anyone could cheer him up it would be Camilla, for whom nothing had changed. Knowing that Camilla had always been able to make him laugh, Patti put them in touch.

He started to laugh again, and slowly began the long haul out of the abyss. Along the way, they became lovers once more. She was interested in him and what he was trying to do with his life; he could speak to her openly and honestly, pour out his heart— and she would listen. She understood him, believed in him, loved him and gently teased him. They had everything in common— children, horses, dogs, hunting, gardening, art, music—and there was no tension, no suspicion, no jealousy, no games, no manipulation. It was an easy, happy, uncomplicated secret relationship that endured the test of time.

Diana's love affair with James Hewitt didn't. In 1991, at the start of the first Gulf War, he was deployed to Iraq following the British invasion. He had been stationed in Germany for some time before that; in his absence, Diana had been seeing someone she had known from her teens, James Gilbey. Despite the risk, she sent Hewitt over a hundred long, loving, handwritten letters. Every day throughout the conflict she anxiously watched the television news, terrified that he was going to be killed, while Harry, not quite seven years old, snuggled on the sofa beside her. William by then was at boarding school, at Ludgrove. Harry would follow in September. But, for the time being, he was at home with his mother, trying to comfort her but no doubt confused by her anguish.

Hewitt returned home safely the following year, ever more besotted. But Diana abruptly ended the affair, as she ended so many of her relationships with both men and women, friends and family. She simply stopped taking his calls. He retired, confused and hurt. Three years later, when Anna Pasternak told him she planned to write a book about the affair, he cooperated with her.

He claimed he made not one penny from the book, but thought that if he cooperated, at least the book would be accurate. Diana saw it as an act of gross betrayal. By the time *Princess in Love* was published, she had moved on to pastures new. There were several men over a period who all seemed to have a claim on her affections and who came and went from Kensington Palace at all hours of the day and night. She appeared to enjoy the power she had over them, telephoning and having them arrive at her bidding and dismissing them when she wanted them gone.

Diana didn't attempt to hide her dalliances—or her emotions—from her children. A friend had once suggested that it was unwise to have hysterics in front of William, who was then a baby, but Diana had replied that he was too young to notice and, anyway, he would "have to learn the truth sooner or later." The children were partially protected by virtue of the living arrangements, and later by being away at boarding school, but even if Charles and Diana had tried to remain civil to one another it would have been impossible for two such sensitive boys not to have noticed the tension, the tears and the absences. By the late 1980s and early 1990s, when Harry was still very young and impressionable, the Prince and Princess could barely tolerate being in the same room together, let alone under the same roof, as everyone who worked for them was well aware. There were blistering rows, tears and hysterics, rage and fury, all heard to some degree by everyone in the house.

What is so surprising is that Diana should have confided in her boys and sought comfort from them when they were still so young. She of all people would have known just how painful it is for a young child to see a parent in distress. She must have remembered how she felt when she saw her mother cry every weekend, knowing that her children were going to leave her, and how it felt to listen to her brother calling out in vain for their mother during the night. These were the very feelings that had led to her sadness and insecurity. Yet now she was a mother, she seemed unconcerned that William and Harry should see the full range of her emotions.

But then everyone who saw Diana behind closed doors

encountered the full range of her emotions. In a good mood, she couldn't do enough to help people, be they friends, family, strangers or staff. But that could change within seconds. If she took against someone or suspected them of disloyalty or of plotting against her, they were cut out of her life. Even her own mother suffered long periods of estrangement from Diana.

William and Harry were, arguably, the only people Diana loved consistently. She would repeatedly say, "They mean everything to me." They undoubtedly did, and their sense of security today must be partly down to that; but it wasn't entirely healthy: she couldn't leave them to be quietly confident of her love for them. It was as if she was afraid that if she didn't demonstrate it with treats and hugs or verbalize it, it might not be real, they might not be aware of it. Her love for them was almost obsessive, and it was possessive. Another of her favorite phrases was, "Who loves you most?"

The real problem was that Diana had never been properly mothered herself and therefore didn't know how to be a mother. She behaved more like a big sister to William and Harry—at times, the nannies must have felt as though they had three children to look after. She told Andrew Morton, "I want to bring them up with security, not to anticipate things because they will be disappointed. That's made my own life so much easier. I hug my children to death and get into bed with them at night. I always feed them love and affection. It's so important." What psychologists might say is that it is equally important for a mother to protect her children from emotions that they are too young to be able to process safely.

Their nannies could keep them occupied and their PPOs could keep them safe, but no one could protect them from the emotional extremes of their mother.

THE THREE Rs

Throughout his childhood, Harry followed everywhere in the wake of his big brother, who for so many years overshadowed him. He found himself constantly compared to William, from his nursery school to his public school and, academically at least, he was found wanting. There were tears when his parents took him to Mrs. Mynors' nursery for his first day, in September 1987, as there are with so many children on their first day at school. He started off doing just two mornings a week; he was just three, still very unsure of himself and probably already feeling unease at the domestic situation. Barbara Barnes had vanished and his father had been absent for long stretches. Charles had left in March for a walk in the Kalahari Desert with Sir Laurens van der Post; no sooner was he back from that than he was off on a week's painting holiday in Italy, followed by his usual stint at Balmoral. Diana had stayed firmly in London. The press, ever vigilant, had calculated that they had spent one day in six weeks together. It was not surprising that Harry tried to run after them when they left him that first morning at Mrs. Mynors,' but he was quickly lassoed and distracted. School did not come easily to him.

Harry didn't yet have his brother's outgoing nature and didn't find it easy to mix with other children. They very swiftly picked him out as different and, in those early years, he was not up to defending himself from bullies. He had never been without his brother, his wingman. He might have driven his brother mad at times, and vice versa, but they had been a unit; suddenly for the first time he was having to face life and other children without his protective shield. But he had his moments. In the Christmas play one year he was a goblin, dressed in green tights with a red hat and tabard. He pulled the role off with aplomb, except for the moment when he stuck his tongue out at the expectant photographers. It was a sign of things to come. The next year he had his first speaking role, as a shepherd in the nativity play.

From Mrs. Mynors' he progressed aged five to Wetherby in 1989, starting with mornings only for the first few weeks. Having a September birthday, he was younger than most of the other children in the year; but at the end of that first term he sang a solo in the Christmas concert. He would come home most days clutching artwork that his mother proudly put up in her dressing room. Diana tried whenever possible to take him to school in the mornings, but getting home in time for the afternoon pick-up after a day of engagements was more difficult. On the way home she would stop and pop into the local supermarket to buy Twiglets or some other treat. "I know they're not good for them," she would say, "but they do love them." It was at Wetherby that Diana first showed off her athleticism—and her competitive nature—when she kicked off her shoes at sports day and triumphed in the mothers' race, while Charles, to her glee, came last in the fathers' race.

Charles was no runner but, like Diana, he was an avid skier. It was one of the few activities they enjoyed together, and every year they went with friends to Klosters in Switzerland. It was the backdrop to a photo-opportunity that had become something of a tradition. The media got some good colorful shots, and sometimes a few words, and in return the photographers undertook to leave the couple alone to ski and enjoy their holiday in peace. In 1991, the press were only too delighted to learn that William and Harry would be joining them. What came as a surprise was that their father would not.

Charles had promised the boys that now they were old enough, he would take them skiing. He was looking forward to introducing them to one of his favorite sports, to watching them experience the thrill of the mountains. And thrill it was, especially for Harry.

He took to skis like a duck to water, and with the fearlessness that only a six-year-old can muster. By the end of a week he was whizzing down the runs, while William approached the whole exercise with infinitely more caution. But what should have been a happy family break—and a happy, united family photo-opportunity—was sabotaged. There had been a terrible accident in Klosters three years before when an avalanche had killed one of their party, Major Hugh Lindsay, and badly injured Patti Palmer-Tomkinson. It had narrowly missed the Prince. He had no qualms about going back but Diana, understandably, didn't want to go to Klosters ever again. Without telling Charles, Diana quietly settled on the Austrian resort of Lech and booked a holiday for herself and the boys with a few other friends and alerted the press. The booking was for half-term, when she knew Charles would be unable to come. He was hosting a shooting weekend for eighteen friends at Sandringham, which she knew he would never be able to call off. It was not the first time, nor the last, that the boys would be used as pawns in their ongoing war.

The year did not improve as the months passed. There was a summer holiday in the Mediterranean on the *Alexander,* a superluxurious yacht that the late Greek shipping magnate, John Latsis, frequently lent the Prince. It was the third biggest yacht in the world and had a room full of computer games, which the boys fell on with delight—but nothing could entirely distract them from the tension that pervaded the ship. A tour of Canada followed, where the family stayed on the Royal Yacht *Britannia*, but by now they were communicating through their Private Secretaries. They hadn't shared a bedroom in years. The wheels were rapidly falling off the marriage, as a tense and difficult Christmas at Sandringham heralded 1992, the year that the Queen, in her Christmas address to the nation, would call her *annus horribilis.*

In June, *Diana: Her True Story* was published, but not before its serialization in the *Sunday Times* had received massive publicity. Under the headline, "Diana driven to five suicide bids by 'uncaring' Charles," the first installment revealed her bulimia, her husband's indifference towards her, his obsession with his mistress, his shortcomings as a father, and the loneliness and isolation she had felt for so many years, trapped in a loveless marriage within a hostile court and a cold and disapproving bunch of in-laws. No one knew at the time that it was the handiwork of the Princess herself, but it had a compelling authority and many of her closest friends and family members were openly quoted and thanked in the acknowledgments.

Diana denied any involvement, which prompted her brother-in-law, Sir Robert Fellowes, by this time the Queen's Private Secretary, to appeal to the Chairman of the Press Complaints Commission, who publicly condemned the serialization as an "odious exhibition of journalists dabbling their fingers in the stuff of other people's souls in a manner which adds nothing to the legitimate public interest in the situation of the heir to the throne."

Diana's response was to pay a very public visit to Harry's godmother, Carolyn Bartholomew, one of the most quoted sources in the book, and in front of the waiting photographers to give her old flatmate a big hug. The Queen refused Fellowes' immediate offer to resign. All sorts of stories in the book pointed to Diana, stories that were almost true but never quite as everyone else involved remembered them, but it was not until years later that the whole truth emerged: that Diana had actively sought out the journalist via an intermediary to kick her husband where it hurt. Yet in doing so, she had failed to consider how hurt and humiliated William and Harry would be by this attack on their father and by this exposé of their private life.

Diana had lived a charmed existence as far as the newspapers were concerned. She lived dangerously but she got away with it. Given the men who came to visit her by day and night, the love letters she wrote, the phone calls she made, the restaurants she openly ate in with male friends, the late-night hospital visits to see a doctor on the pretext of visiting patients, there was surprisingly little negative gossip about her in the press. And Morton's book firmly established her as the injured party.

This was because she had wooed a number of key figures, not least the late Sir David English, who ran the highly successful *Daily Mail* and *Mail on Sunday*, which between them accounted for the biggest middle-market circulation in Britain. He basked in the warmth of her charms, but he also recognized that both titles had a high proportion of female readers, so taking Diana's side against her husband's was sound business. There were other editors she targeted, my own father—Sir John Junor—among them, plus one or two influential journalists, including Richard Kay at the *Daily Mail*. She rang them with stories, invited them to lunch and flattered their male egos.

But no amount of wooing could have prevented "Squidgygate," the transcript of a flirtatious thirty-minute telephone conversation between Diana and James Gilbey, which originally appeared in the *Sun* but was immediately reproduced elsewhere. The *Sun* set up a telephone hotline and for thirty-six pence a minute callers could hear the tape for themselves. He called her "Darling" fourteen times and "Squidgy" or "Squidge" fifty-three times, hence the name. Aside from the romantic endearments, Diana said Charles made her life "real, real torture," and described the look the Queen Mother had given her at lunch: "It's not hatred, it's sort of interest and pity...I was very bad at lunch and I nearly started blubbing. I just felt really sad and empty and thought, Bloody hell, after all I've done for this fucking family."

The transcript appeared at the end of August 1992. It could not have been more upsetting or humiliating for everyone involved—although Diana's PPO, Ken Wharfe, said she had raised the subject with him "in a fairly light-hearted way—the fact that it had reached the front of a national tabloid newspaper." She admitted she had even rung the *Sun*'s hotline, which allowed readers to hear the tape for themselves. "When I asked if it was her, she said, 'Of course it was.'"

It was less funny perhaps for Harry, who just a few days later began his first term at boarding school. The phone conversation had taken place some time before its publication, late at night on

New Year's Eve in 1989. Diana was on a landline at Sandringham and Gilbey in a car parked in Oxfordshire. It was said a radio ham in Oxford picked it up, but some suspected GCHQ, MI5's listening post in Cheltenham was involved. In the light of the phone-hacking trials, in which journalists and former executives of two News International newspapers were on trial for intercepting mobile phone messages, it is perfectly possible it was neither.

Harry was still just seven when he arrived at Ludgrove in September 1992. As before, his birthday made him young for his academic year but, because of the atmosphere at home, the move away came not a moment too soon. Boarding came as a shock, as it does to most children, whatever age they start, but Ludgrove provided a safe environment for both boys during this period when their family life was disintegrating and the people they loved most were tearing each other apart. Ludgrove is a small, family-run private preparatory school set in 130 acres of Berkshire countryside near Wokingham. It has been in the same family for three generations: today Simon Barber is headmaster and his wife, Sophie, is responsible for the pastoral care of the boys. In William and Harry's day it was Simon's parents, Gerald and Janet Barber, and a co-headmaster, Nichol Marston. Charles and Diana had their differences, but they were united in their choice of schools for the boys and they always put on a show of unity for school events.

Ludgrove is about as homely as a school could be. One little boy remarked, "It's like having a giant sleepover." In the first year there are plenty of female staff around, the dormitories are full of soft toys, posters and superheroes adorn the bedding and the emphasis is not on work, but on settling in, making friends and having fun. The boys have their lunch ahead of everyone else, they go to bed ahead of everyone else and they go down to the headmaster's homely sitting room in their pajamas every Sunday evening for stories. Simon Barber readily acknowledges that some boys miss home, but says, "when they're busy, all together, all doing the same thing, full boarding, they have such fun. And if they are homesick, there's a massive support network from their own peer group and the adult population. The boys form very close and loyal friendships because they're all in it together and remain friends for life, a lot of them. They have a common bond and when they have reunions they become prep school boys again."

The Barbers senior kept a watchful eye on both Princes. They didn't give them special treatment but they were well aware of the difficulties at home—there was scarcely a man or woman in the country who wasn't. With just over 180 boys aged between eight and thirteen, the school is small enough and the staff ratio high enough for them to know exactly how each boy is faring inside and outside the classroom. Janet was like a mother to "my boys," as she called them—and still calls them when she meets an old Ludgrovian today, no matter what their age. She quickly picked up on problems and if a child was unsettled for any reason, she stepped in straightaway to help, as if he were her own son. It is unlikely that she ever had to support another child through the particular difficulties Harry was experiencing. But she and her husband were key to helping Harry survive those years.

Harry did not shine academically. But it was clear from early on that he had a talent for sport and some of the other extracurricular activities. Ludgrove offers every sport imaginable. As well as the more usual ball games—cricket, football, rugby and tennis—at which Harry excelled, they play squash, Eton fives and golf on their own nine-hole golf course. The boys make dens in the woods and in summer occasionally camp on the golf course and have singsongs around a campfire. The school is also big on music, theater and art, and an old milking parlor has been turned into an art block where boys can also do ceramics and carpentry. Newspapers were delivered daily and every morning they discussed current affairs, with a test every Saturday. It was not unusual during William and Harry's years at the school for the Barbers to pretend that the papers hadn't been delivered to protect them from the skirmishes in the War of the Waleses that were being played out on the front pages.

During that first term, the papers were full of a disastrous trip his parents took to Korea. Diana refused to go at first, but it had been arranged months in advance, as all royal tours are, and the Queen intervened. Only then did she agree—but she didn't go with good grace. She made no attempt to disguise her feelings. A performer of the first order, she looked sad and miserable and frequently on the verge of tears. The Prince looked no happier and, although he worked hard to cover up for her by doing all the talking and smiling, nothing could salvage the situation. In private, they could not bring themselves to look at each other, let alone exchange a civil word. They even stopped pretending in front of their staff. The media talked about nothing but the state of the marriage. Peter Westmacott, the Deputy Private Secretary (now British Ambassador in Washington) with the unenviable task of accompanying them, took aside the *Daily Mirror*'s royal reporter, the late James Whitaker, to complain. Whitaker was sympathetic but commented, "Peter, you really can't say this is a marriage made in heaven."

"I am not saying it is," said Westmacott. "What I am saying is that you guys are getting it so grossly wrong, you're misreporting what's going on and ignoring the substance of the visit."

Two hours later *Sky News* was interrupting broadcasts to say, "Palace official confirms marriage is on the rocks." The next day the tabloids were full of the story: "Palace official in gaffe," "Palace office confirms marriage over." When a horrified Westmacott tried to explain to his boss what had happened, the Prince was understanding. He had always felt, he said, "It was a waste of time trying to talk sense to these people."

As for the Princess, she was hell-bent on separation. Westmacott spent the flight to Hong Kong trying to talk her out of it. It would be best for everyone, he argued, if they could find a *modus vivendi*. She had her own friends, her own life, the children had the stability of two parents and she was good at her job. Why did she want to destroy it all? His words fell on deaf ears. She was determined.

SEPARATION

William was ten, and Harry just eight and still struggling to settle into the alien world of boarding when the Princess made her move. It was very soon after the Korean fiasco and once again she used the children to outmaneuver Charles. Every year the Prince and Princess had hosted a shooting party at Sandringham for sixteen friends, who came to stay for three days with their children, and the Prince had organized it, as he always did, around the children's half-term. In 1992 that was the weekend of 20 and 21 November, William and Harry had been looking forward to it and so had the Prince of Wales; the boys loved Sandringham, loved shooting with their father and were excited about seeing their friends. But it was not to be.

Less than a week beforehand, Charles discovered that Diana had decided to take the children to stay with the Queen at Windsor Castle instead. (Friday 20 November was, coincidentally, the date of a devastating fire at the castle, which occurred while the Queen was in residence, raged for fifteen hours and caused millions of pounds' worth of damage.) Charles explained the situation to his mother who then spoke to Diana, but the Princess announced that if she couldn't go to Windsor then she would take the boys to Highgrove. Charles asked whether she might not at least let the boys come to Sandringham, even if she was determined to stay away herself, but she refused. On the advice of her lawyer, she wrote a careful letter of explanation in which she said that she felt the atmosphere at Sandringham would not be conducive to a happy weekend for the children. Nor could she be sure that he would not expose them to guests whose presence would be unwelcome to her (she meant Camilla). The Prince's patience finally snapped. Painful though it would be for everyone, there was no alternative but to call a halt to the marriage.

Thus, on the afternoon of 9 December 1992, John Major, then Prime Minister, stood up at the dispatch box in the House of Commons before a packed but silent House and read aloud the following statement: "It is announced from Buckingham Palace that, with regret, the Prince and Princess of Wales have decided to separate. Their Royal Highnesses have no plans to divorce and their constitutional positions are unaffected. This decision has been reached amicably and they will both continue to participate fully in the upbringing of their children."

The Prince was on a Business in the Community visit to Holyhead that day, accompanied by its Chief Executive, Julia Cleverdon. They had worked together closely for ten years, and that afternoon he told her about the separation. In all the years she had known him, she had never seen him so deeply miserable.

It was a Wednesday, the day of the nativity play at Ludgrove, which for the First Years was held in the afternoon. Prince Charles was there for Harry.

He and the Princess had both been down to Ludgrove in advance of the Prime Minister's statement to explain the situation first to the Barbers and then, in the homely surroundings of the headmaster's sitting room, to break the news to their sons. William's rather grown-up response was to hope that they would both be happier now. He let more of his feelings be known, perhaps, in a letter to his trusted nanny, Olga Powell. She wrote him a very personal letter back consoling him about the impending separation. Harry had always managed to take these emotional tsunamis in his stride—at least on the outside.

The households were swiftly divided. Diana took sole possession of Kensington Palace and kept the two senior butlers, Harold Brown and Paul Burrell. Charles took butler number three, Bernie Flannery, and continued to live at Highgrove; he took over

York House, within the St. James's Palace complex, as a London home. They kept their joint office at St. James's Palace, where the two teams were united and cooperative with one another, particularly over arrangements for the children, whose time was divided between the two of them.

That Christmas, just two weeks later, in her traditional television broadcast to the nation, the Queen described 1992 as "a somber year." In the space of eight months, The Duke and the Duchess of York separated, the Princess Royal divorced her husband Mark Phillips, Andrew Morton's book was published, the Duchess of York was photographed having her toes sucked by her financial advisor, there was the fire at Windsor Castle—which of all her residences is the one the Queen most regards as home—and her son and heir separated from his wife.

Diana turned down the Queen's invitation to spend Christmas at Sandringham and went instead to her brother at Althorp. It was the first time the boys had been without her on that most special of all days and, although she rang them on Christmas morning, it was not the same. However, five days later they were jetting off to the Caribbean with Diana's friend Catherine Soames and her son. It could and should have been a glorious holiday, but they were followed by the press. It was the same when they went skiing in Lech a couple of months later. Everywhere they went with their mother, the cameras went too, and she insisted they smile for them. Even the excitement of hurtling down hair-raising rides with their mother on outings to Thorpe Park were marred by the ubiquitous bank of lenses.

It was no coincidence the cameras knew where to find them. Diana tipped them off. She was heavily engaged in a campaign to win public approval. She was seen to be the one who took the boys to theme parks, cinemas, McDonald's and on foreign holidays—with her they had fun. All Charles was ever seen to do was take them hunting, shooting or fishing—all of them elitist sports—or to church dressed in suits and ties. With her they looked like children, decked out in jeans and baseball caps. The public was left to draw its own conclusions.

No sooner were William and Harry back at school for the spring term, in January 1993, than another tape recording was making news. This time it was the *Daily Mirror* that led the field in publishing the intimate late-night telephone ramblings between Charles and Camilla. It was the ultimate invasion of privacy and humiliation. Though she must have enjoyed a little *Schadenfreude*, even Diana was embarrassed on his behalf. Eleven minutes of tape could be distilled into one: the Prince of Wales musing the possibility of turning into a Tampax so as to always be close to the woman he adored.

Dubbed Camillagate, it provoked a puritanical outburst that verged on hysteria. Questions were asked about his fitness to be King and, in the mounting fever, there were demands from Cabinet ministers that he give up Mrs. Parker Bowles. Meanwhile the cartoonists went to town.

The Prince of Wales was mortified and not just for himself—for Camilla, who was bombarded with hateful letters and accused of breaking up the royal marriage, for his children, for her children, for everyone inadvertently dragged into this horrible mess, and for the monarchy itself. His private life had yet again damaged the institution that his mother had dedicated her life to protecting, and that he in turn must protect for his son. He was furious that his phone had been illegally bugged and furious that the press had published the tape; but he was also humiliated beyond words.

Unlike the Squidgygate tape, this was not just one conversation but a compilation of several they had had over several months around Christmas 1989—shortly before Diana's conversation was recorded. Where it came from and who made it has never been determined but, like Diana's, it wasn't published until four years later. In response to calls for an investigation, the Home Secretary, Kenneth Clarke, told the House of Commons, "There is nothing to investigate…I am absolutely certain that the allegation that this is anything to do with the security services of GCHQ…is being put out by newspapers, who I think feel rather guilty that they are using plainly tapped telephone calls."

Diana had always believed that her telephone conversations were being listened into—she suspected the Buckingham Palace switchboard—but her concerns were, not surprisingly, dismissed as paranoia. However, ten years later, stories were again inexplicably appearing in the tabloids, so much so that William and Harry began to think their friends were responsible. They began to feel they couldn't trust anyone. It was another ten years or so after this that the phone-hacking scandal came to light, suggesting that Diana's fears might not have been so paranoid after all. In 2007 Clive Goodman, the former *News of the World* royal editor, and Glenn Mulcaire, a private investigator, were sent to jail for hacking William and Harry's voicemail, but the practice turned out to have been far more widespread. Police investigations culminated in the trial in 2014 of two former editors, Andy Coulson and Rebekah Brooks (née Wade) and five others. During the trial it transpired that Goodman had been in possession of a copy of the Green Book, a telephone directory containing all the home numbers of the Royal Family.

William had made very good friends when he started at Ludgrove with another new boy called Thomas van Straubenzee, whose younger brother, Henry, began at the same time as Harry. Henry and Harry also became very close friends and, although the two sets of brothers went on to different schools after Ludgrove (William and Harry to Eton, the van Straubenzees to Harrow), for the next few years the four boys moved as one. And, true to Ludgrove form, formed friendships that lasted into adulthood. They visited each other during the school holidays, they went on holidays together and very much became part of each other's families. There was an extra bond, perhaps, because Tom and Henry were two of the few friends who had known Diana.

By coincidence, Tom and Henry's parents, Claire and her husband Alex van Straubenzee, had both known the Spencer family for many years. Claire had worked with Sarah at *Vogue* in the early 1970s, and Diana had been one of Claire's sister's best friends. Alex subsequently stayed in Sarah's flat in Fulham for a while when he first came out of the Army in 1979. She shared it with three or four other girls, and Diana was their cleaner, coming in two hours a week. Schoolfriends say she had been obsessively clean and tidy; on weekends out when she stayed in her sisters' flats in London, she had happily done their washing and housework—with hindsight, all classic psychological symptoms that might have indicated an eating disorder.

Every year the Vans, as they were known, took a gang of boys to Polzeath in north Cornwall. Each of their sons—Thomas, Henry and Charlie, the youngest—invited their closest friends, and William and Harry were always among them. They always rented the same house on the cliff top and always went in the same week, immediately after the public schools broke up and before the state school holidays began, when it was slightly less crowded. Polzeath is very popular, like many of the resorts along that north coast. It has a generous sandy beach with a Kelly's Cornish Ice Cream van invariably parked on it and it's known as a good safe place for surfing.

The boys were very young when they first went—ten and eight—and their policemen were almost like nannies. Once, Harry cut his leg on some barnacles and started to cry. The child was clearly in agony. His leg was bleeding profusely and the salt water was making it sting. "Harry, pull yourself together and stop whingeing," said his PPO, Graham Cracker. "It's just a scratch." When a concerned Mrs. Van tried to intervene, he batted her away. "He's perfectly all right."

What both boys liked about going to Cornwall with the van Straubenzees was that it was a perfectly normal English family holiday. It was what all the other boys at Ludgrove did as well, so they felt normal. It was bucket and spade, sandcastles, cricket and volleyball on the beach; they could walk down to the center of the village from the house, and go into the shops or the little Spar supermarket, and with baseball caps pulled down low, nobody noticed them. In any case, the shopkeepers were all used to seeing them. They could catch shrimps in the rock pools at low tide, which they barbecued, and they could put on their wetsuits, take their boards and surf when the wind was up. It was organized chaos, and in the mornings they would all eat Mrs. Van's famous cooked breakfasts (as they still do when they visit). Sometimes, when they were a bit older, the boys would go to the Mariners, the pub at Rock that became the mecca for drunken, rowdy and mostly underage public school children, but they didn't much enjoy it because they were usually recognized and pestered. Conversely, although they were often spotted in the garden by people walking their dogs past the house, they were never pestered or photographed there.

Later in the summer, all four boys would exchange surfboards and barbecues for sumptuous luxury and gourmet cuisine with the Prince of Wales on the Latsis super-yacht; and swap the cold Atlantic breakers for the still warmth of the Mediterranean. And then they would all go to stay with the Princess at Kensington Palace, which was much more informal. The van Straubenzee boys loved going there. Diana was good fun and full of laughter and smutty jokes. And among other treats, she would take them all to the Royal Tournament, which, until its demise in 1999, was held every summer at Earls Court in London. It was a military tattoo on a huge scale, the largest in the world—an extraordinary spectacle involving two and a half thousand servicemen and women, rousing music, bagpipes, flags, military bands, and awesome displays of horses, tanks, guns, motorbikes, field carriages, and everything military; it was noisy and thrilling. William and Harry had been taken to see it since they were very young, and it's perfectly possible that Harry's childhood fascination with the Army and his ambition to be a soldier began right there.

A SIGNIFICANT OTHER

Being a single parent presented the Prince of Wales with the sort of dilemma that faces every working parent who must suddenly start taking turns with the child care following a separation. Diana still had Olga Powell to look after the boys; and that continuity of love and care will have helped them through the separation and all the difficulty that surrounded it. For while they were always their mother's top priority, they must sometimes have felt that her own problems took precedence, and that maybe she was the one that needed looking after, not them. It is very easy for a child, of any age, to slip into a parenting role in such circumstances, and it would be surprising if William and Harry hadn't.

At ten and eight, they were too old for a traditional nanny. What Charles wanted was someone who was more of a companion and big sister; someone who could take them riding, or to meets, or to the fairground, to drive them to their friends' houses, or to the dentist or the hairdresser. He wanted someone who would generally look after them and keep them entertained in his absence and exert some discipline over them, which Charles signally failed to do. By very good fortune, a splendidly ditzy young aristocrat called Alexandra Legge-Bourke, known as Tiggy, had been taken on in the Prince's office as an aide to his Private Secretary, Richard Aylard. Charles had known her family for years; her mother, Shân, and aunt, Victoria, were both Ladies-in-Waiting to Princess Anne. Tiggy, who was and is the biggest bundle of fun, was twenty-eight and perfectly qualified, having previously run a nursery school of her own called Tiggywinkles.

She was given the job of looking after the boys and it could not have been a more successful appointment. They adored her from the very start, especially Harry, who is still extremely close to her. She was an overgrown tomboy, totally on their wavelength, and loved all the outdoor things they loved. She told ridiculous jokes and laughed at theirs; she liked the same kind of music they did, watched the same videos and television programs, yet at the same time she managed to get them to do what they were told, without ever being officiously strict. If their father told them to go to bed, they would ignore him or wheedle him round. If Tiggy told them, they would call her a "Bossy Old Bat," but go.

She once said of them, "I give them what they need at this stage: fresh air, a rifle and a horse. She [their mother] gives them a tennis racket and a bucket of popcorn at the movies." Diana looked upon the blossoming relationship between her sons and Tiggy Legge-Bourke with horror and jealousy.

The years of separation were not happy ones for the Princess. She developed a passion for Oliver Hoare, an art dealer friend of the Prince of Wales, whom she had met through her husband. He was often seen arriving at Kensington Palace and there was much gossip. Hoare was married and not inclined to leave his wife. He tried to cool the relationship, at which Diana started making silent telephone calls to his wife at their family home. Eventually his wife contacted the police and the calls were traced to Kensington Palace. The story found its way into the press, much to the fury of the Princess, who immediately blamed her husband and one of his staff for leaking it, convinced that they were out to smear her name. It had actually been leaked by a boy who was at school with one of the Hoare children.

There was no campaign to discredit Diana following the separation. In fact, quite the reverse. Charles had given specific instructions to his staff to say and do nothing to reflect badly upon the Princess. Shortly after the split, he had declared independence from Buckingham Palace and, with the Queen's agreement, formed his own press office to which he had recruited two highly experienced press officers, both from solid civil service jobs: Allan Percival and Sandy Henney. He made it blindingly clear to them both that no matter what Diana did or said, she would always be the mother of his children and anything that hurt the Princess would hurt them.

For all that, Diana saw conspiracies everywhere and sent anonymous, unnerving and sometimes poisonous messages to a range of people, including Patrick Jephson and Tiggy. Even Camilla had threatening telephone calls in the dead of the night. "I've sent someone to kill you," she would say. "They're outside in the garden. Look out of the window; can you see them?" For a woman on her own in a house in the country in the middle of nowhere and with no protection, it was frightening. But no one dared confront the Princess about the messages for fear of provoking a scene or, in the case of staff, being sacked and joining the long list of people—cooks, housemaids, dressers, secretaries and butlers—who had unfairly and peremptorily been shown the door.

The Prince picked up many of Diana's casualties, even Diana herself. She drove him to distraction in many ways. He was angered by some things she did, not least her decision to retire from public life, which she did dramatically on a public platform, despite pleas from him, the Queen and the Duke of Edinburgh to withdraw if she liked, but to do it quietly so that she could change her mind at a later date if ever she wanted to. She ignored them all. At a charity luncheon in December 1993, to the dismay of all those charities who relied upon her patronage for their fundraising, she said, "Over the next few months I will be seeking a more suitable way of combining a meaningful public role with, hopefully, a more private life. I hope you can find it in your hearts to understand and give me the time and space that has been lacking in recent years... Your kindness and affection have carried me through some of the most difficult periods, and always your love and care have eased the journey."

Charles found conversations with her difficult and upsetting. He seemed to do nothing more than provide a focus for her anger; but he did care very much that she should be looked after. He worried about her and was always there at the end of a telephone, right to the end, when things went wrong with a love affair or the children or even the press. She would ring him up in tears and he would do whatever needed to be done to sort out the problem.

She also shared her emotions and confidences with her sons, particularly William, laying far more on his young shoulders than was good for him. He was very caring, very protective, always keeping an eye to see she was all right, always there with boxes of tissues or chocolates when he knew she was unhappy. Harry, younger and less burdened with responsibility of the firstborn, was more carefree, busy with his games and toys and his own affairs, but taking it all in nonetheless.

There was one problem that Charles couldn't sort out. No longer able to go to Highgrove, Diana wanted a house in the country. The boys loved getting out of London, and at times she felt they were like caged animals in Kensington. She approached her brother Charles Spencer who, after their father's death in 1991, had inherited the earldom along with the family home. She had identified a house on the estate—which had two hundred-odd cottages and farmhouses on it—that would suit them perfectly: far enough away from the big house to leave him undisturbed, but safely within the grounds to afford her and her children privacy. He said she couldn't have it; he didn't want the media circus that her presence would attract. The real reason only came out after Diana's death when Paul Burrell was tried for allegedly stealing some of her possessions. Diana, whose relationship with her family was as volatile and unpredictable as with her friends and staff, had randomly cut her brother out of her life and he had been very hurt. She, in turn, was very upset to be refused the house. Sadly, the relationship was never repaired.

Instead, Diana relied on friends with houses in the country to take the boys to when they were sick of London, or had an exeat from school. She loved the normality of her friends' houses, and immediately got stuck into domestic chores, encouraging the boys to do the same. She'd unload the dishwasher, chop onions, peel potatoes, lay the table, do all the ordinary tasks that go on in ordinary households. One of those friends was Julia Samuel (who is now one of Prince George's godmothers). She and her husband, Michael, have four children, two of whom were the same age as William and Harry, and at the time their country house was very close to Ludgrove. Diana often took the boys there for weekends out—or they would meet up in London, where the Samuels had a house in Hyde Park Gate, opposite Kensington Palace. They would go to the movies together or to a concert at Wembley. For many years they couldn't have been closer, but suddenly the calls stopped coming—for some reason Julia never understood—and for a year there was very little contact. Then, as suddenly as the friendship had stopped, it started again, and she and Diana were once again close.

Another friend was Lady Annabel Goldsmith, who lived in a beautiful Queen Anne house on the edge of Richmond Park, where Diana occasionally took the boys. It was a colorful and rather chaotic household with lots of barking dogs and, on Sundays, her large family, into which William and Harry folded comfortably. Annabel wrote in her memoirs, "She would ring and ask if I was going to be at home and if she could come and join me. She would land like a butterfly, have lunch and dart off again, sometimes bringing the boys with her, sometimes not. She would drive herself down... dash through the back door often clutching a present, greet the staff who all loved her, try to evade the mass of dogs yapping at her feet and settle down to amuse us... Her repartee became an essential part of these Sunday lunches, interrupted occasionally when she vanished to the kitchen to do the washing up."

The last person who might want to rock the boat at this stage was the Prince of Wales, but to mark twenty-five years since his investiture as Prince of Wales, he had authorized a biography by the respected writer and broadcaster, Jonathan Dimbleby, and an accompanying documentary for television. Dimbleby was given unrestricted access to the archives at St. James's Palace and Windsor Castle, the freedom to read and quote from the Prince's journals, diaries and the many thousands of letters he had written since childhood, and permission to speak to his family and friends about him, openly and at length.

The consequences were catastrophic. This well-intentioned venture caused terrible upset within the Royal Family and led directly to Camilla's divorce from Andrew Parker Bowles, Richard Aylard's departure, Diana's *Panorama* interview, and yet more debate about the Prince's fitness to be King. And it was yet another embarrassment for two young boys.

The documentary was called *Charles: the Private Man, the Public Role*. It aired in July 1994, and provided a useful insight into the Prince of Wales and how he spent his time. It ran for two and a half hours, but what most of the fourteen million viewers remembered about the film ran to no longer than three minutes.

Dimbleby asked the Prince about his infidelity: "Did you try to be faithful and honorable to your wife when you took on the vows of marriage?"

"Yes," replied the Prince, "until it became irretrievably broken down, us both having tried."

Camilla, he said, was "a great friend of mine...she has been a friend for a very long time."

At a press conference the following day, Richard Aylard, who had presided over the project and encouraged the question, confirmed that the adultery was with Mrs. Parker Bowles.

His reasoning had been sound, if flawed. The Prince had to be asked the question in the light of the Squidgy and Camillagate tapes, and of Andrew Morton's book. He could confirm it (the truth), deny it (thus lying) or say he was not prepared to comment, which would lead to further harassment by the paparazzi, who had already made their life hell. The decision was made to tell the truth. Charles wasn't the first man to have found comfort in another woman after his marriage had irretrievably broken down, but no one heard the justification. All they heard was the confession.

"NOT FIT TO REIGN" screamed the *Daily Mirror*. Other headlines were similar.

Diana drove down to Ludgrove to talk to the children; there was only so much the Barbers could do. William was more vocal than Harry. As Diana later said in her *Panorama* interview, "William asked me what had been going on and could I answer his questions, which I did. He said was that the reason why our marriage had broken up? And I said, well, there were three of us in this marriage and the pressures of the media was another factor, so the two together were very difficult. But although I still loved Papa, I couldn't live under the same roof as him, and likewise with him."

The book, simply called *The Prince of Wales*, followed in the autumn and was serialized in the *Sunday Times*. The book itself was a comprehensive portrait of a very complex man, but the extracts gave the impression that Charles was a whiner.

What could have been an excellent vehicle for the Prince turned into an own goal. His parents were deeply hurt by his account of his childhood, and Andrew Parker Bowles was left with little alternative but to bring his marriage to Camilla to an end. They were divorced the following January and he subsequently married his long-term girlfriend, Rosemary Pitman.

Sir John Riddell, who had left his role as Private Secretary to the Prince in 1990, was surprised that his advisors had let it happen.

"They released Jonathan Dimbleby and the Prince of Wales on to the Scottish moor together at 9.30 and they came back breathless and excited at 4.30; and when you go for a very exhausting walk with anybody—if you went with Goebbels—after a time the blood circulates, the joints ease up, the breath gets short—you'd pour out your heart to anyone, even Goebbels. Jonathan Dimbleby's charms are huge so the Prince of Wales gave him all that stuff about how unhappy he was when he was a boy—the Queen never spoke to him, the Duke of Edinburgh was beastly to him—and it very much upset them.

"Everyone was told this book would finally show what a marvelous person he was; and people were bored out of their wits by Business in the Community and the Prince's Trust; they wanted to know about their private life. We're interested in who they're going to bec with, except we got rather bored by that because we couldn't keep up with it."

No sooner had the excitement over Dimbleby's book started to fade than Anna Pasternak published *Princess in Love*, her saccharine account of James Hewitt's five-year love affair with Diana.

The Queen had called 1992 her *annus horribilis*, but she maybe should have held her breath. And it wasn't over yet. There was still more to upset a small boy's security.

THE FINAL STRAW

In September 1995, at the age of thirteen, William arrived for his first term at Eton College, one of the best—and certainly the most famous—public schools in the world, having successfully passed his common entrance exam. The whole family turned out to take him, Charles, Diana, and Harry, putting on a display of unity and smiles for the inevitable press and the curious public. It was a daunting prospect for William. He was not just leaving the security of Ludgrove, which he knew so well, for a school that was almost ten times the size, but he was leaving his brother, whom he relied on as much as Harry relied on him, and the reassurance of all his friends and teachers. He knew he was going to be an object of interest from locals, boys and "beaks" alike (Eton-speak for teachers); everyone would be looking at him, wondering what he was like, and, what's more, knowing all the lurid details of his home life.

That very day the Princess had been on the front pages again with yet more revelations about her love life. After Oliver Hoare, she had fallen for the England rugby union captain, Will Carling. She had met him at the Chelsea Harbour Club, the exclusive gym where she used to go to work out in the early mornings. Harry was mad about rugby, William was more interested in football; nevertheless, Carling was a hero to both boys and suddenly he was in their lives. Diana had taken them to watch him play, he was a regular visitor to Kensington Palace and he had given them each rugby shirts that were no doubt their pride and joy. Who knows whether they had known the true nature of their mother's friendship with him. But on that first day of the Michaelmas term, every man and woman in the country was left in little doubt. Oliver Hoare's wife, Diane, had threatened to divorce her husband only when his affair with Diana became public knowledge. Julia Carling was less tolerant. She had no proof, but was convinced Diana and her husband were more than just good friends and ended her marriage to Will in a bitter, protracted and very high-profile way that ensured the tabloids had plenty of material to keep their readers titillated and Diana's name in the news.

A few days after saying goodbye to his brother, Harry went back to Ludgrove for the start of the new term, no doubt relieved to be back with his friends and the safe cocoon that the routine of school provided. What neither he nor William knew (nor anyone at Buckingham Palace or St. James's Palace, nor even the Chairman of the BBC which screened the program) was that their mother had plans actively under way for one final bombshell that would hit right at the heart of the institution that was her children's future.

On the evening of 5 November, a small film crew from the BBC flagship current affairs program, *Panorama,* including the journalist Martin Bashir, visited Diana at Kensington Palace posing as hi-fi salesmen. It was a Sunday when all her staff were off. Only a handful of people knew who they really were, or why they were there, and it was kept that way until shortly before the program aired at 9:30 p.m. on 20 November, fifteen days later. Viewers watched transfixed as one of the most explosive and deadly fifty-eight minutes of television unfolded in front of their eyes.

HRH Diana, Princess of Wales, sitting forlornly in Kensington Palace, wiped away the occasional tear as she talked about her marriage, her in-laws, her love affairs and her children.

She described her feelings of isolation and emptiness, of being a strong woman, a free spirit. She talked about her bulimia, her self-harming, her cries for help. She talked about the Prince's friends who waged a war in the media against her, indicating that she was "unstable, sick and should be put in a home." She talked about his obsession with Camilla—"There were three of us in this marriage,

so it was a bit crowded"—and "the enemy," her "husband's department" that tried to undermine her. She had held those telephone
conversations with James Gilbey, she admitted, and she had made
calls to Oliver Hoare, but not three hundred. She had had an
affair with James Hewitt, whom she had adored, and she had been
devastated when his book came out "because I trusted him, and
because...I worried about the reaction of my children...and it
was very distressing for me that a friend of mine, who I had trusted,
had made money out of me...The first thing I did was rush down
to talk to my children. And William produced a box of chocolates
and said, 'Mummy, I think you've been hurt. These are to make
you smile again.'"

For someone whose first instinct had been to rush down and
make sure her children were all right when Hewitt's innocuous
book hit the shelves, this was an inexplicable interview to have
given. A few hundred people might have seen Hewitt's book, a few
thousand at most. This interview was seen by over twenty million
viewers; it was picked up by just about every newspaper and news
magazine in the world, and by every radio and television news
bulletin. This was dynamite, and she knew it. She knew that the
media would go crazy; she knew that it would strike the man who
had spurned her where it hurt most. But was she forgetting that
that man was also her children's father? In those fifty-eight minutes
she had taken a swipe at all the people William and Harry loved
best. And she had talked about things that neither ten-year-olds,
nor even thirteen-year-olds, want to hear, and certainly don't want
their friends to hear either.

But at times like this, Diana wasn't thinking like a mother.
She was the child still nursing those feelings of abandonment
and emptiness that she had carried for so much of her life; hell-
bent on self-aggrandizement and self-justification and ultimately
self-destruction.

The most damaging remarks in the interview had to do with her
doubts that their father should ever be King. She had been devastated, she said, when she heard on the news that he had disclosed

his adultery to Jonathan Dimbleby, but she had admired his honesty, which for someone in his position was "quite something." When asked whether the Prince of Wales would ever be King or would wish to be, she said, "being Prince of Wales produces more freedom now, and being King would be a little bit more suffocating. And because I know the character, I would think that the top job, as I call it, would bring enormous limitations to him, and I don't know whether he could adapt to that."

And for the final deadly twist of the knife, when asked if, when he came of age, she would wish to see Prince William succeed the Queen rather than his father, she said, "My wish is that my husband finds peace of mind, and from that follows other things, yes."

It was pure, unadulterated theater, as those who knew her recognized, but the wider audience saw her as a victim; a sinner perhaps, but a sinner whose only sin was to love—and certainly more sinned against than guilty of any crime herself. She had used Bashir and the BBC just as surely as she had used Andrew Morton.

Patrick Jephson, her Private Secretary, only knew a week before transmission that she had filmed an interview—she hadn't been able to resist telling him—and he managed to establish it was for *Panorama*, which set alarm bells screeching, but she'd refused to tell him any more. "It's terribly moving," was all she would say. "Some of the men who watched were moved to tears. Don't worry, everything will be all right…" He immediately alerted Buckingham Palace and everyone from the Queen to Diana's lawyer, Lord Mishcon, tried to persuade her to reconsider, or at least to let them know what she had said, but they too were left to wait until the credits rolled that November night, to find out just what she had done. Geoff Crawford, Diana's Press Secretary, watching the program in the press office at Buckingham Palace with a group of courtiers, had jovially bet everyone a bottle of champagne that it would be a "damp squib." He handed in his resignation on the spot.

Patrick Jephson hung on a little longer. "*Panorama* . . . was only one (albeit a heavy one) of the several straws that ultimately broke the camel's back of my loyalty," he wrote. "With several years' close-hand experience of my boss's capricious and occasionally cruel approach to personnel management, I was more than ever aware of my professional mortality. However much I might appear to be in favor, I knew my shelf life was akin to that of the organic yoghurt with which the KP fridge was so well stocked."

He tried to broker a reconciliation with Buckingham Palace but it was too late. The Queen had seen and heard enough. Her main concern was for William and Harry, and the effect that all this public point scoring between their parents was having on them, not just the *Panorama* program and its subsequent publicity. The time had come to bring the marriage that had caused such grief, heartache and humiliation to an end. After consulting with the Prime Minister and the Archbishop of Canterbury, she wrote formally and privately to her son and daughter-in-law asking them to divorce as soon as possible. Negotiations began but, while they were still in the early stages, Diana made a premature and unauthorized statement to the press. Calling it "the saddest day of my life," she said she had agreed to Prince Charles's request for a divorce. She would continue to be involved in all decisions relating to the children and would remain at Kensington Palace with offices in St. James's Palace. She would be giving up her title and in future would be known as Diana, Princess of Wales. She made it clear that she had agreed to this last term under pressure.

The Queen, who had kept her lips sealed throughout the years of provocation and the assaults on the institution she had given her life to, was incensed, not least that Diana had broken the confidentiality of the meeting. She immediately issued a statement. "The Queen was most interested to hear that the Princess of Wales had agreed to the divorce. We can confirm that the Prince and Princess of Wales had a private meeting this afternoon at St. James's Palace. At this meeting details of the divorce settlement and the Princess's future role were not discussed. All the details on these matters, including titles, remain to be discussed and settled. This will take time. What the Princess has mentioned are requests rather than decisions at this stage." And more specifically on the question of titles, her Press Secretary, Charles Anson, continued, "The decision to drop the title is the Princess's and the Princess's alone. It is wrong that the Queen or the Prince asked her. I can state categorically that is not true." Adding, "The Palace does not say something specific on a point like this unless we are absolutely sure of the facts."

The months of negotiations that followed could not have been more difficult or acrimonious. Diana was represented by Anthony Julius, a celebrated divorce lawyer from the firm Mishcon de Reya, and the Prince by Fiona Shackleton from the royal solicitors, Farrer and Co. It was Julius who encouraged Diana to give up the title—a move she later regretted and tried unsuccessfully to reverse—in return for a better financial deal. It was said she had first asked for £46 million. The settlement they finally reached in July 1996 gave Diana a financial package thought to be a lump sum of £17.5 million and £350,000 a year to run her private office. Both parties signed a confidentiality agreement so the precise deal was never known but, according to Geoffrey Bignell, who acted as the Prince's financial advisor for ten years, it cleaned Charles out. "I was told to liquidate everything," he said, "all his investments, so that he could give her the cash. He was very unhappy about that. He had no personal wealth left; she took him to the cleaners."

As regards the children, the Prince and Princess retained equal access and responsibility for them. Diana would carry on living at Kensington Palace, but her office would be there rather than at St. James's Palace, as she had wanted. Importantly, she was still to be regarded as a member of the Royal Family and be invited to state and national occasions, which was entirely fitting for the mother of a future King. But there were many who felt that the mother of a future King should also have remained Her Royal Highness. And no matter which of them had been the first to suggest losing the title, taking it away turned into an own goal for the monarchy, and gave Diana's brother emotional ammunition for his eulogy at Westminster Abbey a year later.

As for the future King himself, when Diana asked William if he minded her losing her royal status, he replied, "I don't mind what you're called—you're Mummy."

Ironically, by the time of the *Panorama* interview, she had become quite relaxed about Camilla Parker Bowles. The person she was now fixated on was the effervescent Tiggy Legge-Bourke, who she thought was stealing her children's affection. She started a smear campaign, bombarding Tiggy's answering machine with disturbing messages, and suggesting that Charles might be having an affair with her.

At the office Christmas lunch party at the Lanesborough Hotel in Knightsbridge, she went up Tiggy, who had just been in hospital for a minor operation, and whispered in her ear, "So sorry about the baby." Devastated, Tiggy rushed out of the room in tears, leaving everyone else to party on with Diana in their midst. It was only when libel lawyer Peter Carter-Ruck was instructed by Tiggy four days later that anyone realized what had happened. Just one person already knew. As they were leaving, Diana told Patrick Jephson what she had done. She was "exultant"; and *that* was the straw that finally broke the camel's back.

"I *knew* I was right," she said, and explained to him that Tiggy had practically fainted after she'd told her, and had to be held upright.

"Ma'am, have you any evidence?" he asked.

"I've just told you. Anyway, I don't need evidence. I *know*..."

HUMANITARIAN CRUSADE

Harry wasn't the only boy at Ludgrove whose parents had divorced but not many had done so in such a high-profile way. And not many had mothers who caused such a stir. Diana had no plans to retire from public life and fade quietly into the background after her divorce, as some might have hoped. She was on a roll, buoyed up by a raft of therapists of one sort or another; she saw herself as someone who could save the world, help the sick and dying, support the destitute, the homeless, the addicts and the starving.

She had once said of her visit to Mother Teresa's mission home in Calcutta in 1992, "That was when I found my direction in life." Martin Bashir had asked her if she thought she would ever be Queen. She'd replied, "No...I'd like to be a queen of people's hearts, in people's hearts...when I look at people in public life, I'm not a political animal but I think the biggest disease this world suffers from in this day and age is the disease of people feeling unloved, and I know that I can give love for a minute, for half an hour, for a day, for a month, but I can give—I'm very happy to do that and I want to do that...I think the British people need someone in public life to give affection, to make them feel important, to support them, to give them light in their dark tunnels."

What she did do after the divorce, however, was scale down her support—she dispensed with a Private Secretary, whose role was to offer strategic advice and guidance as well as organize her diary, she dispensed with Ladies-in-Waiting, who would accompany her to events along with the Private Secretary, and she dispensed with Police Protection Officers, who were with her twenty-four hours a

75

day and who would never have allowed her to be driven by someone who had been drinking.

Asked by Bashir whether she thought the monarchy should change, she had said yes, that monarchy and the public "could walk hand in hand, as opposed to be so distant," and in taking William and Harry round homelessness projects, she said she was trying to effect that change. "I've taken William and Harry to people dying of AIDS—albeit I told them it was cancer—I've taken the children to all sorts of areas where I'm not sure anyone of that age in this family has been before. And they have a knowledge—they may never use it, but the seed is there, and I hope it will grow because knowledge is power...I want them to have an understanding of people's emotions, people's insecurities, people's distress, and people's hopes and dreams."

As for her future, she said she saw it as being "an ambassador for this country...When I go abroad we've got sixty to ninety photographers, just from this country, coming with me, so let's use it in a productive way, to help this country."

William and Harry were rightly very proud of their mother and all her achievements. She probably told them too much about everything but, in talking about her work, particularly the less glamorous side, she was preparing them and hoping to mold them for the future. But by the second half of the 1990s, the sixty to ninety photographers were more interested in Diana's love life than her humanitarian expeditions.

A particular focus, in the last few months of her life, was on her involvement with the Al Fayed family. Mohamed Al Fayed, the wealthy, controversial, Egyptian owner of Harrods department store, had been a friend of Diana's father, Earl Spencer, and his wife Raine. Diana didn't know him well but, whenever she shopped at Harrods, Al Fayed would appear at her side. Every Christmas he sent a hamper to Kensington Palace. On birthdays he sent the Princess and the boys generous gifts, and he had issued several invitations to stay with his family in St. Tropez in the South of France, which she had always declined. This year, she had decided to accept; as a result, Al Fayed had specially bought a new yacht—the 200-foot, £14-million *Jonikal*—to accommodate his royal guests.

So on 11 July, once the summer term was over, the Princess and two Princes, plus two PPOs for William and Harry, were collected from the helipad at Kensington Palace by Al Fayed's private helicopter and taken to lunch in Surrey with his family. He, his wife, Heini, and three of their children, then boarded his private Gulfstream IV jet and flew to Nice, where a private yacht took them the remainder of the way to St. Tropez. Diana and the boys had been to St. Tropez the previous summer with Sarah Ferguson, the Duchess of York, and her daughters, their cousins, Princesses Beatrice and Eugenie. The holiday had been ruined by the paparazzi. This time, Al Fayed promised total privacy. There was a sumptuous villa on the coast that was closely guarded, and several yachts, including the newly acquired *Jonikal*. It promised to be an exciting trip with the prospect of jet-skiing, speedboats and scuba-diving.

What they didn't realize was that Al Fayed had organized another plaything for the holiday. Four days later his eldest son, Dodi, joined them on *Jonikal*, attracting a boatload of photographers, who had already spotted Diana with Al Fayed.

Diana and Dodi hit it off and, during the next five days, as they cavorted on and off the boat, the long lenses sensed a romance. Dodi, a playboy film producer with a jet-set life, was engaged to American model, Kelly Fisher, but soon called that off. Diana's two-year affair with Hasnat Khan, a Pakistan-born heart surgeon, had come to an end. Friends say she had been very much in love with Khan and wanted to marry him. She would have converted to Islam for him and moved to Pakistan, but he knew it could never work. He had been to Kensington Palace on many occasions and had met William and Harry. William was always uncomfortable about meeting his mother's boyfriends, but Harry, as ever, was more relaxed about it. She was devastated when Khan ended the affair, so when Dodi wowed her with his considerable charms and extravagant gestures, Diana was receptive.

No one could have been happier about the liaison than Mohamed

Al Fayed. For years he had tried to ingratiate himself with the establishment and for years he had been denied British citizenship. A Department of Trade investigation in 1989 into his takeover of Harrods had condemned him as a serial liar with "a capacity for fantasy." What could have given a better two-fingered salute to the country that spurned him than for his son to be courting the Monarch's ex-daughter-in-law and the mother of a future King?

William and Harry were only too pleased to get away from the Fayed set-up—they were looking forward to Balmoral. They had not felt comfortable with either the company or the lifestyle and they hated the publicity. Harry had clashed with Mohamed Al Fayed's youngest son, Omar; William and his mother had had a row; and Fayed's bodyguards had attempted to give their PPOs envelopes stuffed with notes. And no sooner were they back in London than Dodi was on the phone to their mother, whisking her across the Channel in a helicopter to dinner in Paris, a night in the Imperial Suite of the Ritz—his father's plush hotel—and a visit to the house Mohamed owned in the Bois de Boulogne that had belonged to the Duke and Duchess of Windsor. She had rung home squealing with excitement; Dodi had given her a gold and diamond watch, and her head was spinning. No sooner was that jaunt over than she was off again, back for a second holiday on board *Jonikal*, this time cruising between Corsica and Sardinia, and this time alone with him.

The paparazzi shots of the two of them entwined was too much for some commentators. "The sight of a paunchy playboy groping a scantily-dressed Diana must appall and humiliate Prince William," wrote the late Lynda Lee-Potter, doyenne of columnists, in the *Daily Mail*. "As the mother of two young sons she ought to have more decorum and sense." While in the *Daily Express*, Bernard Ingham, Margaret Thatcher's former Press Secretary wrote, "Princess Diana's press relations are now clearly established. Any publicity is good publicity...I'm told she and Dodi are made for each other, both having more brass than brains."

Meanwhile, William and Harry, who had been left at Kensington

Palace with their nanny Olga while their mother shot off to Paris, were now with their father and preparing to join *Britannia*, the royal yacht—a far cry from *Jonikal*—for her last-ever cruise of the Western Isles before being decommissioned. First there was lunch at Clarence House with the Queen Mother, their great-grandmother, to celebrate her ninety-seventh birthday on 4 August, and the traditional birthday photo call. Then it was Balmoral and hundreds of acres of heather and moorland, hills and crags, rivers and lochs, and all manner of sport and fun to be had with not a paparazzo in sight.

To ensure the paparazzi left them in peace, Sandy Henney, their father's Press Secretary, had organized a photo call for all three Princes. It was always an ordeal for her to find suitable settings for interesting photographs, one for the daily papers, one for the Sundays; she also had to persuade William to cooperate. Harry didn't hate the cameras any less than his brother, but he was more cooperative. William, by then a bit of a sulky teenager, had to be persuaded and cajoled, whereas Harry, outgoing and uncomplicated, and always eager to please, was Sandy's ally. The Prince of Wales, while never finding it comfortable, was the ultimate professional and simply did what was asked of him.

The first set-up was at a cabin by the River Dee. The idea was that the three Princes and William's black Labrador, Widgeon, the sister of Tiggy's dog, would walk down to the river and meander along the bank, stopping every now and again to throw the odd stone into the river for the dog. "The dog saved the day," says Sandy. "William was throwing sticks for him and you could see Harry was egging his brother along."

She had decided to use a weir as the location for the Sundays but couldn't think how to use it. "So I said to Tiggs, 'Have you got any ideas?' And she said, 'God no, let's go out in one of the jeeps with Harry.' He was hanging off the back of the jeep like kids do and he said, 'I've got a couple of ideas. How about doing this, this and this.' I said, 'Not sure that would work, Harry.' Then he said, 'I've got another idea,' so off we go. The third idea was brilliant, it was all Harry's. There was a salmon ladder in the river. 'Okay Harry, how are you going to make this one work?' 'Well, William and I can run down here...' and Tiggy's up there with a cigarette, and Harry's clambering down and I'm thinking, Oh my God, we're about to lose Number Two, and he came up and he said, 'Right that's what we're going to do.' And I said, 'Well done, Harry, that's going to work. Now you've got to sell it to your father and your brother—and bless this young man's heart—what was he, eleven? Coming up twelve? He briefed the Prince, my boss. I had the radio and we were on the other side of the weir with the press and I said, 'Right,' to the police, 'get them to get out of the car and walk down and Harry will take it from there'; and you could see him directing his father—you couldn't hear because of the noise of the weir—but Harry directed the whole thing and it worked. He was brilliant."

TRAGEDY IN PARIS

Less than three weeks after a happy, carefree day on the River Spey, Diana was dead and life would never be the same again for any one of them. It was Sunday 31 August 1997, and later in the day, William and Harry had been due to join their mother in London for the last few days of the summer holidays. Tiggy Legge-Bourke "by the grace of God," as the Queen so rightly said had just arrived in Scotland to take them south. They never made that journey and they never saw their mother again.

In the initial call, which came at one o'clock in the morning, the British Ambassador in Paris, had only sketchy news. There had been a car crash. It was thought that Dodi Fayed was dead; Diana had been injured but no one knew how badly. Their car had hit a pillar in a tunnel under the Seine, during a high-speed chase. A group of paparazzi had been in pursuit on motorbikes.

Sir Robin Janvrin, then the Queen's Deputy Private Secretary, took the call in his house on the Balmoral estate and immediately woke the Queen and the Prince of Wales in their rooms at Balmoral Castle. He then phoned the Prince's Assistant Private Secretary, Nick Archer, as well as the Queen's Equerry and PPOs and they quickly set up an operations room. In London, the Prince's team had individually heard the news in their homes at much the same time, ironically, from the tabloid press. They were immediately on the phone to Scotland.

The plan was to get the Prince of Wales on to a flight to Paris as soon as possible to visit Diana in hospital, but that was superseded by another call from the embassy at 3.45. Robin Janvrin had the unenviable task of updating the Prince. "Sir, I am very sorry to have to tell you, I've just had the Ambassador on the phone. The Princess died a short time ago." She had suffered serious chest and head injuries but mercifully had lost consciousness very soon after the impact and never regained it. Doctors battled to save her life, both at the scene and for a further two hours at the Pitié-Salpêtrière Hospital four miles away, but they fought in vain.

Transporting her body home was no simple matter and it was a source of heated debate. No longer a member of the Royal Family, she was not automatically entitled to a plane of the Queen's Flight. The suggestion that the alternative might be a Harrods' van clinched the matter and "Operation Overload" sprang into action, a plan never previously needed, to repatriate the body of a member of the Royal Family to London.

Thus at 10 a.m. a BAe 146 plane from RAF Northolt was in the air with the Prince's London team—Stephen Lamport, his Private Secretary, Mark Bolland, his Deputy Private Secretary and Sandy Henney—on its way to Aberdeen to collect the Prince of Wales. It flew via RAF Wittering in Rutland, where it collected Diana's sisters, Lady Sarah McCorquodale and Lady Jane Fellowes. Robert Fellowes had broken the news to the Spencer family and both women had wanted to go with Prince Charles to collect the body. He had decided not to take the boys. The shock, horror and grief felt by everyone in the castle that summer's night can only be imagined, but the Prince's first thought was for William and Harry. Should he wake them or let them sleep and talk to them in the morning? Like every father who has to tell his children that their mother is dead, he was dreading it. He didn't know what to do for the best but the Queen strongly recommended leaving them to sleep which he did but he sneaked into the nursery and removed the radios and televisions from their rooms lest they woke early and switched something on.

What the Prince of Wales said to his sons when he woke them at 7.15 that fateful morning, and how they processed the news, no one but the three of them will ever know. He had spent a lifetime visiting the bereaved in times of national disaster, and being stead-fast in the face of tragedy, but nothing could have prepared him for the terrible task that faced him that morning. Any father who has ever had to break such news will share his pain. Just as any child who has lived through that unique loss will identify with William and Harry. There can be no easy consolation, no easy explanation, no way of softening the blow or easing the pain and the anger. And for Harry, still just twelve, still a child, still emotionally dependent on his mother, still vulnerable, it must have been almost impossible to absorb.

Just hours later, William said he would like to go to church "to talk to Mummy." Harry agreed, so the Queen took them that morning, along with the rest of the family, to the little kirk at Crathie. There is something deeply comforting in the traditional ritual and language of a church service for those who have been brought up with religion in their lives, as they all had—and some-thing deeply spiritual about a building that over hundreds of years has witnessed every stage of life from birth to death, and absorbed in its very fabric every emotion known to man.

William was newly confirmed into the Church of England—of which he will one day be the Supreme Governor. The ceremony at St. George's Chapel at Windsor Castle just five months earlier was the last time the entire family had been together, although his grandmother, Frances Shand Kydd, had sadly been missing. Diana had not been speaking to her mother at the time, so had not invited her; she had also forbidden Tiggy to attend. After months of reli-gious instruction, William would have had his faith to lean on. Harry, two years younger, and not yet in that zone, might have struggled more. Though not even faith can take away the agony of loss, the hollowness, the numbness, the inevitable rewind of last conversations, last thoughts, last memories, the words left unsaid and the guilt—whether real or imagined—that most of us feel when someone so close to us is unnaturally snatched away. But for those who believe in God, there is great catharsis in prayer.

The secular media saw none of that. They were outraged that

William and Harry should have been taken to church—one news-paper described it as a public relations exercise—and they were out-raged that Diana wasn't mentioned by the minister in his prayers. It had been the Reverend Robert Sloan's decision, but the media blamed the Queen. "My thinking," he told reporters, "was that the children had been wakened just a few hours before and told of their mother's death." But what outraged the media the most was that not one member of the Royal Family shed a tear.

The Royal Family, and the Queen in particular, became the focus for the nation's anger as it fell into a period of deep (and, to some, entirely incomprehensible) mourning for the Princess who, with her mixture of vulnerability and beauty, had tapped into the nation's psyche. And in a week that saw the most extraordinary outpouring of grief from people, most of whom had never met or known Diana, the Queen's absence from Buckingham Palace became a lightning rod. At every other national disaster, she or a close member of her family had been one of the first to visit, the first to offer words of commiseration and comfort and to be present alongside ordinary people, doing what royals do best, spearheading national sentiment, representing the nation to itself. Yet, in this greatest hour of need, there was no sign of them. And there was no visible sign that they were in any way grief-stricken.

It was not the reality. This is a family that for generations has been brought up to keep their emotions in check—not in private, but in public. It is part of the training, part of the job—and quint-essentially British. But in the touchy-feely, confessional world that characterized modern Britain—and that Diana had been so much a part of—their restraint was anathema. But it is a family that has suf-fered its fair share of grief. The Duke of Edinburgh's early life was punctuated by loss. By the age of seventeen his mother had been admitted to a mental asylum, his father had virtually disappeared from his life, one of his sisters and her entire family had been killed in a plane crash and his guardian and favorite uncle had died of cancer. Prince Charles, too, had suffered shocking losses, including the sudden death of his influential great-uncle, Lord Mountbatten, killed in 1979 by an IRA bomb; and that of his cousin, Prince William of Gloucester, after whom William was named, who was killed aged thirty when his light aircraft crashed.

But if ever there was a place conducive to the healing process it was Balmoral, a spiritual haven among the hills and the heather where, for the next week, while preparations were under way in London for the funeral, William and Harry were supported by loving family and friends, including their cousin Peter Phillips, aged twenty, who immediately flew up to join them, and by the routine of life that they had enjoyed every summer. It was familiar to them and thereby safe and reassuring. They could go for long, long walks, they could be kept busy, or they could be given the space and time to talk, to reminisce, to ask questions and to begin to take in the enormity of what had happened. The boys' welfare was the prime focus of everyone there in Scotland that week, on helping them get through each hour of each day.

SPEAK TO US MA'AM

That Sunday morning, Tony Blair had caught the mood of the nation perfectly. His voice cracking with emotion, he had said, "I feel like everyone else in the country. I am utterly devastated. We are a nation in a state of shock, in mourning, in grief. It is so deeply painful for us. She was a wonderful and a warm human being. Though her own life was often sadly touched by tragedy, she touched the lives of so many others in Britain and throughout the world, with joy and with comfort. She was the people's Princess and that is how she will remain in our hearts and memories for ever."

In the healing calm of the Scottish Highlands, the Queen was insulated from what was going on elsewhere in the country. She and the whole family were getting news from every quarter—politicians, friends, historians and VIPs from all over the world—and they saw the newspapers screaming at her to come back to the capital, but none of them could feel the raw emotion that those in the streets could feel, especially in London where the piles of tributes, flowers and teddy bears were growing by the hour. There were said to have been a million bouquets outside Kensington Palace alone and countless other offerings. Sandy Henney was sending graphic updates to the Prince of Wales via Stephen Lamport. "You can't read about this," she said. "You can't even see it on television. There is real hatred building up here, and the public is incensed by your silence."

But Charles knew he was not the one to take the lead, it was his mother's call; and for once in her long reign, she put her family before the nation she served. She took the view that this was a private tragedy and that her priority was her grieving grandsons. And in the long run, and in human terms who is to say she was wrong? The fact that William and Harry survived the trauma of their mother's death so successfully, and are now happy and focused working royals, is in no small part due to the love and support of their grandmother and everyone else at Balmoral that August who helped them through those early days.

"They're up in bloody Scotland; they should be here. Those children should be here," was the common cry in the pubs up and down the country, fueled by increasingly angry headlines. "Charles weeps bitter tears of guilt," proclaimed the *Daily Mail* over a photograph of the Prince taken some months before. "Show us you care," demanded the *Express*. "Your subjects are suffering, speak to us Ma'am," railed the *Mirror*. "Where is our Queen: Where is her flag?" shouted the *Sun*.

There was no flag. All over the country, flags were flying at half-mast, but at Buckingham Palace there was nothing—just mountains of flowers and messages piling up outside the railings. The reason was protocol. The only flag ever to fly at Buckingham Palace is the Royal Sovereign, and then only when the monarch is in residence; it never flies at half-mast, because technically the monarch is never dead. As the adage goes, "The King is dead, long live the King!" Faced with the clamoring of the tabloids, the Queen, in consultation with her advisors, clung to what she knew best: tradition.

The flag became the embodiment of all that was out of touch and irrelevant about the monarchy in the 1990s, and stood in stark contrast to the warmth and compassion of the Princess whom the Royal Family had spurned. It caused a furious row internally, and in the heat of the moment it was suggested that Sir Robert Fellowes might "impale himself on his own flag staff." Eventually the Queen was persuaded, and on the Thursday, in the nick of time, a Union flag was raised to half-mast.

That day the family ventured outside the gates of Balmoral for the first time since Diana's death. William and Harry had expressed a desire to go to church again, so the Prince took the opportunity to give them a small taster of what awaited them in London. The funeral was just two days away and, in preparation for it, the Prince had asked Sandy Henney to come up to Balmoral to speak to the boys. He often asked for her help when there was something difficult or confrontational to impart to his sons. She explained about the extraordinary scenes that they could expect to see on the streets of London. "Mummy's death," she said, "has had the most amazing impact on people. They are really sad because they loved her very, very much and they miss her, and when you go down to London you will see something you will never, ever, see again and it may come as a bit of a shock. But everything you will see is because the public thought so much of your mummy, it is the sign of their grief for your loss. We want you to know about it so you will be ready for it." William absorbed everything she was saying in silence; Harry was curious and wanted answers. Why was she telling them this? Why were people behaving in this way?

Later, she was up in the tower at Balmoral, where letters were pouring in by the hundreds and thousands. "Harry arrived with Tiggs," she recalls. "'What are you doing?' he asked. I explained that all of these people wanted to say how sorry they are that your mummy's dead and that they're thinking of you.

"'Can I open some?' said Harry, snatching up some envelopes. 'Of course you can. Go on, help yourself'—and just sit there, I thought, and break my heart."

Sandy was a warm, empathetic figure, with no children of her own, but with stepchildren—the perfect person for the sensitive task of coaxing the boys out of their shell. "I think he was slightly overawed. They are who they are, she was who she was and yet I don't think there was that realization when they were small just what an effect their mother had on people.

"He didn't just lose a parent, he lost *that* parent and in such a spectacular way. I think they did a marvelous job at Balmoral. That blanket that went around them, just to give them some breathing space to begin to understand that she wasn't going to be there any-more. No matter what anyone says about how the Queen should have come down to London, I don't care; they got it right for the boys and we should be forever grateful for that because they've turned into two reasonable, decent human beings."

About sixty members of the press were waiting outside the gates of Balmoral that Thursday, a crowd for the Highlands, yet they uttered not a single word as the Queen, the Duke of Edinburgh, Peter Phillips, the Prince of Wales and the two boys stepped out of their cars to look at the flowers and the tributes. There were hundreds, but nothing compared to what awaited them in London. The only sound to be heard apart from the clicking of the camera shutters, was the voices of the royal party. It was the first time in the five days since Diana's death that the country had seen her sons. It was a touching scene. All three Princes, father and sons, were visibly moved by what they saw and taken aback by the messages attached to the bouquets.

"Look at this one, Papa," said Harry, grabbing hold of his father's hand and tugging him down. "Read this one."

Of all the criticism that Diana leveled at the Prince during their bitter war of words, nothing could have been more hurtful, or less truthful, than the suggestion that Charles was a bad father. And the sight of him that day with Harry, and the obvious bond between them, was a revelation to a lot of people who had thought him cold and heartless. It was a bit of a game-changer. And when the Queen made a surprising live television broadcast the following evening, the mood in the country softened further and the very real danger that hung over the future of the monarchy that week was averted.

"Since last Sunday's dreadful news we have seen throughout Britain and around the world an overwhelming expression of sad-ness at Diana's death.

"We have all been trying in our different way to cope. It is not easy to express a sense of loss, since the initial shock is often suc-ceeded by a mixture of other feelings: disbelief, incomprehension, anger—and concern for all who remain.

"We have all felt those emotions in these last few days. So what I say to you now, as your Queen and as a grandmother, I say from my heart.

"First, I want to pay tribute to Diana myself. She was an exceptional and gifted human being. In good times and bad, she never lost her capacity to smile and laugh, nor to inspire others with her warmth and kindness.

"I admired and respected her—for her energy and commitment to others, and especially for her devotion to her two boys.

"This week at Balmoral, we have all been trying to help William and Harry come to terms with the devastating loss that they and the rest of us have suffered.

"No one who knew Diana will ever forget her. Millions of others who never met her, but felt they knew her, will remember her.

"I for one believe that there are lessons to be drawn from her life and from the extraordinary and moving reaction to her death."

A LONG WALK

The Spencer family had initially wanted a small, private funeral—and the Queen had been inclined to agree; but, as the public mood intensified, they all came round to the Prince of Wales's view that Diana should have nothing less than a full royal number at Westminster Abbey. And so it was; but it was not without complications. Charles Spencer wanted to walk behind the cortège on his own. The Prince of Wales wanted to join him, and he felt Diana's sons should be able to walk too if they so chose; he felt it might help the grieving process. Downing Street meanwhile was suggesting a "People's Funeral" with the public following the coffin.

The Prince of Wales and his former brother-in-law got into a bitter war of words over it, but the matter was finally settled by the Duke of Edinburgh who announced that he would also walk. So it was that William and Harry walked alongside their father, grandfather and uncle.

Alistair Campbell, Tony Blair's Press Secretary, claimed in his diaries, *The Blair Years*, that Sandy Henney had been asked by the Prince to talk the boys into walking with their father because he was afraid that without them he might be attacked by the public. That was not true. "At no time," says Sandy, "was there ever a question of using the boys as a barrier against possible reaction from the public towards my boss. But there was genuine concern as to what reaction the public might have to the Prince of Wales—and indeed any member of the Royal Family from a highly emotionally (and some may say irrationally) charged public. The boys talked about walking with the cortège to close members of their family and only those they trusted, and no one they talked to at that time would ever speak to a third party about what the children said."

They joined the cortège at St. James's Palace, and for the long walk to Westminster Abbey, past hundreds of thousands of people lining the route, some of them sobbing openly. They walked knowing that the cameras and the eyes of the world were upon them. It is hard to imagine an experience that could have been more intimidating for a fifteen-year-old, let alone a twelve-year-old child but, flanked by his uncle and his father, Harry bravely kept his composure. So too did William, who walked between his uncle and his grandfather; and it was only once they were in Westminster Abbey, out of sight of the cameras, when at times the occasion got to them, that they allowed the mask to slip.

But the most heartbreaking of all the sights that day was the white envelope tucked into a bouquet of white freesias on top of the coffin with the simple word: MUMMY. Sandy had rightly guessed that the boys might want to write their mother one last note. "I remember ringing Tiggy. 'The boys are going to put some flowers on their mother's coffin?' 'Of course.' 'And they're going to write a note aren't they?' 'Yes.' 'Right, could you do me a favor? Please make sure that whatever they say is in an envelope.' 'Okay. Why?' 'Because one of the first things the cameras are going to do is zoom in on their words.'"

Her foresight that day protected them from the most basic violation; but no one could protect them from Charles Spencer, their uncle's hostile words.

"Diana was the very essence of compassion, of duty, of style, of beauty. All over the world she was a symbol of selfless humanity," he said in his tribute that was broadcast all over the world. "Someone with a natural nobility who was classless and who proved in the last year that she needed no royal title to continue to generate her particular brand of magic...

"She would want us today to pledge ourselves to protecting her beloved boys William and Harry from a similar fate, and I do this here, Diana, on your behalf. We will not allow them to suffer the anguish that used regularly to drive you to tearful despair.

"And beyond that, on behalf of your mother and my sisters, I pledge that we, your blood family, will do all we can to continue the imaginative way in which you were steering these two exceptional young men so that their souls are not simply immersed by duty and tradition but can sing openly as you planned."

It was an extraordinary insult to the people that William and Harry, now motherless, loved most: their father and their grandparents, the Queen and the Duke of Edinburgh, who were right there in the abbey. The Prince of Wales was particularly galled that it was coming from a man who'd had a disastrous marriage of his own and who had brought his latest mistress to the funeral.

Diana had said she wanted to be interred in the family crypt at Great Brington alongside her father and grandmother, Cynthia, but it was deemed that the small churchyard would be unable to cope with the anticipated volume of visitors. So, after the funeral, her coffin was driven slowly to Althorp, her ancestral home in Northampton, past thousands of spectators on the roadside, while the Prince of Wales, William and Harry and the Spencers all made the journey in the Royal Train. Diana was buried instead on an island in the middle of a lake on the estate where, in life, she had been refused a home. It has become a shrine and her brother has turned the old stable block into a permanent exhibition in her memory, which the public can visit. But there are some who think her body was later quietly placed where she had wanted to rest.

In the aftermath of the funeral, Earl Spencer was feted for his speech and the Prince of Wales criticized for having "forced" his sons to walk behind the cortège. Stuart Higgins, editor of the *Sun*, refused to believe it was the boys' own choice. Sandy Henney nearly came to blows with him.

"When she died, the country may have lost a Princess but two young boys lost their mum and I'll never forget saying to Stuart, who I actually like a lot, 'Who is anyone to tell those boys what they should do? I'm sick of this Our Princess has died Their MUM has died; they should choose where they walk.' All this nonsense of the children being forced to protect Charles. Right up until the last minute when the boys decided to walk behind the coffin there was a plan that if they couldn't do it—entirely their choice—I would go, take them from the Prince's apartment at St. James's across to Clarence House and they would go to the funeral with their great-grandmother. It was their choice and it angered me that everyone was saying what the boys should and shouldn't do in relation to their mother's funeral."

GETTING ON WITH THE DAY

Two days after their mother was buried, Tiggy took William and Harry to the Monday meet of the Beaufort hunt. Charles was hugely grateful to have Tiggy around to help keep everyone's spirits up.

As soon as they arrived, Captain Ian Farquhar, the Master went over to them. 'It's good to see you, sirs," he said. "I just want you to know that we are all very, very sorry about your mother. You have our deepest sympathy and we were all incredibly proud of you on Saturday. That's all I'm going to say, and now we're going to get on with the day."

"Thank you," said William. "Yes, you're right. We all need to get on with the day."

And metaphorically as well as literally, that is exactly what they did. Whether by nature or nurture, both boys had even then that Windsor ability to keep their emotions in check. Charles, rightly afraid that he would be blamed for Diana's death, was dreading his first public engagement after the funeral, which included a visit to a Salvation Army drop-in center in Manchester, in one of the most notorious estates in the city. Walking into a hall full of cameras, he discarded his prepared speech and spoke about his two sons.

"I think they are handling a very difficult time with enormous courage and the greatest possible dignity," he said. "I also want to say how particularly moved and enormously comforted my children and I were, and indeed still are, by the public's response to Diana's death. It has been really quite remarkable and indeed in many ways overwhelming. I think, as many of you will know from experiences of family loss in your own lives, it is inevitably difficult to cope with grief at any time. But you may realize, it is even harder when the whole world is watching at the same time. But obviously the public support, and the warmth of that support, has helped us enormously. I can't tell you how enormously grateful and touched both the boys and myself are."

One can only guess about whether, in their determination to get on with the day, they grieved sufficiently, but what is certain is that the bond between them after their mother's death grew ever stronger. They were there for each other, then and in the weeks, months and years that followed. It was not just William for his little brother. Harry was very much a support for William, and has remained so. Sandy thinks he knew at an early age that his role was to support his brother. "I can't think of another spare," she says, "who's ever supported the heir in the way that Harry's supported William. Whatever people say, both the Princess and the Prince got it right in terms of bringing up those two boys, in that they actually loved each other. Of course there was rivalry, they are just like normal siblings, and Harry was a typical younger pain-in-the-arse brother but adored by William. There's a deep love and respect there—and what bonded them even more was that their mum died."

William went back to Eton and to the care of his exceptional housemaster, Dr. Andrew Gailey, and Harry went back to the embrace of Ludgrove, where he was doing an extra year. It had always been the intention to keep him at Ludgrove for that extra year, so that he would move on to his senior school as a rising fourteen-year-old, rather than a rising thirteen. This meant that most of the friends in his year had moved on, including his closest friend, Henry van Straubenzee. Henry had joined his elder brother, Thomas, at Harrow. But it also meant Harry knew the school inside out, and most of the boys, so he wasn't an object of curiosity, and he had other friends.

At half-term, when he would have been with Diana had she been alive, the Prince of Wales was committed to a five-day tour of

South Africa, Swaziland and Lesotho; rather than cancel it, or leave Harry at home with Tiggy, he decided to take Harry and Tiggy with him, along with a schoolfriend called Charlie Henderson. Also in the party was Mark Dyer, a friend of Tiggy's and a former Equerry to the Prince of Wales. He was brought in to be her male counterpart, and was another hugely significant figure in William and Harry's life after their mother's death. Harry and his father flew out on separate flights, and while Charles and his entourage carried out his program of engagements, Tiggy, Mark, Harry and Charlie and a few others all went off on safari in Botswana on a trip organized by Mark. It is a country Harry has been back to again and again, but that was his very first taste of Africa and the beginning of a love affair with the continent, its people and its wildlife.

It was a trip filled with magical and unforgettable moments. From Botswana they met up with the Prince of Wales at Fugitives' Drift, a lodge perched above the Buffalo River, in a remote and beautiful part of KwaZulu-Natal in South Africa. From there they were taken to Isandlwana and Rorke's Drift, the sites of the two greatest battles of the Anglo-Zulu War of 1879. Their guide was David Rattray, an electrifying storyteller and expert on the war, who was sadly murdered ten years after the Princes' visit. The battle of Isandlwana was arguably the most humiliating defeat in British colonial history—and the basis for the iconic 1964 film *Zulu*. Eleven days after the British commenced their invasion of Zululand, a Zulu force of 20,000 warriors, armed with their traditional assegai spears and cow-hide shields, attacked a group of about 1,800 British soldiers armed with state-of-the-art weaponry. Some 1,300 British and native troops were killed; the Zulus lost about 1,000 men. Rattray interpreted it not as a British defeat but as a Zulu triumph. But the tables were turned just a few hours later, at Rorke's Drift, a few miles away, where just 139 British soldiers successfully defended their garrison against an almighty assault by 3,000 Zulu warriors. Rattray, who spoke Zulu fluently, had an extraordinary ability to transport his audience back to the day of the battle and to recreate its sights and sounds. As one commentator said, "To listen to David Rattray narrate the story of Isandlwana was akin to watching the best-scripted, best-directed and best-produced movie Hollywood's finest studios could put out. It was goose-bump stuff." For a thirteen-year-old wannabe soldier, it was mesmerizing and, in June 2014, Harry was at the fiftieth anniversary gala screening of *Zulu* at the Odeon in Leicester Square to raise money for the David Rattray Memorial Trust, Sentebale and Walking with the Wounded. He told the daughter of the film's director that it was one of his favorite films. He watched it every year before Christmas, "Maybe once; maybe twice."

The significance of meeting President Nelson Mandela for tea at his residence in Pretoria would not have been lost on Harry, even at the age of thirteen, but nothing could have been quite as exciting for a thirteen-year-old as meeting the Spice Girls at the height of their girl-power fame. President Mandela had paid a State Visit to Britain the previous year and, during it, Prince Charles had taken him to a particularly good Prince's Trust event at a leisure center in Brixton. The two men had got on famously, and Mandela had been inspired to set up something similar in South Africa, which became the Nations Trust. Charles had asked the Spice Girls if they would fly to South Africa to sing at a Two Nations fundraising concert.

It was a star-studded evening held at a huge stadium in Johannesburg, and Sandy Henney, who had the usual task of organizing a photo call, asked the Prince of Wales whether she could include Harry in it. The press, she argued, had been good in leaving him alone on the rest of his holiday. He told her to ask Harry. "So I said to Harry, 'Would you like to meet the Spice Girls?' and typical boy, 'Oh yeah; can Charlie come too?' 'Of course he can.' I remember going into the girls and saying, 'Harry would like to come over and meet you and I know he's larger than life but don't forget his mum's not long dead,' and they said, 'No, no bring him.' I got Harry and Charlie and took them in, 'Harry, Charlie; Spice Girls. Spice Girls; Harry, Charlie.' Baby Spice said, 'Come and sit over here,' with Posh Spice the other side and the little boy sat down and he was absolutely beaming. 'Oh, isn't he lovely?' They were doing the same to Charlie too, they were excellent." Afterwards, Harry and his father and the girls went outside for the photo call, and again Baby and Posh tucked him between them, and Sporty fussed over him. He stood grinning, like a cat who'd got the cream, and was declared the star of the show. "He was just like any kid meeting his heroines, these gorgeous girls who had just been singing and were going to go and sing for him again."

Mark Dyer was the perfect appointment: having been an Equerry, he knew the whole family, and they him. The Prince's idea was that he would work alongside Tiggy to be a friend, companion, role model and a bit of a mentor—all the things a responsible older brother might be—and to provide some healthy normality. Since working for the Prince, he had left the Army and started a wine bar in Chelsea. Mark, or Marco as he is widely known, was a Welsh Guards officer. He is tall, good-looking and red-haired; colleagues describe him as a Captain Hurricane figure. He proved to be all that the Prince hoped he would be, and more; like Tiggy, he has been loyal to his bootstraps and is still very close to Harry. "He was a rugby player, a good egg," says one of Harry's team who knows him well. "He's a very straightforward, hard-drinking, hard-living adventurer, and a great soldier. He was also somebody the Princes could relate to at that age; and they remembered him from their childhood when he'd shown them guns and tanks and things and taken them rock climbing. The press thought he was a bad influence but he did a bloody good job for them. He had huge integrity, and he was around when they needed advice that didn't come from their father."

It must have been a relief to Tiggy to have someone to share the responsibility with. Tiggy had a nose for trouble. She had already been rapped over the knuckles by the Prince of Wales for a paparazzi shot of her driving her car with a cigarette in her mouth while Harry hung out of the passenger window shooting rabbits; but when the *News of the World* published a dramatic photo of

Harry abseiling down a dam wall in Wales, wearing no safety gear, they were both in hot water. "MADNESS!" screeched the headline. "The boy dangling 100 feet up with no helmet or safety line is PRINCE HARRY." As Sandy says, "Tiggy and Mark got the bollocking of a lifetime and were told this must never happen again."

Sandy had taken a call from Clive Goodman, the *News of the World* royal editor, saying he had a set of photos and wanted her to comment on them. They had been taken by a tourist at the Grwyne Fawr dam in Monmouthshire, near Tiggy's family estate at Crickhowell, where she often took the boys. She insisted he bike them over so she could see them for herself first. "An hour or so later, I see them," she recalls. "No crash helmet, no safety line and I'm thinking, Oh my God. First of all, get hold of Tiggy. 'Tiggy.' 'Yes, Granny,' which was their nickname for me, 'what have I done now?' 'I don't know yet but I want to know the circumstances behind these photos,' and she said, 'Mmmmmm, yes we were there.' So I said, 'Where was bloody Mark Dyer? He's supposed to be in there acting like the big brother and sorting all this stuff out,' and she said, 'He was asleep on a rock somewhere.' That's a fat lot of good."

Since November 1997 there had been new rules of engagement for the press. The day Diana's brother had heard the news of her death he had said, "I always believed the press would kill her in the end but not even I could imagine that they would take such a direct hand in her death as seems to be the case." At the time it was thought the paparazzi were entirely responsible for the accident and he went on to say that the editors and proprietors of every newspaper that had paid money for intrusive pictures of his sister had "blood on their hands." The paparazzi were subsequently exonerated but the industry took the message to heart and, after much debate, opted for self-regulation rather than a privacy law. The Press Complaints Commission, previously regarded as toothless, drew up a strict Code of Conduct designed to prevent all the excesses of the previous ten years and to guarantee the boys' privacy during their school years. The abseiling photos were clearly in breach of the privacy rules but they did demonstrate that those responsible for the Princes' safety were failing to protect them. Sandy's dilemma was that, if she suppressed them, a more damaging story could have followed.

It was not always Tiggy and Mark who were *in loco parentis*. After the breakup of their parents' marriage, Hugh van Cutsem, an old university friend of the Prince of Wales, and his wife Emilie, had scooped up William and Harry, and they were there for them again now. The Princes slipped seamlessly into their family; the four van Cutsems sons—Edward, Hugh, Nicholas and William—all a little older than William and Harry, were like brothers to them. Hugh was a wealthy banker and businessman, but also a passionate countryman and conservationist, and one of the best shots in the country.

When the Princes first used to go and stay in the 1990s, the van Cutsems were renting Anmer Hall from the Queen, the ten-bedroom Georgian house on the Sandringham estate that was refurbished for William, Kate and Prince George to live in. They then built a magnificent neo-Palladian house on a big estate about twenty-five miles away, near Swaffham, where there were big shoots that Harry enjoyed. As a passionate conservationist, it was not surprising that, after Diana's death, Hugh van Cutsem chose to take his family, including its two honorary members, on holiday to a pioneering wildlife conservancy in Kenya. Called Lewa, and owned by the Craig family, it lies on the northern foothills of Mount Kenya.

Their guide was Geoffrey Kent, a polo-playing friend of the Prince of Wales and founder of the luxury travel company Abercrombie and Kent. He had grown up in Kenya and knew the country and Ian Craig and his family well. It was on this holiday that William first met Jecca Craig, Ian's daughter, with whose name his was intermittently linked before his marriage to Kate.

Southern Africa is a very special part of the world, as Harry had already discovered. Now it was William's turn to fall in love with it. They stayed in a tented camp—canvas tents raised up on stone decks, luxuriously equipped yet just feet from the bush, where some of nature's most magnificent creatures roamed free. Each morning before dawn they set off in open-topped jeeps, wrapped in blankets against the cold, looking for game before the heat of the sun drove them and the animals they sought in search of shade, and in their case, breakfast and a day in the swimming pool. In the evening, animals and the jeeps set out again.

One day Charlie Wheeler, one of Ian Craig's colleagues on Lewa, took them out on foot on a camel safari—the camels carry the lunch. When they stopped at noon in the middle of nowhere, a makeshift camp was fleetingly erected (from the backs of the camels) and lunch was served as it might have been in a five-star hotel, with a troop of servants to prepare and serve it.

There is no twilight in Kenya—when the sun goes down it is pitch dark and it happens with astonishing speed. On their way back, the sun set and, in the darkness, they walked into a herd of elephants. It's the sort of experience that either thrills or terrifies. William was exhilarated; Harry, still only thirteen, clung to Charlie's shirt, wisely sticking close to the expert, not to say the man with the gun. The night was saved when they rendezvoused with some vehicles and were driven safely back to camp, to enjoy supper under the stars round the blazing fire.

The whole trip was a great adventure. Out there in the bush, no one knew or cared who they were, and the press was nowhere to be seen. It was a revelation and a liberation for the Princes. The anonymity they enjoy there is a significant part of their passion for Africa to this day.

MRS. PB

The newspaper-reading public knew about Camilla Parker Bowles—more, probably, than she would have liked—but William and Harry knew surprisingly little. They knew their mother's view of her, and that inevitably colored their own view, but they had never met her. Charles had deliberately bided his time for the right moment. However, in the summer of 1997, two months before Diana's death, when the relationship between him and his ex-wife had become more civilized, the Prince of Wales felt the time had come. He sat both boys down and tried to explain a bit about the situation, but they were very quiet, and it was clear to him that William, in particular, didn't want to know, and so he left it.

Since the divorce, he had begun the slow process of trying to restore his tattered reputation, and gradually to introduce Camilla, known by most of the Prince's staff as "Mrs. PB," to the public. To this end, in July 1996, he had taken on Mark Bolland, to whom he had been introduced by Camilla's divorce lawyer, Hilary Browne-Wilkinson. Mark was thirty years old and had been head of the Press Complaints Commission for five years. He was very impressive: clever, confident and entertaining—also very single-minded. William and Harry referred to him as "Blackadder" after the scheming character played by Rowan Atkinson in the television series of the same name. For the next six years, Bolland was the Prince's blue-eyed boy, who could do no wrong. His methods caused havoc but he achieved what he set out to do and, without him, it is unlikely that the Prince of Wales would now be enjoying such widespread popularity and be happily married to the woman who so many people believed had broken up the royal marriage.

"Mark had incredible contacts," says Sandy Henney, "and balls to do some of the things he did. Whether or not you agreed with some of his methods, he got results. He was incredible fun to work with. He had an incisive brain, which made him very scary sometimes. My view of him was that he was working primarily for Mrs. Parker Bowles and then the Prince. He wanted to make Mrs. Parker Bowles acceptable; but you can't treat the institution of monarchy as individuals, you need to treat it as a whole. They weathered the storm and the damage is behind them now but at the time, the public became almost indifferent to the institution and some of the stuff was very damaging."

Colleen Harris, who joined the press office as Sandy's deputy early in 1998—the first black member of the Household—agrees. "Mark was a spin master, but if you look at what he inherited and where the Prince was, in terms of reputation, image etc., he had to turn it around and he did turn it. It wasn't easy some of the time and some of our decisions in the press office may have caused some emotional upheaval, but I don't think the Prince of Wales could have married Camilla without that groundwork. There's payback each time—and sometimes we got that a bit out of kilter."

But, as she says, "Without Mark, the Prince would have been unhappy and the boys would have been unhappy as a consequence, and it would have been damaging to the monarchy as a whole, so he did help."

After Diana's death that process had to be put on hold. Charles had openly held a big, glitzy party at Highgrove for Camilla's fiftieth birthday in July 1997 (when the boys were with their mother), and there had been plans for them to be seen together for the first time in public in September at a big National Osteoporosis fundraising event, but that had to be scrapped; and while the nation and the family mourned for the Princess, Camilla remained very firmly out of sight. Charles knew that any move to introduce her to William and Harry must now wait until they initiated it. He did, however, invite her children, Tom and Laura, to stay with him and the boys when they were at Birkhall, the Queen Mother's house, in Scotland during the Easter holidays in 1998; another house guest was Ted Hughes, the Poet Laureate. The young people had got on well together and are very good friends to this day.

Also early in 1998, William and Harry began plotting a surprise fiftieth birthday party for their father. His birthday is in November, but they decided to hold the party on 31 July in the school holidays before the summer migration to Balmoral. It started out as a party for his godchildren and their parents; they decided that if Camilla was, therefore, going to be a guest because Tom was a godson, they should meet her beforehand. William was the first. They met in his flat at York House one Saturday afternoon, 13 June, when he was home from school. A month later, Sandy had a call from Rebekah Wade (now Brooks), then Deputy Editor of the *Sun* (and one of the defendants who was acquitted in the 2014 trial for conspiracy to hack phones). She had heard there had been a meeting. "Rebekah, I'm not going to deny it," said Sandy, "but the shit's going to hit the proverbial fan when the young man finds out about this because he will think that someone's been spying on him. And anything we've done in terms of trying to persuade him that the media has a place, etc...it ain't going to work. I'm really pissed off with this." A couple of hours before the *Sun* went to press, she had another call from Piers Morgan, editor of the *Daily Mirror* who, like Wade, was a good friend of Mark Bolland's.

When the story appeared, an internal inquiry was launched. Ten days later, Camilla's PA, Amanda McManus, whose husband was a *Times* executive (owned, like the *Sun*, by News International), fell on her sword. Sandy had told William the full story and how they might limit the damage. He wasn't happy, but she was impressed by how grown-up he was. "He could have gone into a real teenage-boy sulk but no—he said, 'I understand' and accepted it." But she was dismayed that he should have been used so cynically: if William likes Camilla, then the public will like her too.

Harry was much less tortured about the whole process. He met her a few weeks later over tea at Highgrove with Tom and Laura one Sunday afternoon. It would be wrong to think that after one or two meetings they were all the best of friends, but it was a start. "Harry was just Harry," says a friend of the meeting. He just got on with life. He had no qualms about meeting Camilla.

The birthday party wasn't quite the surprise they had planned. One of the guests inadvertently tipped off the *Sunday Mirror*, but despite that disappointment, it was a huge success. Guests partied until 4 a.m., and, while Tiggy and the Prince's former valet, Michael Fawcett, helped bring it all together, the evening was entirely driven by William and Harry. The highlight of the evening was a review—their own take on *Blackadder*—in which both brothers appeared, alongside actors Stephen Fry, Emma Thompson and Rowan Atkinson, whose help they had enlisted. The stars were all friends of the Prince of Wales through the work they'd done for the Prince's Trust.

At the end of the evening, their father, who was moved to tears by the whole event, gave an emotional vote of thanks to them and to everyone involved. What touched him most was their acceptance of Camilla. They had seated her in pride of place. They couldn't have given him a more precious birthday present.

Tiggy was only around in an official capacity for another year after the party. In October 1999, she married Charles Pettifer, a former soldier, and now runs a bed and breakfast business in Wales, but she has been there at all the major events in their lives and she and the Princes are still the best of friends. She's still that big sister, particularly to Harry, who is godfather to her eldest son, Fred.

THE PLAYING FIELDS OF ETON

On the first anniversary of Diana's death, in August 1998, there was to be a service of remembrance for her at Crathie Church, which would be the focus of the day's media coverage. As well as the Queen and senior members of the Royal Family, Tony Blair and his wife Cherie were to attend. William was adamant that if the press were going to be there, he didn't want to go. Sandy understood his position, but it was inevitable that the press would be there. "The Prince of Wales asked me whether I would come and talk to them both," she says. "I said, 'Okay, but I'm not going to say "You've got to go." I'll give the pros and cons to them but they make up their own minds.'

"We went for a walk round Loch Muick and I said, 'Okay guys, why don't you want to go?' 'Well, you know, the press are going to be there and we don't want to be gawped at.' This was a year after their mum died and bloody right boys, but then you say, 'Well don't you think it would be a bit funny if everyone else turns up for a remembrance service for your mum and you don't?' 'Well, yes,' says William, 'but I still don't want to go.' 'Okay, but this is how it's going to be played out in the newspapers, but it's up to you to decide. I'm not telling you either way.' And it was Harry who said, 'I think we should go. We need to be there and we need to support Papa and to support everyone else. I think I'm going to go, William,' and William then said, 'Yes you're right.' I left them and said to the Prince, 'I've talked to them and they may well go but, if so, it's their choice; no one will ever say they were forced into doing it.'"

They weren't forced, but William did make one condition. He would go, he said, if Sandy would issue an announcement calling for an end to the mourning. In this both boys were united. They agreed a text with her and she read it out on their behalf during the photo call on the first day of the Michaelmas Half, on 2 September 1998, the day Harry joined his brother as a pupil at Eton College.

"They have asked me to say that they believe their mother would want people now to move on—because she would have known that constant reminders of her death can create nothing but pain to those she left behind. They therefore hope very much that their mother and her memory will now finally be allowed to rest in peace."

Eton was the school that Diana had chosen for her sons. Founded in the fifteenth century, it boasts an impressive list of old boys; Diana's own father and brother had been there. By now almost fourteen, Harry was more than ready to move on from Ludgrove, but with 1,200 pupils and buildings that were spread across an entire town, it was a big change. And with that change came a new vocabulary that needed to be learned: a "Half" was a term (actually one of three in a year), a "school" was a class but more commonly called a "div," a teacher was a "beak," homework was an "EW," "chambers" were elevenses, and the blazer and trousers he wore when he arrived on his first day, marked with his name and laundry number, were called "formal change," although they were actually less formal than the outfit he would wear for lessons. That was called "school dress," and consisted of a black tailcoat, waistcoat, a stiff white collar with a paper tie and pinstriped trousers, which were adopted to mourn the death of George III in 1820.

Eton is one of the wealthiest schools in Britain and has educated some of the wealthiest and most privileged boys in its long history. Ironic really, given that the school was founded by King Henry VI in 1440 to provide free education to seventy poor boys, who would then go on to King's College, Cambridge, which Henry also founded. By the time Harry arrived, there were around 1,300 boys, most of them paying nearly £30,000 a year (before the cost of uniform and extras); although there were still seventy who were King's Scholars, attending on scholarships. By then, the focus was very much on academic excellence, but there were also great sporting facilities and clubs to cater for every interest and activity known to boy, and it had strong links with the military. The school has produced an astonishing roll call of prime ministers, statesmen, diplomats, actors, artists, directors, writers, soldiers and adventurers—and the City of London is thick with Old Etonians. It has also educated a fair number of princes from around the world.

Charles and Diana had agreed on the choice of Eton for their sons. The Prince of Wales had been sent to Gordonstoun, in the north of Scotland, his father's old school, where he had been bitterly unhappy. He was not going to subject his sons to that. But he had liked his English and drama teacher at Gordonstoun, Dr. Eric Anderson, who had gone on to become Head Master at Eton and then Provost of the school, and they had remained in touch. He and Diana both had friends and knew sons of friends who had been to Eton, and Tom Parker Bowles had just left. Before making their final decision they had canvassed opinion from a range of people connected with the school, asking about the teachers (beaks), the boys and, most particularly, the privacy. One of those they asked was Lord Hurd, then Foreign Secretary, who "was struck," he says, "that they were both, separately singing from the same hymn sheet."

The school is huge but it is divided into twenty-five houses, each with about fifty boys, and roughly ten to a year group, and that is where most of them eat, sleep, socialize and study, each of them with a study/bedroom to themselves. Lessons, or "divs" are held in classrooms, "schools," around the town. Each house master has a dame, whom the boys address as "ma'am," to look after the pastoral welfare of the boys and deal with laundry, administration, catering and domestic issues. Harry's was Elizabeth Heathcote, who was said to be "a bit firm but very nice." Although the boys have to change their own sheets and make their own beds, the rooms are kept clean by "boys' maids," who are local women, inured to the smell of dirty socks, who often become very fond of the boys they look after.

Pubs are out of bounds, but otherwise boys have the run of the town in their spare time. Harry often used to walk across the bridge into Windsor and have tea with his grandmother at Windsor Castle. And, in the final two years, they can go to the school's own pub, called Tap, down an alleyway off the High Street. It serves beer, cider and snacks, but no one's allowed more than two pints and being drunk is a punishable offence.

Harry followed William into Manor House, known as ALHG after house master Andrew Gailey's initials, which is located in the center of the school, next to the College Library and "the Burning Bush" (an elaborate wrought-iron street lamp). College is where the scholars live, and Bekynton is a canteen, where those boys in houses with no dining rooms go for their meals.

Every boarding house has two entrances, the Boys' Door, leading into the boys' living area, and the door to the Private Side, where the house master lives with his wife and family, if he has one. Dr. Gailey was Irish, as was his wife, Shauna, and they had a young daughter, and several pets including a couple of springer spaniels, Rosie and Jenny. Eric Anderson would no doubt have been key in suggesting Andrew Gailey as house master for the Princes: a historian, a man of great humanity and humor, whom everyone agrees played an enormous role in their lives. He was crucial in supporting and steering them both, with their very different needs, through some nightmarish times, without short-changing the other forty-eight boys in his care.

As Colleen Harris says, "He's a very, very special man, absolutely adorable and he's had an enormous influence on them and has been there for some of the really difficult times in their lives and helped them through. Andrew was there day in day out helping them. When the papers were bad he prepared them, he didn't remove them. You can't move on if your mother's there in the newspaper every day." He was the right man in the right place at the right time; he remains a friend, confidant and mentor, and guards their secrets faithfully.

Harry didn't find Eton easy—and the chances are that Dr. Gailey didn't find Harry all that easy at times either. The other new boys in his year didn't immediately warm to him; he gave the impression of being pleased with himself, which may have been nothing more than a defense mechanism, but it didn't go down well. He struggled with the academic work and found it hard being compared yet again to his brother, who was the all-round model student: William was popular among his peers, the teaching staff liked him, and he was as successful in the classroom as he was on the playing fields.

Being at the bottom of the academic heap in any school is difficult, and at that time Eton had a very questionable policy of openly listing every boy's overall marks at the end of the term, so it was no secret where anyone came. One way and another, they were not his happiest years, but Harry went some way to rescuing his reputation and self-esteem on the sports field. He could also release some of the anger that contemporaries say raged inside him, particularly during his early years at Eton. Where that anger came from is pure speculation; there were plenty of possible causes. It could have been that he felt he didn't fit the Etonian ideal; it could have been the abnormality of everything about his life, the feeling of living in a goldfish bowl, of being an object of constant fascination. It could have been the feeling of being second best—the spare. It could have been a reaction to the upsets and difficulties of his childhood. It could have been the stories about his mother that still filled the newspapers and the whispering about who his father really was. Or it could quite simply have been grief—the loss of his mother—and maybe anger that the whole nation had hijacked something that to him was intensely personal and private. Everyone seemed to feel entitled to an opinion about his mother, a woman they had never met—despite Sandy's plea on his behalf to move on and let her memory rest in peace, it hadn't happened. He would find sanctuary in the calm of the Drawing Schools, where he spent a lot of his time with equally angst-ridden teenagers, and transferred his feelings onto canvas.

The more physical outlet for those feelings was sport, in which Harry excelled, becoming House Captain of Games. He was widely regarded as a formidable opponent, fiercely competitive. In the Michaelmas and Lent Halves he played football, but his passions were rugby and the Wall Game. The Wall Game is a fearsome and largely inexplicable hybrid unique to Eton (and apocryphally perhaps, Ford Open Prison, where it has been known for Old Etonians to stay from time to time). It is played between Collegers and Oppidans—that is to say, scholars and the rest of the school—and since College owns the wall the game is played against, their team usually has the upper hand. The two teams of sweaty boys covered in mud form a "bully" or a scrum up against a high redbrick wall and push against each other, endeavoring to free the ball. It rarely happens; goals are scored every hundred years on average, and if the scrum moves more than a couple of feet in either direction it's considered an exciting match.

During the summer, the main sports Harry played for the school were cricket, which made him a "dry bob"—as opposed to rowers who were "wet bobs"—and polo, which he often played at the Guards' Polo Club over the bridge at Windsor, where his father and grandfather used to play.

His other great enthusiasm at Eton was the Combined Cadet Force, which he signed up for in "D block," his third year, as soon as he could, and where at last he was able to indulge his childhood fantasies about becoming a soldier. He learned weapon handling, foot drill, first aid, battle skills, signals, navigation and field craft in the basic training, and then went on to the advanced course, which included leadership exercises, shooting, writing and delivering orders, advanced infantry tactics and close target reconnaissance. In every Half he went off on a weekend exercise or "corps scheme," where the boys did more intensive training, and in the Summer Half they went to a range and fired live ammunition.

He was awarded the highest rank of Cadet Officer in his last year, and in May 2003 he led the annual CCF Tattoo, which is the highlight of the year. It takes place on the evening before the

THE PLAYING FIELDS OF ETON

"Fourth of June," Eton's equivalent of speech day (which rarely actually happens on 4 June) when parents, grandparents, siblings and Old Etonians descend with picnics, to wander around the school looking at exhibits of work, to watch cricket and other games, have Pimms with their boys' house masters, and line the riverbank for the traditional parade of boats In front of an audience of over 800 people, eighteen-year-old Harry as Parade Commander, with ceremonial sword in hand, marched straight-backed on to College Field, after hours of rehearsal, and commanded the forty-eight-strong Guard of Honour.

Harry's greatest disappointment at Eton was that, unlike his brother, he didn't become a member of Pop—but it's a disappointment he honorably shares with most Old Etonians, including his former Private Secretary, Jamie Lowther-Pinkerton. Pop, more properly known as The Eton Society, is highly coveted, and only bestowed on nineteen of the most popular and successful boys in their final year. It used to be a debating society, but today it consists of prefects elected by their peers, and with the title comes all sorts of privileges. including the right to wear wing collars, white bow ties, spongebag trousers and colorful waistcoats of their own choice. Harry had to wear black to the bitter end.

THE FOURTH ESTATE

Harry left Eton in the summer of 2003 with two A levels—Grade D in Geography and B in Art. He was never destined for university; having set his sights on an Army career long ago, all he cared about was getting good enough grades to get him over the first hurdle towards an officer training course at Sandhurst. And he did.

The only sour note was that as he began his first week at Sandhurst two years later in May 2005, a former art teacher at Eton, Sarah Forsyth, accused him in an employment tribunal of having cheated in the course work for his A level and thereby not having earned the B he had been awarded. Her allegations had already been published in the *News of the World*. She claimed she had been asked to write the text for his Expressive Project and had secretly tape-recorded Harry admitting it.

Clarence House issued a statement saying: "It is not true that Harry cheated in his exams. These are unfounded allegations by a disaffected teacher in the context of her dispute with the school. A full investigation into these allegations was held by the relevant exam board which found no evidence to support the claims." This was confirmed by a senior Edexcel examiner, who double-checked the work, which made up around 20 percent of the final grade, and concluded that the anonymous candidate had not cheated.

A spokesman for Eton College said: "We believe these allegations to be absurd. They are not just untrue—the exam board confirmed this—but are of no relevance to the tribunal case whatsoever. Eton refused to give in to what appeared to be a crude attempt to embarrass the college into paying money. That is why we are determined to fight this matter in tribunal."

After the tribunal, Paddy Harverson, who had been brought in as the Prince of Wales's new PR supremo in 2004—one of many changes—told the media that the allegations had previously been disproved and it was unfair for the teacher's lawyers to give the court only a small portion of the tape. He accused them of having "placed their own interpretation upon it."

He went on. "The tape . . . contains barely audible half-sentences, and it appears to have been edited," he said. "It is also difficult to tell what Harry is saying and what he is referring to, due to the poor quality of the recording and the disjointed nature of the tape. The fact remains Harry did not cheat."

To mark the end of his five years at Eton, Harry had agreed to a pose for a set of photographs showing him engaged in various activities around the school during his final term. They were the quid pro quo for being more or less left alone by the press during those years.

Maintaining a good relationship with the media was—and still is today—vital. But it has always been a balancing act for those employed by the Household to manage it. The monarchy relies upon the oxygen of the media for its life blood (it must not just be relevant, it must be *seen* to be relevant), but as William and Harry saw so painfully when they were growing up, if the balance is upset, and the boundary between their private and public personas is badly violated, then the result can be catastrophic. The PCC Code of Conduct covered the boys to the age of eighteen, after which it was a constant battle to keep stories out of the press, and for every one that appeared, many more were suppressed; and much of the time it was the result of good old-fashioned horse-trading.

"We'd say, 'Okay, you've got that, but let's go with this, if you don't say anything about that.' There was a lot of negotiation like that going on," says Colleen. "There were many times when we managed to protect William and Harry and keep them out of the media when they were up to mischievous things. Nothing terrible, nothing criminal, but things they wouldn't have wanted the media to write about." Their success was partly down to good relationships with the press, but partly because she and Sandy discussed things with the boys ahead of time. " 'What could happen if you did this, and what might happen if you did that?' They might not have always agreed but we worked through scenarios." Sandy would always say to them, "Don't ever do anything that you don't want to see in a newspaper at some stage." One can only conclude that William heeded her advice more than Harry.

But Harry was always more of a risk taker; he was a typical last-born child in that respect and, being the spare, always had more freedom to behave as he wanted; he could get away with misdemeanors that William, as heir, could never have contemplated—or, as a typical, cautious, respectful firstborn *would* never have contemplated. Not that William was a saint. There are plenty of stories about him at local pubs and parties that never went any further. As a friend who knows them both well says, "The idea of Harry being the wild one and William the good one is nonsense. They were both wild; Harry was just the one who got caught." Harry didn't do things in half-measures; he didn't share his brother's sense of responsibility or decorum. He loved being the center of attention, the clown, the one who made everyone laugh. He was a party animal, he was rebellious and no great lover of authority; but Harry always, always had a kind heart.

As Sandy says, "He was quite amazing. He'd go from this naughty child that one minute you wanted to throttle, to this quite compassionate grown-up person. He is one of the nicest kids I've met. Yes, he was a bit of a rebel and don't you love a boy who's a rebel? Everyone does. But inside there was something about him, he could always see another person's point of view at a very young age."

Colleen vividly remembers the first year she had to organize the annual skiing photo call at Klosters. It was a year when there was no snow on the mountains, so she postponed it, but by that time the media had all arrived in the village. Most of them were more than happy to hang around and wait for snow, but some couldn't and so, as an interim solution, she found a location outside the hotel. William, Harry and their father all duly performed for the cameras. But she had made it clear to them that once the snow arrived, they would have to do it all over again for all the other photographers. "They didn't hear that bit," she says with a laugh, so when she told them, after a night of heavy snowfall, that they were needed up the mountains, it took some negotiating.

"My God. I asked the Prince of Wales and he said, 'Yes, absolutely fine, go ahead. You talk to William.' So I had to go and chat to William. Harry was there as well—they were watching something on the telly. It was hysterical, a program called *Banzai* which they would shout every so often. Harry kept bursting into laughter; the Prince of Wales was sitting in the corner reading, looking up at me. So I said, 'We've got to do this photo call.' William said, 'No, we've done a photo call.' 'No, that was only for some of the media, the ones that had to leave. Now we need to do another one, otherwise you're going to have all the paparazzi following you around for the rest of the week. So let's just go and do a nice big one up the mountain.' 'No, I'm not doing it.'

"Now, I've got 150 media," says Colleen; "it's my first trip, Sandy's sick so I can't ring her and I'm sitting there with this belligerent young man. This carried on backwards and forwards for a bit and in the end, I just lost it, the mummy in me came out and I said, 'Look, you're doing it, otherwise you're all going to be in trouble and it will be a rotten week for everybody. It won't hurt you, it'll be good for you, dah, dah, dah, dah,' and went mad, and he just sat there.

"Then Harry said, 'Yeah, let's do it William. Get out the way, Colleen, I'm watching something,' and that was it. So Harry got the deal signed for me. What a nightmare. I couldn't believe it. If you look at the photos now, that was the photo shoot where the public first heard William speak. Up on the mountain at Klosters with Harry and his father and I asked an ITN guy to ask him a question, 'Say "How's it going?,"' and he responded. It was a great photo call. They laughed, they chatted, they did it brilliantly; the best one they'd ever done. And it was a turning point. The media went crazy because they'd never heard him speak on camera before. It was a kind of two fingers up to me I think, it was like, 'Yeah, I can do it if I want to, when the mood takes me. I can deliver.'"

But she doesn't think the press office always got it right. She remembers Harry breaking his arm at Eton and her and her colleagues not letting the media report it. "We said it was a private matter because it happened at school and the media were saying, 'Hang on a minute, this is of public interest,' and we said, 'Yes, but it's not a proper break so it doesn't count.'"

The most extraordinary examples of horse-trading that ever went on was in January 2002 when Harry was thrown to the lions in order to make his father look good. The *News of the World* (with Rebekah Wade now at the helm) ran a seven-page exclusive story under the headline, "HARRY'S DRUG SHAME." According to the story, Harry, then sixteen, had been smoking cannabis and drinking heavily underage and after-hours in the Rattlebone Inn, a pub in the village of Sherston, just a few miles from Highgrove. He had been so drunk that on one occasion, at the end of a lock-in, when asked to leave, he had called the French under-manager, "a fucking frog." All of this had come to light in August or September 2001. He had confessed to his father, and his father had taken him for a short sharp shock to Featherstone Lodge, a drug rehabilitation center in south London, to spend a day talking to recovering drug addicts.

"Worried Charles chose to 'terrify' Harry away from drugs by sending him to therapy sessions with hard-core heroin addicts," claimed the *News of the World*, but a "family friend" said that Charles remained "very calm. He didn't confront Harry aggressively but sat him down and asked him to tell the truth." Later, after the visit to the Featherstone Lodge, Harry had "returned to Highgrove for a heart-to-heart that he will never forget." Adding, "He has never done drugs since. William is such a steadying influence. The two of them have had detailed discussions and Harry has changed his ways. He now understands the very real perils of drug-taking and excessive drinking. He has a lot to be thankful for. If his brother and father did not care so much about him there might well have been a different end to this story."

The Prince of Wales was widely applauded for his action. "The way Prince Charles and the Royal Family have handled it is absolutely right," proclaimed Tony Blair, "and they have done it in a very responsible and, as you would expect, a very sensitive way for their child." Peter Martin, Chief Executive of Addaction, Britain's largest drug and alcohol treatment agency, said, "The Prince of Wales has acted with deep sensitivity and very quickly, which is exactly what is needed." To which the Department for Education added, "Parents play a very important role, as demonstrated by Prince Charles, who has set an extremely good example."

The story, as it appeared, was not strictly true, while suppressing a more damaging story. Harry *had* visited Featherstone Lodge, but he had gone with Mark Dyer, not his father, and they had gone in the summer of 2001, at least two months before the *News of the World* published the story about the Rattlebone. The visit had absolutely nothing to do with his own behavior.

As Mark Bolland subsequently admitted in an interview with the *Guardian*, "Presenting the center as the great solution to the problem was something that I was embarrassed about. It was misleading." But it had come about because, "We had been wrestling every two weeks for about nine months with several newspapers, principally the *News of the World*, on stories about William and drinking and/or drugs, all of which were untrue, and then Harry—drinking and drugs—as well. We were going to the limits to stop newspapers writing things about Harry.

"There . . . was a particular incident that summer in Spain, photographs that allegedly showed Harry in a drunk or drugged condition. That particular incident went on for most of the summer and the *News of the World* pushed very, very hard to run that story and didn't because we just said it was untrue, that all the information they had, the witness statements they had [were false].

"We pushed it to the limit that time with the *News of the World*. It was a screaming match. I think [they] thought that we had misled them. I think that provoked the *News of the World* to take a very close interest in Harry. They then had a big investigation down in Gloucestershire and confronted us with what they had found. Their dossier of evidence was compelling. We had to make a choice. Did we fight again to stop these allegations appearing in the newspaper, or did we accept that the *News of the World* was going to print something and make the best of it?"

He decided to make the best of it. He told the paper about Harry's visit to the rehab center and, instead of an unremittingly negative story about drink and drugs, it turned into a heart-warming story about Charles's sensitive and responsible parenting. Even the Queen publicly praised the way he had handled the problem.

According to locals, the *News of the World* had sent a couple of young reporters to live in the village for a month and infiltrate the Rattlebone. They had been introduced as relatives of a regular customer and a sum of £35,000 is rumored to have changed hands.

Steve Hoare, half of a rock band called Nobodys Business, which used to play in the Rattlebone, admits that the lock-ins certainly happened, but never saw any drugs in the pub when William or Harry were around—and, if there had been some, their older friends from the polo club would have been on to it like a flash. As for the incident with the Frenchman, François Ortet, known to everyone as "French Frank," Steve was there that night and says it was just playful banter. They were friends and the Frenchman gave as good as he got.

Harry was at school when the *News of the World* story appeared and it was Andrew Gailey who once again had to pick up the pieces. William had left Eton in the summer of 2000, so was no longer on hand to help. After a gap year spent traveling with Mark Dyer and working in Africa and Central and South America, he had gone to St. Andrews University in Scotland. But even when they were thousands of miles apart, they were only a phone call away, and they did speak frequently. William took every blow that

Three Princes: two heirs and a spare. Harry, a year old at
Kensington Palace with his father and brother.

Aged three secure in the calm
and capable hands of nanny
Olga Powell.

Swapping places with his police escort—
the perks of being a little Prince.

But underneath it, no different from any cheeky four-year-old.

Mother and son on
holiday, August 1987.

First day at school.
There were tears when
his parents left him.

Trooping the Colour
in June 1990—a small
face at the window of
Buckingham Palace.

No escape from the cameras—even on holiday.

Boy soldier. A taste of
things to come.

With Tiggy Legge-Burke, a hugely
important figure in his life.

4 August 1997,
aged 12. The
Queen Mother's
97th birthday

16 August 1997,
Balmoral photo-call,
Harry calling
the shots.

6 September 1997,
Diana's funeral.

The cat that got the cream. Surrounded by Spice Girls at the Two Nations concert in Johannesburg.

Rugby has been an abiding passion. It was also an outlet for his teenage anger.

New boy timidly signing the register on his first day at Eton September 1998

What a difference five years makes. Harry in his room at Eton, personalized with wall hangings and a framed photograph of his mother on the desk.

Father and sons at the start of their skiing holiday at Klosters.

Has hat will travel. Sydney Zoo in September 2003. First stop on his gap year.

With Mark Dyer, the Captain Hurricane figure, close friend and mentor.

Team Highgrove. A rich man's sport but the Princes have raised millions of pounds for charity on the polo pitch.

A natural sportsman—and fiercely competitive.

Camilla made his father happy and that was the important thing.

Sovereign's Parade at Sandhurst. One very happy Cadet H. Wales being inspected by his grandmother.

Harry suffered very much to heart, as his tutors knew only too well. Just as Harry too felt every knock and setback that William experienced.

"Harry really resented the way he was made to look bad so that his father could look good," says a friend. "He understood why it happened, and I don't think he blamed his father, but the idea that Harry had gone to a rehab center a year before because Prince Charles had seen the way things were going is a blatant load of bollocks. Prince Charles didn't have any idea what his son was up to. It was PR panic and spin and he really resents that he was made to take the rap for that."

That same friend doubts that William would ever have taken drugs. "He's quite canny, quite square in that way. I'd bet a lot of money he never has. He would never have been bullied into doing it because everyone else was. He would know absolutely if he was caught taking drugs it would be a catastrophe. He lets his hair down and puts down some serious drink on occasions, he certainly did as a student, and he likes a good night out with his friends, but he's always quite careful to protect his image and not do anything that would really damage him. You get pissed, so what? Nobody cares; you take drugs, it tarnishes you for ever, and if you're going to be King? No. But the idea of a good Prince, bad Prince was always a load of rubbish."

What upset both boys, however, was that the *News of the World* placed the blame for Harry's cannabis use on a mutual friend, Guy Pelly. He was said to "have encouraged Harry to experiment with the drug at a private party in Tetbury," and taken it into Highgrove so Harry could smoke it at parties there. The Prince of Wales had done up the basement as a den which was known as Club H. A family friend was quoted as saying, "Prince Harry fell in with a bad lot. Guy Pelly, who has a drink-drive conviction and is a student at Cirencester, was the worst influence. It was Pelly who introduced Harry to cannabis in June last year." It's more likely Harry was introduced to cannabis at Eton, where, despite a policy of zero tolerance, it was plentiful, as it was in most schools.

Pelly took the hit for his friend, and his name and reputation were trashed by the media; he was even forced to give up his farm management course at the Royal Agricultural College because of the row. Yet, in all the years, he has only once made any comment about it. "I have never dealt in drugs at Highgrove, at the Rattle-bone Inn or anywhere else," he said. "I have never taken drugs with Prince Harry or supplied any drugs to him. I have never used drugs at Highgrove or the Rattlebone Inn. I would like this categoric statement to put an end to the matter." It's a measure of the depth of loyalty and affection that he—like all of Harry's close friends—feel towards the Prince that he was prepared to put up with the slur on his reputation and never attempt to clear his name further.

Five weeks later, although the newspapers reported that the Prince of Wales had forbidden Harry to see Guy Pelly again, he and his brother very publicly stood shoulder to shoulder with him on the terraces at Twickenham for a high-profile international rugby match.

ROCK 'N' ROLL

Steve Hoare and his partner in Nobodys Business, Frank McQueen, had just set up their kit to play at an eighteenth birthday party in a village near Swindon. They were sitting on their upturned speakers, their guitars propped beside them, chatting, when suddenly a bread roll came hurtling through the air and missed Frank's ear by a millimeter. Shocked and surprised, they scanned the room looking for some explanation. Nothing looked out of the ordinary. Then they spotted a familiar mop of ginger hair behind one of the tables, the crouched figure laughing and pointing at Frank. "Right, I thought, he's going to get that back," he says, and immediately re-launched the roll. It missed Harry by a whisker, whereupon he leapt up and there were handshakes and hugs all round.

Steve and Frank were local, loud and gutsy—and Harry used to impersonate their broad Wiltshire accents. They sang songs by Eric Clapton, The Rolling Stones and The Beatles, and played electric guitar to backing tracks. For many years they played at parties in north Wiltshire and Gloucestershire, and some of the pubs, including the Rattlebone, as well as at The Beaufort Polo Club. They rapidly became everyone's favorite band, including William and Harry's. They had met William first, after playing at a twenty-fifth birthday party in the neighboring village of Crudwell; he had sat around on hay bales afterwards, chatting to them with some friends. Steve remembers watching him on the dance floor, as his friends instinctively formed a protective barrier around him to fend off some young girls who were trying to muscle in. The next time they saw him, he was wearing one of the band's T-shirts, which they often saw him in. He once told Steve he'd been wearing it over the weekend and "Granny asked what the logo was."

They first met Harry a few weeks later at the Rattlebone. He came in with William and their cousins, Peter and Zara Phillips, and two of their regular companions from the polo club, Richard Skipper, known as Skip, who was a groom, and Caspar West, who was an instructor. It was August 2000 and Harry was not quite sixteen. "I remember him looking so young and trying to act all grown up," says Steve. "He was very friendly and you could instantly tell he had a mischievous streak about him. During the break I was chatting to Skip and I remember Harry walking over and joining in the conversation. He asked me how everybody knew the words to the songs we were playing and admitted he didn't know many of the tunes at all." When Steve started playing again, Harry came and stood in front of him, staring at him, his nose about six inches from Steve's face as he sang into the microphone. When Steve turned his head, Harry lent forward and kissed him mischievously on his cheek. Steve was nonplussed and very nearly lost the plot. He told Harry afterwards that he'd feared he might turn into a frog.

Throwing bread rolls and behaving in this rather odd and immature way was typical of Harry during his teens and it hadn't endeared him to his peers in his early years at Eton. But beneath the immaturity was a boy with a very sweet nature, and impeccable manners, which most people warmed to.

Steve and Frank's music always raised the roof and they ended the gig that night, as they invariably did, with the Status Quo number "Rockin' All Over the World." "Harry certainly knew this one and was joining in with Skip, Caspar and Will and the whole manic crowd on backing vocals to finish the night off in fine style." As often as not after a gig, the landlord had an after-hours lock-in with only friends and regulars, and they would all sit around drinking and chatting until the small hours.

Both Princes enjoyed acting as the band's roadies. Once Steve and Frank arrived to play at the polo club close to midnight, having already played an earlier gig in a pub. The clubhouse was packed and the party in full swing; everyone had spent the night waiting for them. As they drew up outside, William and Harry both came out to help them carry their guitars and amps and all their kit from their cars. "Excuse me, excuse me, move aside, the band's coming through," shouted Harry above the din and cleared an instant path to the front that they could never have managed alone. On another occasion, as they arrived to play at Victoria Inskip's eighteenth birthday party (Victoria is the sister of Harry's great friend Tom), Harry was standing with his back to them and, by way of greeting, Frank kicked him up the backside. Harry spun round indignantly, then saw who it was and was immediately all smiles and hugs.

Guy Pelly was one of that crowd of horsey, public-school-educated teenagers who hunted and played polo at The Beaufort Polo Club. He was originally William's friend—he is three years older than Harry—but, as with many of their local friends, there is no real distinction about who is whose friend. The Glosse Posse, as these privileged inhabitants of Gloucestershire came to be called (the abbreviated Glos for Gloucestershire rhyming with Posse), were a close-knit group who had known each other for most of their lives and who, as they grew older, spent much of their time hanging around the bar at the polo club—with Westonbirt, the girls' public school across the road, providing plenty of love interest—and at the local pubs. They frequented the Rattlebone, the Vine Tree at Norton (where Nobodys Business also played) and the Cat and Custard Pot at Shipton Moyne. These were the places where the Princes trusted the landlords and the locals and felt safe; and it is a measure of how polite, charming and loved both boys are, that although stories abound of late-night drunken antics, they normally go nowhere. Stories of Harry's teenage romances are similarly circumspect, but there is no doubt he had a healthy appetite for pretty girls and that there was no shortage of choice. Girls threw themselves at both brothers, but Harry was the more reckless and he left a trail of them in his wake. To his credit, they were not always Sloane Rangers with double-barreled surnames.

In April a very pretty, tired and tearful young Swiss waitress was serving dinner at the Hotel Walserhof in Klosters where Harry had just been staying. In between sobs, she kept repeating, "Prince Harry has gone home." The maître d', Herbert Moser, apologized to the guests and explained that for the last two nights she and Prince Harry had been out partying at the local nightclub, Casa Antica, and hadn't been back until 4:00 in the morning. Before he left, Harry had pressed a piece of paper into the girl's hand with his contact details at Eton. Klosters in mid-season was little short of paradise for an attractive and adventurous sixteen-year-old, and it was not surprising that Harry should have explored the possibility of working at the hotel for part of his gap year, but he swiftly changed his mind when he was offered a highly unseasonal slot in October.

The annual Hunt Ball in December, a very swept-up, expensive, black-tie affair, was also fertile ground for attractive females, and the highlight of the horsey social calendar for young and old alike. That same year, 2001, it was held at Badminton House, and Nobodys Business were asked to play there for the first time. The Chance Band, which had come down from London, was the main attraction, playing in the main marquee, while Steve and Frank were in a small side marquee. But no sooner had they started to tune their guitars than their faithful polo club followers moved in to join them, including William and Harry. Within minutes the small tent was bursting at the seams, leaving the Chance Band to play to a decimated audience. Very soon Luke and Mark Tomlinson and William and Harry Wales were their self-appointed backing singers, belting out all the songs at the tops of their voices until Mark inadvertently hit the Stop button on the mini-disc player halfway through a song. At which point Frank and Steve threw them all off the stage.

That night Harry was knocking back champagne with the best of them and took a shine to a pretty 34DD blonde girl on the next table. Her name was Suzannah Harvey; she was a twenty-four-year-old model and TV presenter who, after a couple of intimate dances and few more glasses of champagne, was only too happy to be taken outside into the cold night and appreciated by the seventeen-year-old Prince. When they returned both of them were covered in muc—and the tale of their exploits were in the *Sunday People*. Fortunately for Harry, not many of the girls he has taken a fancy to over the years have been so keen to "kiss and tell," which again speaks volumes about how well he must treat women; clearly he is usually able to inspire loyalty.

As Sandy says, "If you are a Prince and you're straight, you are going to have women throwing themselves at you, but if you're a decent human being, which he is, and you treat women with respect, which he does, they don't tell. He made a mistake in judgment, oh dear. Get a life, people. He's got an eye like his father. He's attractive, he's got a twinkle in his eye, let him get on with it. As long as he doesn't hurt anyone, and from what I can gather he hasn't."

YET MORE LOSS

No twelve-year-old should ever have to lose a mother, and no eighteen-year-old should ever have to lose a best friend. But Harry did—and both of them in tragic and unnecessary accidents.

Just before Christmas in 2002, Harry heard the devastating news that his friend Henry van Straubenzee had been killed in a car crash. Because Harry had been held back a year at Ludgrove when Henry had gone on to Harrow, they were out of sync academically; after their usual holiday together in Polzeath that summer, Harry had gone back to school for his final year at Eton, while Henry had embarked on a gap year. He had won an Army scholarship to read Business Studies at Newcastle the following year, and before that had plans to work with children at a school in Uganda. His brother, Thomas, had been to the same school on his gap year two years earlier. After Newcastle Henry was destined for Sandhurst and his father's old regiment, the Royal Green Jackets (now The Rifles) continuing a family tradition that hadn't been broken in 150 years. But before any of that, he was earning some money by working at Ludgrove, their old prep school.

The term was over and members of staff were having a farewell Christmas party. The next day he was going home to Hertfordshire and flying out to Uganda straight after Christmas. In the early hours of the morning, the sound system stopped working so he and a friend drove down the drive to borrow a CD player from a friend. It was a foggy night, they had both been drinking, and because they were on a private road, neither of them was wearing a seat belt. On the way back, doing no more than 27 mph, the car collided with the only tree in the driveway. Henry was killed instantly and his friend, who had been at the wheel, was gravely injured.

Words cannot adequately describe how Harry must have felt when he heard the news. Shock, disbelief, anger, emptiness, grief. He must have felt that he was in danger of losing everyone close to him. That year alone he'd lost two members of the family and, although those deaths had not been sudden or unexpected like this, for someone so young and as sensitive as Harry, it was a lot to process.

He had been just a few weeks into the Lent Half in February 2002 when he was told that his great-aunt, the Queen's seventy-one-year-old sister, Princess Margaret, had died. She had suffered a series of strokes and been unwell for some years but, in such a close family, it was still a great sadness. She had been a neighbor at Kensington Palace, had befriended the Princess of Wales when Harry was young, and had been at every family get-together. They all attended her funeral at St. George's Chapel, Windsor—including Queen Elizabeth, the Queen Mother, now aged 101. Despite her own failing health, and a fall just a few days earlier in which she had damaged her arm, she was determined to be there to lay her troubled youngest daughter to rest. She was flown from Sandringham to Windsor by helicopter and carefully helped into a car for the last part of the journey. She was very frail and hidden behind a black veil but, as Margaret's coffin was taken away, she struggled to her feet. It was the last time Harry saw his great-grandmother.

Six weeks later, in the early evening of 30 March 2002, she died peacefully in her sleep at Royal Lodge, Windsor. No one, possibly, felt her loss more acutely than the Prince of Wales. He had been exceptionally close to his grandmother and was said to have been "completely devastated." He had been in Klosters with William and Harry and a group of friends when they heard the news, and this time it was the boys' turn to do the comforting. The whole family, indeed the whole nation, was again in mourning, but at a hundred and one, the Queen Mother had had a good innings. She had two new hips, her own teeth, a full set of marbles, a very good sense of humor, and liked nothing more than the occasional tipple or two. She was a deeply cool great-grandmother.

Plans for her funeral—Operation Tay Bridge—had been in place for years and were very straightforward. Held on 9 April 2002, it was a full-blown State funeral, the like of which Westminster Abbey had not seen since the funeral of her husband King George VI, fifty years before. Her son-in-law, Prince Philip, her grandsons—the Prince of Wales, the Duke of York, the Earl of Wessex and Viscount Linley (Princess Margaret's son)—and breaking tradition, her granddaughter, the Princess Royal—together with her great-grandsons, Princes William and Harry, and Peter Phillips all walked behind the coffin. It was carried on a gun carriage, drawn by the King's Troop, the Royal Horse Artillery, as Diana's had been. William and Harry looked sad but composed while their father was visibly distressed; but the walk and the crowds and the service in the Abbey—everything about the day— must have brought unbearable memories flooding back.

And now Henry. Henry, who was young, handsome, healthy, mischievous and happy, with everything to live for. Alex and Claire van Straubenzee had heard about his death at 4:30 in the morning, when the headmaster of Ludgrove telephoned—the call that every parent dreads. They envisaged a small family funeral for him, which was held on 23 December in their local parish church. To their surprise, 350 people turned up on the day and squeezed into the little church, among them, William and Harry, also Tiggy, who was now married, and two of the Princes' PPOs, who had regularly been with them in Cornwall and knew Henry well.

Harrow School held a service of thanksgiving for him in the school chapel the following month, which a thousand people attended, including William and Harry. Henry's younger brother, Charlie was only fourteen when Henry died and the Vans say that both William and Harry were enormously supportive to the whole family, but particularly to Charlie. Having been there themselves, they could understand better than most what the family was going through and they are all still very close.

After the memorial service, William went back to St. Andrews and Harry went back to Eton, both of them dealing as best they could with their grief, and having yet another shared experience to bind them. Two boys, so different in so many ways, emotionally fused; their relationship cemented by mutual need for support. Only they had experienced the nightmare of their childhood—the rows, the chaos, the upset; it was nothing unique to their family, except for the fact that it had become public knowledge. Only they had experienced the humiliation of being at all-boy schools when their parents' infidelities were all over the newspapers. They had come to the not unnatural conclusion that no one, apart from each other, could be trusted.

The events of the next few months proved it to them. Ken Wharfe, Diana's long-standing and trusted PPO, who'd been a constant figure throughout their childhood, who they'd treated like a favorite uncle, wrote a book about his years with the family. He knew everything and he told everything. On the fifth anniversary of their mother's death, it was serialized in a Sunday newspaper, supposedly for a six-figure sum. Harry was desperately upset that his mother was yet again being remembered for her private life, and told his father that he wanted to use his eighteenth birthday, just two weeks later, to remind people that she had done a lot of good things too. He didn't want a big party; he wanted to visit some of her charities instead, he said.

As one of Prince Charles's aides explained at the time: "For more than a year now, it has bothered Harry that, in such a short time, many people seem to have forgotten about his mother's charity work. The last straw came when much of the media coverage of the fifth anniversary of her death further eroded what Diana was and what she stood for. Prince Harry has said, 'I want to do something that evokes memories of Mummy's charity work.' Harry, more than William, wears his heart on his sleeve and has been very upset by some of the recent media coverage about his mother. He wants to do something that is tough, cutting-edge and challenging.

"A lot of people look at Prince William and compare him in

looks to his mother but, in reality, it is Harry who is more like his mother in many ways. Like his father, Prince William's future role is clearly defined but Harry, like his mother, needs to find a pathway for himself that is fulfilling and makes a contribution to society. Harry is his mother's son and he wants to carry on his mother's mantle. His mission is to remind people of some of the good things that she did and how she took on 'lost' causes that other people wanted nothing to do with."

In October 2002, Paul Burrell, who also knew every intimate detail of the family's life, went on trial at the Old Bailey. He was accused of stealing several million pounds' worth of items belonging to the Princess of Wales's estate, most of which had been found at his home. It was one of a series of revelations that made both William and Harry feel that the people they had grown up with, who had been trusted wholeheartedly and treated as though they were part of the family, had, in fact, been on the make in some way or another.

What had not been found when police raided Burrell's house was a mahogany box containing a tape recording Diana had made that her sister Sarah had told them contained "sensitive" material. Spurred on by the Spencer family, who were Diana's executors, the Crown Prosecution Service prosecuted and the case came to court—only to come to a screeching halt a month (and £1.5 million) later, when the Queen mentioned in passing to the Prince of Wales that Burrell had been to see her privately soon after Diana's death and told her that he was taking a number of papers from Kensington Palace for safekeeping. It was never quite explained why Burrell telling the Queen about a few papers should have exculpated him from having over three hundred items found in his house and under his floorboards. Be that as it may, he walked away a free, if embittered man. And a lot of people were left wondering why so much time and public money had been wasted on so flimsy and inconsequential a case.

The Prince of Wales had been against this prosecution from the start, afraid that it would be upsetting for the Princes, particularly

Harry, who was so sensitive about his mother's memory. And Harry was, predictably, very upset; some of the details that emerged reduced him to tears. Burrell had been closer to Diana than almost anyone: she had trusted him, relied upon him and confided in him. He had been a friend as well as a servant, and he was Harry and William's friend too. And for the three weeks that he was on trial at the Old Bailey, they watched one close relative after another step into the witness box and recall intimate details of their mother's behavior and the ups and downs of her dysfunctional family relationships, while the media and the public gorged on the disclosures.

Nothing could have been more damaging to the memory of the Princess. These were not just the exaggeration or lies of the tabloid press, the memories of disloyal bodyguards, or the fanciful writings of people who didn't know her. These were testimonies delivered under oath. And they painted a very disturbing picture.

Harry found it hard to understand why the trial had happened in the first place; why the man he regarded as a trusted friend has been treated in this way. The truth was that the Prince of Wales had tried to sort it all out privately at the very beginning. He liked Burrell and was grateful to him for the support he had given Diana after their divorce. He knew that life had not been easy for him, and had planned to see Burrell, ask for an explanation and tell him to give back the items he had taken and that would be the end of it. He had made an appointment to meet him one Friday afternoon in August—a meeting that the police mysteriously seem to have known about, because that very morning two detectives paid a visit to Highgrove to tell the Prince of Wales and Prince William that they had evidence that Burrell was profiting from Diana, selling some of the items that he had "stolen" abroad. Prince Charles was left with no alternative but to let justice take its course.

No fewer than four hundred media organizations approached Burrell for his story. He went with Piers Morgan, editor of the *Daily Mirror*. Announcing the deal, Morgan said, He will protect the memory of Princess Diana and will honor his pledge to always protect the Queen. But I think there will be many others in the

Royal Family and close to the Royal Family who will be quaking in their boots tonight." His story ran day after day and opened an unpalatable can of worms about unwanted gifts to the Prince of Wales either going to charity, exchanged, or given as a perk to a member of the Household. And the Prince's valet, Michael Fawcett, who handled the disposal, became known as "Fawcett the Fence."

Hot on its heels was another damning revelation in the *Mail on Sunday*. "I WAS RAPED BY CHARLES'S SERVANT" screamed the headline. It was an unreliable story from an unreliable witness—George Smith, a former valet who had suffered from alcohol problems. It was common knowledge that his allegations were on the tape that was in the missing mahogany box. It prompted the Prince to set up an inquiry into the probity of his Household, which threw up plenty of room for improvement in creating systems, but found no fundamental dishonesty.

The following year, 2003, Paul Burrell's memoirs, *A Royal Duty*, were published about his time in the Wales Household, in which he all but accused the Prince of Wales of murder, and revealed intimate details about William and Harry and their mother, also detailing her love affairs, quoting letters and notes she had written over the years and conversations they had had. It was serialized in the *Daily Mirror*. William, up at St. Andrews, read the installments day after day with mounting fury; by the end of the first week he had had enough. He rang Harry, who was by then on his gap year in Australia. He no longer felt sorry for Burrell; he was furious. Between them they agreed on a statement that Colleen released on their behalf. Many were shocked by the vehemence of their words.

"We cannot believe that Paul, who was entrusted with so much, could abuse his position in such a cold and overt betrayal. It is not only deeply painful for the two of us but also for everyone else affected and it would mortify our mother if she were alive today and, if we might say so, we feel we are more able to speak for our mother than Paul. We ask Paul please to bring these revelations to an end."

Paul issued his own statement. "I am saddened at the statement issued on behalf of Prince William and Prince Harry. Saddened because I know that this book is nothing more than a tribute to their mother. I am convinced that when the Princes and everyone else read this book in its entirety they will think differently. My only intention in writing this book was to defend the Princess and stand in her corner. I have been greatly encouraged by calls of support from some of the Princess's closest friends within the past forty-eight hours I would also like to point out that, following the collapse of my trial at the Old Bailey last year, no one from the Royal Family contacted me or said sorry for the unnecessary ordeal myself, my wife and my sons were put through..."

Speaking on the BBC's *Real Story*, he said he would never have written the book if the boys had contacted him after the trial. "I was saddened but slightly angry because I know those boys. I felt immediately that those boys were being manipulated and massaged by the system, by the palace, by the gray men in suits—whatever you want to call them. By those people who did exactly the same to their mother. The spin machine has gone forward again. Too many people busy spinning and William and Harry sent out as the emotional cannon."

HERE TODAY, GONE TOMORROW

There were all sorts of people William and Harry were attached to who provided stability and continuity in their lives. They were not as close as friends and family, but their disappearance (or, in the case of Burrell, betrayal) was not insignificant.

Sandy Henney was one, and the manner of her leaving was as sudden as it was reprehensible. She had been the Prince of Wales's Press Secretary for seven years and been key at the time of Diana's death and thereafter, along with Colleen Harris, in protecting both boys and guiding them through various media minefields. She had been there to broach subjects with them that their father had not wanted to do himself and they had had a good, honest and straightforward relationship; they called her "Granny" and teased her rotten—especially Harry. "He was always poking fun at people," she says, "and he expected you to play back."

Nothing illustrates the whole family set-up better than a story she tells of the day she was sitting in her office in St. James's Palace, when the phone rang and it was the head gardener at Highgrove. She was up to her neck organizing an overseas tour. " 'Yes David.' 'I've got a problem.' 'Christ, I need another one. What is it?' He said, 'The moorhen's dead.' I thought, do I give a stuff about the moorhen? I said, 'Right, David, what do you want me to do about it?' 'I want you to tell the Boss.' I said, 'You're down at Highgrove [where he was], you go and tell the Boss.' He said, 'But the Prince of Wales is very fond of this bird.' So I said, 'You want me, who's in London, to ring the Boss to tell him the moorhen's dead because you won't do it?' 'Yes.' 'Well, what's so special about this moor-hen?' 'It's because it's been shot,' and I thought Oh, and laughed. *Now* I know why he wants me to tell him, so I said, 'Okay, but before I do I want you to tell me the full story.' 'Well it's been shot.' 'Yes, but by whom?' 'I don't know.' 'Come on David.' He was just like a policeman; he said, 'The boys were seen walking in the vicinity of the pond.' 'Right, so you're telling me one of the kids has shot the bird?' 'Well, I didn't see it.' 'No, but that's what your understanding is,' and he said, 'Yeah.'

"So I rang the Boss. 'Bernie [the butler], can you put me through to the Boss please?' 'Yes, what's it about?' 'Don't ask, Ber-nie.' 'Your Royal Highness.' 'Good afternoon, Sandy.' 'I'm so sorry to trouble you, sir, but I've got some sad news.' 'Oh, what's that?' 'The moorhen's dead,' and he said, 'Oh my God, I loved that bird.' I said, 'That's just what David said.' One of the things he used to do when he came home from a day out was to go out and feed the chickens and walk down by that wonderful pool. It relaxed him.

"Then he said, 'Those bloody boys!' I hadn't said a word. I said, 'I can't let you say that because I don't know that.' And he said, 'Where were they?' I said, 'Well, they were seen in the vicinity of the pond.' 'Right,' he said, 'that's it. I want you to talk to them. I want you to find out which one of them did it. I want to know what happened, and I want an apology.'

"So I thought, Right, they're at school: and I called my mate Andrew Gailey. 'Hello Sandy.' 'Got a good one for you this time...' It's not funny, the bird's dead, but by this time I'm starting to giggle. 'Would you mind getting the boys into your office, please, because the Prince is really hacked off about this. Could you tell the kids Granny will give them twenty-four hours for one of them to cough to the Boss. Twenty-four hours and that's it.' Some hours later, I'm driving home and Andrew rings and he's giggling before he starts. He says 'I got them into the office and I said, "William. Harry. I've had Sandy on the phone and your father's very upset because someone has shot the moorhen."' They're looking at each other and saying, 'Shot the moorhen? Shot the moorhen?' Then William turns to Andrew and says, 'Which moorhen is that, Dr. Gailey?' And Harry says, 'The one you told me not to shoot!'

"I said, 'Tell Harry he's got twenty-four hours,' and bless his heart he rang his dad and said, 'I'm so sorry Papa, it was me, I shouldn't have done it.' Those boys are so close to each other—the loyalty between them and the mischievousness and sense of honesty, not wishing to tell a lie. Andrew and I were wetting ourselves laughing. The Prince was delighted that Harry had coughed."

What is curious, and speaks volumes, is that their father didn't simply telephone William and Harry and ask them himself.

"Harry's got mischief as his middle name, thank God," she says. "One smile would melt anyone and he's got so much going for him. He has an incredible sense of fun and just naughtiness. But he was incredibly endearing, incredibly loving and wanting to help; always wanting to help."

Another story she tells is of the year they were all in Klosters. Their equally mischievous cousin Zara Phillips was with them. Sandy was warming up in the bar of the hotel after a freezing day, when she noticed Harry and Tiggy waving frantically at the window. "I thought, Oh my God, what's happened? So I ran out—I was just wearing a jumper and it was freezing bloody cold outside and I got outside the door and that little sod Wales—I mean the big one—was pelting me with snowballs. There's me thinking he's fallen over and broken his neck or something... Tiggy and Harry and one of the policemen who were also in on this joke, were roaring with laughter, and I'm chasing William up the road, saying 'Person of doubtful parentage, you wait till I get hold of you.'"

On another occasion, she was having supper with them and their father at Birkhall, the Queen Mother's former home in Scotland, which has eleven grandfather clocks in the dining room—along with tartan walls and carpets. Nothing delights the Princes more than watching the reaction of first time visitors when, on the hour, all eleven clocks start chiming at once. At 10 o'clock sharp, Sandy duly jumped out of her skin, while they roared with laughter.

William and Harry had invented a card game and after supper they asked her to stay and play. "The idea was you were kneeling on the floor and had to get these cards down as quickly as you could and of course they thought it was just hysterical and William was pushing me out of the way and I went flying at one stage—everyone roaring with laughter at me trying to get back into the game to put my cards down. Are they competitive? Not half, they were really going for it—and mischievous too."

In the summer of 2000, when Harry was fifteen, Sandy was gone. She had devised a clever way of getting round William's aversion to the press. Rather than asking him to perform in front of dozens of cameras for his eighteenth birthday, she had hand-picked one photographer and one television cameraman who were both young, sympathetic and good ambassadors for their profession. They got on well with William, worked successfully with him over a period of five months at Eton and produced some intimate and insightful shots that they were to pool with the other print and film media.

Unhappily, the deal with the photographer, Ian Jones, fell apart at the eleventh hour. It was no fault of Sandy's or Ian's. His editor, Charles Moore at the *Daily Telegraph*, had so liked the images that he wanted to break the embargo. Piers Morgan, editor of the *Daily Mirror*, with scores to settle, wound up the rest of Fleet Street to object, and made life extremely difficult. Sandy had relied on a gentleman's agreement, only to discover she had not been dealing with gentlemen. And although she had consulted and informed Stephen Lamport, the Prince's Private Secretary, and Mark Bolland, his Deputy Private Secretary, at every turn, when she offered her resignation, it was accepted. By three o'clock that afternoon, on 9 June 2000, she was gone. The Prince of Wales, for whom she had worked long and unreasonable hours, and been devoted to, didn't even say goodbye, but Prince William—in the middle of his A-level exams—telephoned right away.

She was too upset to take the call immediately but he rang back three times before she finally picked up. "There was no 'Poor me, all this horrible publicity and it's ruined my exams,'" she says. "It was, 'How are you? I am so sorry.' Total loyalty. I didn't hear a word from the Prince of Wales—and there's William, not quite eighteen and in the middle of his A levels, the total opposite.

"I didn't tell him what happened, it was a convoluted story and anyway it didn't matter. I was going and that was it—out, gone, clear your desk, away, there's no looking back—someone else was going to look after him now. The saddest thing was the boys, knowing I would never see them again. I know they're Princes but they were a huge part of my life; I loved them to bits."

Colleen was the one left to look after them, but she too was soon gone, in the autumn of 2003, though of her own volition, exhausted by the demands of the job and needing to look after her own teenaged sons. In the meantime, the Prince of Wales had lost Stephen Lamport, who left in the summer of 2002, after nine years, to join the Royal Bank of Scotland, and Mark Bolland, the master of spin, who left the same year to set up his own public relations consultancy—and write a gossipy column in the *News of the World* under the pseudonym Blackadder. He had done his job; the way was paved for the Prince of Wales to marry Camilla Parker Bowles without there being riots on the streets. Working for the Prince of Wales was never easy, as every past employee will testify. It was not easy being his sons either.

GAP YEAR

Sir Michael Peat, a former partner of KPMG, was appointed the Prince of Wales's new Private Secretary in summer 2002. He came from Buckingham Palace where, as Keeper of the Privy Purse, he had been the architect of a major modernization program there, and his appointment was seen as a way of repairing the relationship between the two Palaces, a relationship that, to quote one member of the Household, "had been comprehensively bulldozed."

The man brought in to mastermind the relationship with the press was Paddy Harverson. A former *Financial Times* sports journalist, he had been at Manchester United since 2000, handling the royalty of the football world—people like David Beckham and Rio Ferdinand—and perpetually managing the tabloids and scandal. He arrived in February 2004 with a brand-new broom and no sense of awe about his employer and his family. Michael Peat's remit was to get the Prince of Wales's private life out of the newspapers and his good works into them, and Paddy's was to rebuild trust and internal bridges. He gives Mark Bolland credit for doing a lot of clever things and achieving what was asked of him, but it did cause damage behind the scenes, and left a sense of mistrust even within William and Harry's own small team. As a former member says of Mark Bolland, "I went to have lunch with him one day and it was in Richard Kay's column in the *Daily Mail* the next day. I can only assume Mark was addicted to the game and it was the only game he knew. He felt that the way to win over the people at the *Daily Mail* was to keep feeding them stuff so that when the big story came around they'd be on his side."

Paddy Harverson made it clear from the beginning that he worked differently: there would be no horse-trading, no favors and that the Palace was no longer going to lie down and take whatever the tabloids threw at it. Scarcely were his feet under the desk than he was busy defending William, accused by the *Mail on Sunday* of spearing and killing a dwarf antelope, known as a dik-dik, during a holiday in Kenya. Clarence House had issued a statement saying the story was untrue but the paper stuck to its guns. So Paddy went on to Radio 4's *Today* program to say, "Now, hopefully, they will understand that we do take things seriously and will hold them to account where we feel that they are wrong and have evidence to prove that they are wrong." He says: "No one had ever stood up for them before."

When Paddy arrived, Harry was already halfway through his gap year. It had got off to a disastrous start in Australia in September 2003, where republicans had recently lost a referendum on replacing the Queen as Head of State. It began with the obligatory photo call, at Sydney Zoo, where he pulled suitably funny faces for the cameras whilst cuddling up to koala bears and other native species. That all went well enough—and the female teenage population of Australia seemed pleased to see him—but there was controversy from the start about Australia having to foot some of the £600,000 bill for Harry's security during his stay; particularly since his only official duty was the photo call. Australia was hosting the Rugby World Cup, so the plan was to watch a lot of rugby, and cheer on the England team—which beat Australia in the final. He also played some polo: captaining the Young England team versus the Young Australians in the Ambassador's Cup. The bulk of the time was to be spent working on a cattle station in the outback. But the paparazzi made life so unbearable for him that, before the first month of his three-month stay was out, he was threatening to come home.

He was based at Tooloombilla Station, a 40,000-acre ranch near Roma in central Queensland, owned by a friend of his mother's who was married to a polo-playing friend of his father's, but instead of herding cattle and mending fences and doing all the things he had gone to Australia to do, he was sitting indoors watching videos, a prisoner in the house because he couldn't leave it without being photographed. "I've got a young man in there in pieces," Mark Dyer told the press. "He can't do his job as a jackaroo, he can't go out, he can't even muster cattle in the yards near the road without having his photo taken."

In one of her last jobs before leaving St. James's Palace, Colleen Harris came to the rescue and, to appease the media, persuaded Harry to perform for a second time. The once compliant little boy was grown-up, angry, and no longer so eager to please. He had already endured a photo call in Sydney and expected that to be that. Begrudgingly he agreed to a second, on the understanding that he would be left alone for the rest of his stay. The media were allowed to film and photograph him as he demonstrated his new-found skills on a horse called Guardsman, but he refused to answer questions. He issued a statement saying, "I have had a great time working out here, meeting people and learning a bit about how to be a jackaroo. And of course the rugby was absolutely fantastic. It's a great country." The photo call didn't go particularly well and there was bad feeling all round, although it did do the trick and he stayed his allotted time until Christmas.

Africa much improved his mood. Harry had longed to go back to Africa. When he'd been plotting his year away, he had said he would like to do something there with children. Mark Dyer had helped him plan the year, and he traveled with him, as he had done with William two years before. Damian West—brother of Dominic West, the actor, and close friend of Mark and Tiggy—had also been involved in the plans. He had known William and Harry for years, through Mark and Tiggy; like Mark, he also knows Africa well. He suggested Harry should go and work with children in the small mountain kingdom of Lesotho, in the middle of South Africa. Lesotho's population of 1.8 million people has been devastated by HIV/AIDS. The infection rate is the third highest in the world and the disease has virtually wiped out a whole generation and left thousands of children orphaned. In 2000, the King, Letsie III, had declared the AIDS pandemic a "national disaster" and the country's "number one enemy."

Damian had been good friends with Letsie and his brother, Crown Prince Seeiso, since their schooldays together at Ampleforth College in Yorkshire. Seeiso was his exact contemporary; they'd first met on the school train from London at the beginning of their first term in the prep school aged seven or eight. "He was a long way from home and he must have been desperately homesick," says Damian. "His grasp of the English language was quite limited and on his first day at boarding school the first class he was asked to attend was French. It must have been terribly difficult for him. He and his brother were great characters; they were very, very popular. When it first snowed in the middle of north Yorkshire, we all said, 'Look it's snow, have you ever seen it before?' We had no idea that it regularly snows in Lesotho."

He knew that in Lesotho Harry would be able to lead a normal life. The children he worked with would only know him as their friend Harry and, because of the remoteness of the places where Harry would be working, there would be relative freedom from the press. It was also a good opportunity to put Lesotho on the map. He spoke to Seeiso about the idea. "Mark and I flew over to Lesotho to discuss matters with Seeiso. On arrival we had an audience with HM Queen Mamohato, Seeiso's mother, who I had known since childhood. She was a wonderful, larger-than-life figure who had been a leader and campaigner in the fight against HIV and in supporting vulnerable children. When I told her what we were hoping to do, she was absolutely thrilled. Sadly, she unexpectedly passed away about a week after we left which was a great shame. It created a huge void in Lesotho and I think Harry came and filled that hole—and what we've done since has been remarkable. She was on such fantastic form when we went to see her—and her death was a big shock. She was the life and soul—and she is greatly missed."

Harry didn't know what to expect from Lesotho, Damian

explains. "He hadn't really heard of the place, so I was doing it on the basis of: one, I knew there was someone there who could look after him—Seeiso, a trusted friend; and two, that he could go somewhere where people didn't know who he was, and in a small enough area where he would be left alone. He had the freedom to move and operate and actually get a real feel for the place and it worked very well.

"He had been plagued by the press in Australia, but I didn't really fear the same, for the simple reason there are only certain places where the press could stay and the rugged country doesn't lend itself, so everything could be kept in check. People absolutely left him alone in Lesotho; and I think that had a huge effect. He could see things unhindered. When you're someone like him who has this massive affinity to children—it is fantastic how they react to him, he has an absolute draw. Only children will tell you why, but it is amazing; he's exceptional at it, he's brilliant with them—you can slot him in anywhere and away he goes."

There could not have been a more perfect place nor people to tap into these extraordinary gifts of Harry's. The experience of his eight weeks working with Lesotho's orphaned children—of which there are more than 220,000, with a further 700,000 children deemed to be vulnerable—was profoundly affecting. He went all over the country, with Seeiso as his guide, meeting children everywhere he went, but he also got stuck into manual labor at the Mants'ase Children's Home in Mohale's Hoek, building rooms, putting up fences, and painting walls. Whatever needed to be done, Harry was game to do it, and the rapport he had with the children was astonishing. He played with them, taught them English and fell in love with them. They all adored him but there was one little four-year-old boy in particular who followed him like a shadow, wearing a pair of big blue wellington boots Harry had given him. In another orphanage, a ten-month-old baby girl lay motionless in his arms. She had been raped by her mother's boyfriend and so badly damaged it was thought she would have to have her womb removed; witch doctors tell men that they will be cleansed if they rape a child, the younger the better. This little girl was so traumatized she couldn't even cry. The good news was that when Harry went back to Lesotho four months later, he found she had made a remarkable recovery, surgery hadn't been necessary and, miraculously, she wasn't even HIV positive. These were the children that ensured his concern for them was not a five-minute, gap-year wonder. They awakened a genuine passion in Harry that has never diminished and will no doubt, in some form or another, be his lasting legacy.

Lesotho is a beautiful country, but it is also one of the poorest and least developed in the world. It is mostly made up of highlands, with very few—and mainly dirt—roads, so most of the villages can only be reached on foot or horseback. Life is necessarily very simple and education is not a priority. In winter most of the country is covered in snow; in summer, families send their young boys—some as young as five—on their own, up into the hills for months at a time to graze the precious livestock. Life expectancy, at forty-one years, is the lowest in sub-Saharan Africa. The decimation of a whole generation has left the grandparents to cope with the orphaned children. "It is a huge crisis," says Damian. "So many orphans being cared for in this rather ad hoc way."

Prince Seeiso had been secretly apprehensive about having to look after Harry for two whole months, but he took to his young guest. He says their relationship got off "to a thunderous start—quite literally." The storms in Lesotho can be fearsome and they met in the midst of an impressive one. They instantly had a good rapport—Seeiso is eighteen years older than Harry, but he is a very likeable and amusing individual with no great sense of self-importance. And there was plenty to bond them—not least the loss of their mothers who had both been active in the fight against HIV/AIDS—and their legendary fondness for a party.

"Before I met him I had total sympathy for him," says Seeiso, "because I am a second son as well. And being number two has an effect on you and the way people perceive you. I knew how it felt to be judged against someone who is squeaky clean, quiet, reserved and perfect. My brother, like H's brother William, ticked all the right boxes, and I ticked all the wrong boxes. Fortunately, we do not have an aggressive media in Lesotho, because I am sure if we had there would have been stories about me rather like the ones printed about H."

"I remember going to Seeiso," says Damian, "and saying, 'We need a program for between one and three months and he sent back one for between one and three days. No, no, didn't you hear me correctly?' He would always say he didn't thank me at all for sending over an eighteen-year-old gap-year student. 'How on earth am I going to fill the time for this young man? It's an awful long time for me to have to entertain someone and organize their program,' but when the two months came to an end, Seeiso would say, 'It was only then I realized, when I looked at him work, how wrong I was, this is far too short.' I think they both saw a huge problem that they could both address."

To stave off any recurrence of the media fiasco in Australia, Paddy Harverson found himself on a plane to Lesotho with Harry to recce a photo call. "It was not something I expected to do in the first few weeks of my job," he says. Nevertheless, he found him "incredibly down to earth but with great natural charisma and charm. I remember him helping the ladies do the washing up after dinner the first night and just showing the qualities of a decent kind person with a lot of spirit. He was young, a typical eighteen-year-old, nothing like a fully formed adult, but he had a natural quality that shone through and ease with his emotions. He was being introduced by Seeiso and you could see everywhere he went he got on with everyone. They liked him, they were drawn to him, particularly younger people. He was a very cheerful and positive young man.

It is a testament to those figures like Tiggy Legge-Bourke, Mark Dyer and Andrew Gailey at Eton—and possibly the school itself—who were there to support him during his teenage years, that the Harry that Paddy found himself with on that trip should have left such a favorable impression on him. The eighteen-year-old Harry was not the finished product but the hurt and anger that had initially alienated him from many of his contemporaries at school had been suppressed. The qualities that were most evident were his charm, charisma, impeccable manners and a natural ability to communicate, especially with children.

"I came back with about forty-odd members of the British press and foreign press and we set up a big photo call. He was fantastic; very good with the media, he played pick-up rugby with the kids or football, there was a lot of laughter. One little four-year-old wouldn't let him go, followed him everywhere wearing wellies. They were great friends and that became the big story of that visit; and he then went back and met him again. He was very enthusiastic and passion-ate. And early on clearly wanted to try and do something for Leso-tho. He was genuinely moved and shocked by the absolutely terrible situation the country faced and still does through AIDS."

The coverage prompted Carol Sarler, writing in the *Daily Express*, to launch a vicious attack on Harry, calling him a "thor-oughly horrible young man" and a "national disgrace," who "rarely lifted a finger unless it's to feel up a cheap tart in a nightclub." His gap year she said, was "a space between no work whatsoever at school and utter privilege at Sandhurst." In Australia, he had spent his time "slumped in front of the television waiting to behave badly at the next available rugby match," while in Lesotho, he was spending "eight lavish weeks... [during which] he has reluctantly agreed to spend a bit of the trip staring at poor people. His exploits have been making headlines for years: the drinking, the drugging, the yobbing, the waste of the costliest education in the land, the explicit disdain for the lower orders, the increasingly sexual public romps—we've seen it all, we've heard it all."

Paddy too had seen it and heard it and had had enough. He wrote a furious letter of complaint to the *Express* that he insisted be printed in full. He took her points one by one. "These comments make it entirely clear that Ms. Sarler has little or no understanding of Harry as a person and how he has spent his current gap year." It was a "very unfair and unfounded attack" full of "ill-informed and insensitive criticism." The next week her column was an out-and-out attack on Paddy Harverson.

UPS AND DOWNS

One of the journalists at that photo call was Tom Bradby, ITN's former royal correspondent. He had filmed both the Princes over the years and had come to know Mark Dyer very well. Mark and Colleen Harris had identified him to William and Harry as the acceptable face of journalism—someone they could trust. Tom was knocked out by what he saw in Lesotho. "The stuff that Harry was doing with African kids was so interesting and he was so amazingly natural with them. There were some fantastically moving stories about that little boy Mutsu who used to follow Harry around everywhere. It was clear that Harry had some kind of natural aptitude with kids, particularly kids who'd had a very rough time. I didn't know whether that was something he innately got from his mother—so in the genes—or from the fact that *he'd* had a very rough time, maybe both. But he was in some ways quite an immature young man and yet here he was, behaving with amazing maturity with these kids and they really took to him. Everywhere he went you could see; there was no invention about that, there were kids hanging off him and they obviously really loved him and he had a really natural talent with them."

Harry agreed to be interviewed. It was the first interview he had ever given and, to Tom's surprise, he spoke very openly about his mother—and, it seemed, somewhat cathartically. Neither boy had ever spoken about Diana; but in Africa, with AIDS orphans, mirroring his mother's work in Africa all those years before, there was no way to avoid asking the question. Tom had talked at length to Mark beforehand, and there was a degree of nervousness about what Harry would say and whether it would upset his father. "I don't think he is now, but in those days Harry was a prisoner of everyone else's worries and nerves, particularly officials at the top of the pile who were nervous of what the Prince of Wales would think. It would have been bizarre and absurd if I hadn't asked about it, so I did, but what was surprising about it was the way it just came spilling out. He obviously wanted to talk about her, he was quite moving talking about her, I definitely had the feeling he wanted to get something off his chest and in fact somebody in the car, Damian or Mark later told me that he was slightly elated as he got in the car. So I got the impression, it bizarrely turned into a bit of therapy. He lived in a world where the Palace was always nervous about the memory of his mother. I think he felt she was in danger of being forgotten and wanted to put his own personal stamp on it, and I think he was pleased to have done so and in a way that's Harry all over. He's very 'shoot from the hip.' Everyone who works for him will tell you the same thing."

For all these reasons, Tom suggested making a documentary about Lesotho. It took months to persuade the Palace to agree but finally *The Forgotten Kingdom*: *Prince Harry in Lesotho* was shown on ITV in Britain in 2004 and sold to America. It incorporated the interview Harry had done with Tom the previous year. "I want to try to carry it [her work] on to make her proud," he said, and in reference to various tape recordings of his mother talking about her marriage that were, coincidentally, being broadcast for the first time, he remarked, "It's been a long time now [since she died], not for me but for most people. The stuff that's come out has been bad...these tapes and everything. Luckily, I've been out here so I haven't really heard about it but I feel bad because my father and brother have been taking the stick instead. It's a shame, it's a shame that, after all the good she'd done, even this far on, people can't bring out the good in her; they can't remember the good. All they want to bring out is the bad stuff. I mean, bad news sells. I'm not here to change that. All I'm out here doing is what I want to do, doing what she'd want me to do and it's not a question of reminding everyone of what good she did, because everyone knows that, hopefully."

Talking about the times his mother used to take him and his brother on late-night visits incognito to meet AIDS sufferers and sick children or to hostels to meet the homeless, he said, "I've always wanted to do this. It's what she was doing when I started off going to Great Ormond Street [Children's Hospital]. I believe I've a lot of my mother in me, basically, and I just think she'd want us to do this—me and my brother. Obviously it's not as easy for William as it is for me. I think I've got more time on my hands to be able to help."

When asked about the criticism of the likes of Carol Sarler he said, "I'd love to let it wash over me but I can't. I don't think anyone can. It's hard but I'm not out here for the sympathy vote. William and I try to be normal. It's very difficult but, you know, we are who we are. I feel that I'm now getting to the age where I can make the most of that. I always wanted to go to an AIDS country to carry on my mother's legacy as much as I can. I don't want to take over from her because I never will. I don't think anyone can, but I want to try and carry on to make her proud."

An appeal was launched on the back of the film and all the money raised went towards supporting the orphans in Lesotho, and ultimately towards founding Sentebale, the charity that he and Seeiso now run between them. There was no way Harry was going to jet home to his privileged, comfortable life in Britain and turn his back on all those children.

In June 2004, shortly before the official announcement that he was planning a career in the Army, he had sad news. His grandmother, Frances Shand Kydd, had died on the Isle of Seil off the west coast of Scotland. She was just sixty-eight, a rather tragic figure, who had last been seen in public at the Burrell trial as a witness for the prosecution, when under oath she had been forced to admit that she and Diana had been estranged for four months before her daughter's death. They had had no contact. Life had been very hard on her: she had endured an unhappy marriage and lost custody of her children when they needed her. Her second husband, Peter Shand Kydd, had left her in 1986; her brother had committed suicide two years before, and she had buried two children—her newborn son in 1960 and Diana in 1997. It was not surprising that she should have turned to two of life's great comforters, religion and the bottle. When she returned to Scotland after Diana's funeral, she was trapped indoors for eleven days by reporters; and, after the Burrell trial, she found she had been burgled in her high-profile absence, and her jewelry stolen. She had been living as a recluse for many years in a two-roomed bungalow, doing relentless charity work, supported by the local community in Oban and the Roman Catholic Church. She once said, "It takes very little to make you happy if you've had real sadness. It makes you take less for granted, and it's a very enriching experience, really."

Her funeral at St. Columba's Cathedral, a big old church on the seafront at Oban a week after her death, was a large gathering of the Spencer clan. The Prince of Wales, her former son-in-law, was not there—not, apparently, invited. William and Harry both looked immensely sad. They hadn't seen much of this grandmother in recent years, but they had happy memories of times with her and holidays spent on Seil when they were younger. She and Diana had been alike in so many ways and just knowing she was there must have been a reassuring link to their mother's memory. Sadly, she would never know that her red-haired "rascal" of a grandson had achieved his ambition to become a soldier.

Harry had passed his Pre-Regular Commissions Board assessment in September 2003 before he went to Australia. In July 2004 he was due to sit his entrance exams, the Regular Commissions Board that—if he was successful—would enter him into Sandhurst. It was not a given that he would get in: many candidates, most of whom are graduates, fail. Lord Dannatt, formerly General Sir Richard Dannatt, says of the process that: "It's four days, and tough, and there is an absolute quality line; you will only go to Sandhurst if you hit the absolute quality line." He was Chief of General Staff, the highest rank in the Army, but his own son, whom he believes would have made a good Army officer, didn't make it through the process. Neither did the son of the Major General who was the Commandant at Sandhurst. "So if Harry had not measured up to the standard, I don't think he would have got through. We're pretty fair and pretty robust in our processes."

In advance of the Board, which is a combination of grueling physical, mental and emotional aptitude tests held over four days, Harry had a bit of coaching from a former instructor. They used to meet at Broadfield, the Duchy Home Farm, near Highgrove, and the instructor helped bring Harry up to speed about what he could expect. "They are not looking to see whether you are a fully rounded leader at that moment," says Dannatt. "They are looking to see whether you've got the potential given a year's training at Sandhurst and continuing training, to become an effective leader and an effective Army officer, of which leadership is the core activity."

Harry was delighted to have passed and intended to start at Sandhurst in January 2005. In the meantime, his plan for the final part of his gap year, starting in November, was to stay on a polo ranch in Argentina, to immerse himself in the sport among the best horses, players and teachers in the world. Unfortunately, a couple of months before he went, he damaged his left knee on a training exercise with the Army, and then compounded the injury on the rugby pitch, coaching children on a Rugby Football Union community program. So when he arrived at the El Remanso polo farm, he disappointingly wasn't able to ride. Instead he saw a bit of the country, did some sightseeing and, among other things, went big game hunting at a private lodge owned by Count Claudio Zichy-Thyssen, who had more than 170,000 acres stocked with wildlife. Little did Harry know that a photograph of him, gun in hand, triumphantly squatting beside a dead water buffalo would come back to haunt him ten years later, the very day he, his brother and father jointly launched an impassioned appeal in London to stop the illegal slaughter and trade in endangered wildlife.

At the time, that wasn't the issue. What was occupying the

British press were cock-and-bull stories about Harry's supposedly drunken exploits and excesses in the local town. The party boy—whose reputation for staggering out of nightclubs was gathering pace—was behaving so badly, they said, that the local police had complained to the Prince's protection team. He had been sneaking out of the ranch at night to go clubbing; the tabloids quoted a local girl who claimed to have danced with him. What's more, a gangland kidnap plot had been discovered that forced him to leave the country early.

Harry, in fact, had never set foot inside the nightclub in question, and the kidnap plot was pure fantasy. Unbeknownst to the media, Mark Dyer had sneaked Harry's new girlfriend, Chelsy Davy, out to the ranch as a surprise, and Harry had no need to go in pursuit of girls. What he and his mates had done for a laugh was let a friend, who was also a redhead, pretend to be Harry—it was the friend who had been out partying and enjoying the attentions of the local talent, who triumphantly thought they'd pulled a prince.

Harry had fallen in love with Chelsy Davy when he had been in Africa earlier in the year. He had first met her a couple of years before that, introduced by mutual friends when she was in her final year at Stowe School, but this time they clicked. Although often portrayed in the press as nothing more than a good-time girl whose love of vodka and late nights was second only to Harry's, she is actually very bright, very ambitious, and, like most girls from southern Africa, fun, sporty and practical. They made each other laugh and had a lot in common and seemed to make a perfect couple. Everyone liked Chelsy; she very quickly became friends with his friends and family, as well as with William's girlfriend, Kate Middleton, and Kate's sister, Pippa.

She was born and brought up in Zimbabwe, but educated in England. Her father ran a game farm in Zimbabwe called Lemco Safari Area, which covered an area of 1,300 square miles—twice the size of Surrey. Charles Davy was one of the largest private landowners in the country, but lost several farms to President Mugabe's aggressive reclamation policy. Chelsy's mother, Beverley, had been

Miss Rhodesia, and was once the face of Coca-Cola locally; her family were also farmers. Like so many white Zimbabweans, they had had their land seized and their home razed to the ground. The Davy family now lives in Durban in South Africa with a holiday apartment at Camps Bay near Cape Town and, over the years, Harry has been a frequent visitor to both.

A longstanding family friend once quoted by a newspaper said, "She's probably never made a cup of tea or a bed in her life. But she could ride bareback, skipper a speedboat across Kenya's Lake Naivasha and all the time match the boys drink for drink. African girls like Chelsey have a lot in common with the upper classes. The bottom line is that these girls are athletic, strong-boned and gorgeous. They have that extra something that comes from being raised in the bush. They have a big appetite for life. These are the kind of girls who'll sleep under the stars without bringing a change of underwear, who aren't afraid of spiders and could strangle a snake. That wins them a lot of respect. They also share the same education, impeccable manners and privileged outlook on life as the British aristocracy." Was it any wonder someone like Harry would find her so irresistible? And her surprise arrival at El Remanso must have been all his dreams come true.

In Argentina, Harry's two PPOs, who had been telling the local police, as is customary, where Harry was going each day, discovered that the police were in dispute with the local municipality over their wages, and to supplement their meagre earnings were getting backhanders for tipping off the local press about where Harry would be. "So the protection officers stopped telling the Argentinean police where they were going," says Paddy, "which really annoyed them. They then leaked a story to the local newspaper that there was a kidnap threat against Prince Harry. A newspaper in Buenos Aires constructed this extraordinary vision of Harry on the rampage, based on the nightclub story and the police stuff, which was picked up by the *Daily Mirror* and run word for word—without any checking—on the front page. He had lived probably the most blameless two weeks of his life; sometimes it's quite comical."

The story appeared the morning Harry flew to Heathrow, under the headline, "OUT OF CONTROL? Harry's home early from Argentine in booze row. Prince picked up girls and was 'ungovernable'—but the Palace say he's just a boy with a bad leg."

The bad leg was on the mend. Harry saw a specialist sports physician and had an MRI scan, but it was a bone bruise inside the kneecap and there was no need for anything more radical than physiotherapy and strengthening exercises. It did, however, mean that his entry to Sandhurst had to be delayed by four months, until May 2005, to make sure he was completely fit.

The delay was unfortunate. During those months, the average tabloid reader might have concluded that the spare did nothing but spend his time in expensive nightclubs, taking a swipe at the waiting paparazzi as he staggered into the street in the early hours of the morning. As one of his team says, "He came back from Argentina and had more time on his hands, which was not a good thing because, like any young man, he kicked around, hung out with his mates and probably spent more time than he might have done out and about when he should have been in Sandhurst."

The tabloids had decided upon a narrative. William was the clean-living Prince and Harry was the wild child, and week after week they produced the photographs that proved Harry was off the rails. He didn't help himself; the photographs didn't lie—he did drink too much, like most of his friends and contemporaries—but, after Christmas that year, the press found a new stick to beat him with. He and William went to a fancy dress party in Wiltshire, given by Richard Meade, the former Olympic show-jumper, for his son Harry's twenty-second birthday. The theme was "colonial and native" and while William went as a lion, Harry dressed in a German desert costume with a swastika on the armband that he had found in a local fancy dress shop. With the typical mindlessness of the average twenty year old, he didn't think, and neither did most of the people at the party—both young and old. But someone took a photograph.

"HARRY THE NAZI" declared the *Sun* headline over

the offending shot—and, of course, true to form, he was holding a drink and a cigarette. Unhappily, the Holocaust Memorial
Day, in which the Royal Family was taking a leading role, was
just days away. Clarence House immediately issued a statement.
"Prince Harry has apologized for any offence or embarrassment
he has caused. He realizes it was a poor choice of costume." There
were calls for him to make an apology in person, and Doug Henderson MP, a former Armed Forces minister, said he was unfit to
attend Sandhurst. "If it was anyone else," he said, "the application
wouldn't be considered. It should be withdrawn immediately."
The outrage was understandable; there's no denying what Prince
Harry did, given who he is, was crass, particularly in the lead-up
to the sixtieth anniversary of the liberation of Auschwitz, but the
media onslaught against Harry outweighed the crime.

"Harry was in bits," says a former member of the Household.
"It was a very bad lapse of judgment, which he knew straightaway, and he apologized. Then all hell broke loose with the media
because they can't just move on; they have to have days and days
of drama. He had the whole world turned against him. The Italian prime minister; the Japanese prime minister was in London
and was asked about it, everyone just took the chance to have a
pop. Michael Howard, who was leader of the Tory Party, was
demanding things. His father weighs in. I don't know about this
grandmother but his father wants to know and talk about it. Harry
said 'Sorry, I'm a fool.' That was it. It was a young man's mistake,
thoughtless. He was upset because he realized he'd made a mistake and here was this pack baying for his blood. Rightly so, in a
way, but as ever these things are enormous storms and you have to
weather them. Young people make mistakes but his mistakes are
on the front page. And a great media trick is you have to apologize publicly, prostrate yourself in front of the cameras for it to be
meaningful. Why can't it be meaningful if he just says, 'I'm sorry,
it was a mistake?'

"'Should there have been someone there to advise him?' they
said. But on a Saturday night members of the Household are not

going to a party with them. There were protection officers, but their job is to protect them from harm, not to say what the Princes should and shouldn't do; and the relationship between them becomes impossible if they become their nannies and protectors of their morals. The policemen have to have a clear job to do. William probably reflected on whether he might have said something."

William was back at St. Andrews when the storm hit, with the first set of his final exams looming, and it is a measure of how affected he was by his brother's distress and embarrassment that it was interfering with his work. He spoke to John Walden, his geography tutor, and told him he was "having a bit of a crisis" and was worried about his exams. "He was really wound up about the way the press was treating his brother," says John. "It was obvious that he was very upset."

A WINDSOR WEDDING

As the media were sating themselves on the story of Harry's Nazi armband, Jamie Lowther-Pinkerton was wondering what he had let himself in for. He had just agreed to take on the job of Private Secretary to both William and Harry, and was horrified by the thought that he might have to deal with this kind of thing every day. His first meeting with Harry had been at the Troubadour, one of the last remaining 1950s coffee houses in London, in the Old Brompton Road. It was owned by Simon Thornhill, a former Scots Guards officer who now sports a pigtail and earrings. He was an old mate and a good friend of Mark Dyer's, and Harry was DJ-ing in the club in the basement. Mark, who was also a friend of Jamie's, suggested he come along and have a beer with the Prince. It was very late at night and Harry was busy with his music. Their second meeting over tea at Highgrove was altogether more conventional, and William was there too.

Some things about Harry, he says, have remained exactly the same since that first meeting. "He's always been incredibly polite and thoughtful about people and their feelings, to the extent that when I arrived he was courteous to a fault. I knew I hadn't got under the skin of him, because he was so charming and so polite and always telling his brother to say thank you to me when his brother *was* saying thank you. That hasn't changed and is a pretty good underlay." By the time he arrived in May to take up his position, the storm about the armband had blown over, William was in his last term at St. Andrews and Harry was just about to begin Sandhurst.

Mark Dyer had been invaluable; he had done a superb job in

supporting and guiding both Princes through their adolescence and showing them something of the world—also introducing them to Africa—and he remains a firm friend and steadying influence. As someone who knows both Mark and Harry well says, "Mark Dyer is incredibly good for him because he's one of the few people who talks some sense into him at times. One of the most absurdly inaccurate things that's ever been written is that Mark Dyer is in some way a bad influence on him; that's the biggest load of crap I've ever heard." But Mark had a business to run and needed to get on with his life. He had been with them on a part-time basis for eight years and, like so many people who work for the Prince of Wales, he had done it for love, not money. Now both boys were about to begin their careers, they needed more than a big brother to advise and guide. Jamie was the man selected for the task of taking them on to the next stage in their lives.

The only other person working exclusively for William and Harry when Jamie arrived was Helen Asprey, a member of the jewelry family, who had previously worked as a PA in the Lord Chamberlain's office and then for the Duke of Edinburgh. She had been brought in to organize their diaries and their personal lives and to answer their correspondence. She was young, pretty and less intimidating than anyone from their father's office. She is what a friend describes as "very old school, very formal, very Buckingham Palace," but also very good fun and utterly devoted to William and Harry, as they are to her. She organized house parties, shooting weekends and birthday parties; she managed big events for them and polo matches; booked flights and holidays; fixed dentists' and doctors' appointments; did their shopping, handled personal invitations, liaised with the police about their plans and helped in their relationships with family friends and other foreign royal families. Moreover, when they first started doing official engagements, she went with them. More than ten years later, she still keeps their personal diaries and manages their personal lives—with such discretion that most of time not even their Private Secretaries know what they are doing in their own time.

Jamie Lowther-Pinkerton, who is a former SAS man, was in his mid-forties when he arrived at St. James's Palace, and could not have been better suited to mentor two Princes about to go into the military. He is an Old Etonian, married with three young children (one of whom was a page boy at William's wedding) and he had been a professional soldier for twenty years. He had served in the first Iraq War and in the Balkans, and had won an MBE in the early 1990s busting drug cartels for the government in Colombia. Those who served alongside him say he was "completely brilliant." As a bonus, he already knew the Prince of Wales and was familiar with Court life, having been one of the Queen Mother's favorite Equerries. No doubt his stories about their great-grandmother will have endeared him to William and Harry; also the fact that he was a friend of Mark Dyer's.

He tells the story of how, as a twenty-three year old, he had been dozing in a frozen trench with a fellow Irish Guardsman somewhere between West and East Germany, when he got a call telling him he had been chosen for the job at Clarence House. Within forty-eight hours he was sitting down to lunch with the Queen Mother, nervously discussing how best to judge distance when flicking peas into a crystal chandelier with a fork. Some time later, after a boisterous stag party, he invited all his friends back to his Equerry's room (with free bar) at Clarence House. It was the night before the Trooping the Colour ceremony, so the Queen Mother was in residence. "The next morning," he says, "with the Private Secretary eyeing me darkly, and my room strewn with empty bottles and glasses, I crawled into my uniform just in time to attend Queen Elizabeth the Queen Mother as she mounted the carriage to take her to Horse Guards. 'Did you have a party here last night, Jamie?' I stared at my boots and mumbled, 'Ma'am, I'm terribly sorry. I hope we didn't disturb you,' knowing full well we had. 'I'm so glad to see the place being properly used,' Her Majesty sparked, hopping into the carriage."

William and Harry had both been involved in Jamie's selection, but the first time he had any dealings with Harry on his own was at a meeting the Prince was chairing with the Red Cross at

Clarence House. He and Prince Seeiso had talked about starting a charity together, but nothing had yet been finalized. In the meantime, the ITV program on Harry's trip, *The Forgotten Kingdom*, had raised a million pounds, which needed to be distributed. The Red Cross came to their aid and set up a Lesotho Fund to administer the money. Jamie had to leave the meeting early, so he excused himself, said goodbye to everyone—"all those very frightening, grand people of the Red Cross"—and set off for what he thought was the door, but which turned out to be a cupboard. "I went as far as almost closing the door behind me and thought, what do I do here? Do I stay in the cupboard and risk someone at the end of lunch following me and finding me standing there in the dark, or do I come out; so I came out of the cupboard and said, 'It's a cupboard' and everyone roared with laughter and Harry, with brilliant timing, said, 'Don't worry, he's new.'"

It was the start of an extraordinary working relationship. Jamie has always said that, had he still been running a Special Forces squadron in Hereford, he would have had Harry in it any day. "He's always been a soldier," he says. "At the end of the day, whether he's on a hill in Scotland or out in the middle of nowhere and it's raining and blustery and cold and miserable and wet, Harry will stay out there because he revels in that sort of environment, physical challenge; he's a tough chap, a natural soldier."

Before Sandhurst, Harry had his father's wedding to attend. More than thirty years after the Prince of Wales had first fallen in love with Camilla Parker Bowles, he finally married her on 9 April 2005 in the Guildhall at Windsor. The Queen had taken a long time to come round to giving her consent. Their relationship had brought the monarchy close to its knees, and while she had no personal animosity towards Camilla, life would have been very much easier for everyone without her. But Charles, normally duty personified, had insisted that Camilla was "non-negotiable." He loved her and he needed her and, as everyone who has known him any length of time will say, he is a different man now that he is married to her; he's happy, relaxed, utterly transformed.

But it was never going to be a straightforward affair. As one of his Household says, "Their marriage was a matter of huge constitutional and political importance and you had to court the approval of the Queen, Number Ten, the Archbishop of Canterbury and arguably a few others besides." Top of the list of the "others besides" were William and Harry, and concern for their feelings was one of the principal reasons why, even after the Queen was on his side, the Prince had taken so long to make Camilla his wife. Mark Bolland had worked so tirelessly (if riskily—sometimes seeming to promote his boss at the expense of other members of the Royal Family) during his six years with the Prince of Wales to make their marriage acceptable to the British public, and had been so successful that large sections of them were baying for him to make an honest woman of Camilla after all these years.

The boys had been unashamedly used as part of the process. William's first meeting with Camilla on 12 June 1998 was leaked to the press, which caused a surge in her popularity. The meeting was known to have been amicable, and Harry's meeting with her a few weeks later was also known to have gone well. The next move was for Charles and Camilla to be seen in public together. It happened in January 1999, when Camilla's sister Annabel Elliot was having a fiftieth birthday party at The Ritz Hotel in London. To their great relief, the majority of the British public scarcely turned a hair.

Their next public get-together included Harry the Queen, the Duke of Edinburgh and twenty-five of the younger members of the Royal Family. It was the Party at the Palace, in June 2002, the biggest and most revolutionary of all the Queen's Golden Jubilee events. For the first time, the gardens at Buckingham Palace were opened up to ordinary members of the public—twelve thousand of whom won tickets in a ballot—for a star-studded evening of rock and pop. A million people watched on giant screens in The Mall and Green Park, and a further 200 million watched it on television worldwide. Brian May of Queen started the proceedings, standing on the roof belting out the National Anthem, and it ended with a spectacular pyrotechnic display and a tribute from Prince Charles

to his mother, which to deafening cheers began, "Your Majesty...
Mummy..."

The Prince's popularity rating was riding high. At the time of
Diana's death it had plunged to 20 percent; by 2002 it was up to 75
percent. They could have married. There would always have been
some people unable to stomach it, but most of the public would
have been supportive, as they were when they finally did marry
three years later.

The reticence was over William and Harry, whose allegiance
was inevitably torn. They had loved their mother and knew that
she had been tormented by the woman she saw as her rival. Equally,
they could see that their father was lonely and that this woman lit
up his life; that he was good fun to be with when she was around,
and sank easily into gloom and despondency when she was not.
And both of them were old enough to know that nothing was as
black and white as it had seemed when they were children.

Camilla had never pushed things. She is a friendly, warm
woman; a great giggler, someone who makes life fun for those
around her, and who has a capacity to make Charles laugh—at
himself as much as anything—and to relax and lighten up. As a
mother herself, she knew only too well what William and Harry's
feelings might be towards her, and had no intention of ever trying
to be a mother to them.

As Colleen Harris says, "Part of the thinking was that in order
for the public to approve of Camilla, she had to be seen with the
boys or it wouldn't work. I think the relationship between them all
is warm now but, if I'm honest, it wasn't then. I think they found
it hard when they were little. I remember Harry being uncomfortable and saying something awkward. It was difficult for them; it
was a natural thing. You want your mum, you don't want her, and
she had her own family. To be fair to Camilla, she never tried to
be Mummy but she was the 'other woman,' and she was there and
taking Daddy's time. It wasn't all happy families for quite a long
time, but William and Harry were happy to see their father happy.

"They have had a tough time. They are royal and it's all lovely but as two young lads it hasn't been that great. In the early days Sandy was very good and she played a slightly maternal role for a while. Tiggy was great for adding spark; I don't think she gave guidance but kept them amused and was there for them. Andrew Gailey played an important part, I think I played my little part, a slightly maternal role on occasion and laying the law down. And they had Mark Dyer, a true friend to them. He's as nutty as a fruitcake but he's been a real support and a chum to them. One harebrained scheme after another; he had this bar, then that bar, he's a live wire character. He is older and has given them that young man steer. And Edward, the big van Cutsem boy, helped. And the Prince of Wales and the Queen and the Duke of Edinburgh. But at the end of the day there's no substitute for Mum, and then to have another woman thrust into it and all in the public eye, it's been very, very hard. It's great that they have turned out the way they have, but they've had a lot of love around them and a lot of support from the staff as well. And their mum did love them and that has stood them in very good stead."

By the time it came to the wedding, both boys had long since put their own feelings to one side and were simply delighted for their father. They released a joint statement saying, "We are both very happy for our father and Camilla, and we wish them all the luck in the future."

After a multitude of obstacles along the way—including postponement for a day because the original date clashed with the funeral of Pope John Paul II in Rome, and arguments about whether it was right or wrong for the country, good or bad for the boys, what kind of service it should be, whether Camilla should be called HRH The Duchess of Cornwall, or something more low key, and what the Princess of Wales would have thought—the marriage finally happened. And, despite their fear that the public would stay away, the streets of Windsor were packed.

Ian Jones was there. "One of the best, best moments was when they came out of the chapel. Having photographed Charles for quite a few years around the world on tours alone, he always seemed to be lacking someone by his side. He was passionate about what he was doing, but he had no one to share it with, no one to appreciate what he was doing and you could see the loneliness. It was so different when she was there with him and able to support him. When you think of all the grief she went through to get to that stage...It was transparent that William was happy for them—and Harry; but more so William. Harry is 'Yeah fine, get on with it, let's have a beer,' but the caring side of William came out and from that first moment, you could see on that wedding day that what mattered to him was the happiness of his father and how good Camilla was for him. You could see the genuine happiness of them all together. There's a lovely moment when the newlyweds are leaving by car and William and Harry are there seeing them off. There's real engagement and real confidence between Camilla and the boys."

During an interview to mark Harry's twenty-first birthday a few months later, Harry said of Camilla, "To be honest with you, she's always been very close to me and William...But no, she's not the wicked stepmother. I'll say that right now. Everyone has to understand that it's very hard for her. Look at the position she's coming into. Don't always feel sorry for me and William, feel sorry for her. She's a wonderful woman and she's made our father very, very happy, which is the most important thing. William and I love her to bits."

SANDHURST

The Royal Military Academy Sandhurst, at Camberley in Surrey, has been training leaders of the British Army—and some distinguished foreigners too—for two hundred years. In the twenty-first century, it is not for the faint-hearted: the sophistication and precision of modern warfare has seen to that. It is forty-four weeks of getting up at dawn, polishing boots, ironing uniform, intensive drill sessions and punishing physical exercise. It is tough, brutal, relentless, intolerant of mistakes, failure or weakness; and there are no concessions for princes. It is not for the proud or the sensitive; it's not for people who might have qualms about killing the enemy, or who don't like being shouted at, sworn at and told what to do— and when and how to do it—without question.

The Prince of Wales delivered Harry to the academy but, once his father had been introduced to all the top brass and given Harry a playful punch on the arm by way of farewell, the third in line to the throne became plain Officer Cadet Wales and there were no dispensations. He was treated no differently from any other recruit—except that not every other recruit was of such interest to the media. He had not been there a month when a cadet, supposed to be him, was splashed over the front page of the *Sun*. "The *Sun* wrongly identified him," says Paddy Harverson. "They smuggled someone into Sandhurst to say the place was a security risk and photographed what they said was Prince Harry and it wasn't him, it was another ginger-haired soldier. I pointed this out and the managing editor went on *Sky News* and said, 'I'll resign if I'm wrong,' and I said, 'Well you're wrong mate!' They didn't bother to ask

Arthur Edwards who's been photographing him since the year dot to see if it was him, or ask the royal correspondent. It was just: tall, red-haired, front-page splash. It caused all sorts of ructions; the Defence Secretary demanding an inquiry into the security lapses and in fact Sandhurst had always allowed civilians in to use the library. The *Sun* journalist had got in disguised as a warfare student on a research assignment. The end result was that Sandhurst had to put a whole clamp down on civilians using the facilities. All that for a cheap front page about a security scare with the wrong guy?"

Everyone arrived that first day with a bag of belongings and their own ironing board. They were all in it together. The belongings had to be arranged in a set pattern in their rooms—toothbrush and toothpaste with exact spaces in between. Every morning, beds had to be made uniformly and flawlessly, boots polished like mirrors, uniforms ironed to perfection, and everything ready for inspection at 5.30 a.m. Mistakes, creases, rumples were met with a terrifying barrage of abuse, and press-ups by way of punishment followed, often for the whole group.

It is an environment in which strong bonds are forged, second only to those forged in actual combat, where the enemy is not simply exhaustion and the Colour Sergeant yelling at you all. Those cadets who come through the forty-four weeks—and a high percentage don't—know that effective teamwork is essential to survival both at Sandhurst and in places like Afghanistan. Active service is what these young men and women are training for, and want. Many choose which regiment they want to join at the end of it according to which will give them the best chance of frontline service. And frontline service was all that Harry was interested in. "I wouldn't have joined the Army unless I was going to [fight]. If they said I couldn't then there's no way I would drag my sorry ass through Sandhurst. The last thing I would want to do is have my soldiers sent away to Iraq or somewhere like that and for me to be held back at home twiddling my thumbs, thinking 'What about David or Derek or whoever?' It's not the way anyone should really work."

Like every recruit, he was confined to barracks for the first five weeks with no visitors, no laptops, no mobile phones and no alcohol. They are renowned for being one of the toughest experiences most people will ever go through. Many of them are begging to leave after the second day and 15 percent drop out by the end of the five weeks.

In his twenty-first birthday interview, Harry admitted "the first five weeks—the infamous first five weeks"—had been "a bit of a struggle." He had lost weight, been treated like a piece of dirt and been shouted at by Sergeant Majors but he said he had got through it and admitted it had done him good. "Nobody's really supposed to love it, it's Sandhurst," he said. "Obviously, you've got a platoon of thirty guys so everyone's going through the same thing and the best thing about that is being able to fit in as just a normal person."

There is no denying Harry found it tough going. At twenty, his body was not as strong as it would have been if he had enrolled a few years later, after university, as most of his fellow cadets had. "You get stronger at the beginning of your twenties," says an aide. "It didn't show but I know he found it physically very challenging. He was a lot less strong than he is now, but he did well there."

A former member of the Household says he got into Sandhurst and immediately thrived. He reckons, "The Army was the making of the man. The man was there, he just needed time to be molded and matured. I'm not going to be a pop psychologist and guess at what his mother's death meant to his maturity but there is no doubt he matured quickly in the forces and prospered; and as we know he loved it because he could be one of the guys, could be 'normal.' He's an absolutely natural soldier, a natural leader."

This same aide remembers going out to organize the media on a skiing holiday one year and afterwards skiing with William, Harry and all their mates. "Almost everyone was older than Harry but he was always the leader down the slopes—there's always someone who decides where to go and everyone follows him. Always the bravest and the first off the edge. Those qualities shone through, you could see he would make a great soldier and he has done. Not a crazy risk taker, just 'Okay, let's go for it.' Physically brave but not foolhardy. He's smarter than people give him credit for. He's not academically smart in terms of degrees but he's got natural street-smart, really good intuitive intelligence. He often comes up with the best idea instinctively. Everyone else is thinking it through, working it out, and he will just come out with something and everyone will go, 'that's not a bad idea,' and it will be the answer."

A friend agrees about the good effect the Army had on him. "I would say Harry was probably a bit of an idiot at Eton; quite a lot of the people I know who were there with him weren't that impressed. He was a bit immature, a bit of a loose cannon. After leaving school, he was good fun but in the slightly edgy way of somebody who's cutting loose and probably is capable of being too immature, too often. And in his gap year he still had elements of that. Somewhere between that period and him becoming an Apache pilot, he settled down into being a really decent guy who people really like. And if you'd asked me in his gap year, do you think he's got the bottle to compete with the best of the best in the Army? I would think, not sure. The Army is great, it knocks the shit out of a lot of people and at some point in there Harry became quite a substantial human being."

In some respects, William, who joined his brother at Sandhurst in January 2006, found the course easier. At twenty-three he was physically stronger and, having heard from Harry about the horrors he could expect, he was better prepared.

Harry and William shared everything with each other. "It's amazing how close we've become," Harry said of his brother. "I mean ever since our mother died, obviously we were close, but he is the one person on this earth who I can actually really, you know, we can talk about anything. We understand each other and we give each other support. Luckily we've had the chance of growing up together, going through the same stuff as each other. If I find myself in really hard times, then at least I can turn to him, and vice versa, and at least we can look after each other."

"Harry has been a rock for William," says a close aide. "It's not just the other way round. He's a very, very cool guy and very good at listening when it matters; very empathetic. He knows when to stop taking the mickey, when someone needs a shoulder to cry on or a helping hand. He will be of immense and immeasurable support to William all the way through, even if sometimes it's perceived as being, certainly early on, the other way round. Harry's a real influence."

A friend of their mother's who has known them on and off for most of their lives, agrees. "Emotionally and empathetically, Harry is amazingly gifted but I think he's much angrier than William and my guess is he hasn't been able to work that through.

"They are amazing with each other, a great duo. They bring the best out of each other; Harry forces William to be more spontaneous and freer, and William helps steady Harry up and protects him from himself. They parent each other and I would have thought they were doing so when their mother was still alive. It can't have been easy with Diana. It's very sad for children seeing their mum unhappy. They played really well together and trusted each other in a way that they couldn't trust anyone else in the world."

Their approach to life could not be more different, but trust has always been an issue with both of them. William is cautious and conservative; and, in his friendships, his tendency is to cling to what one friend calls, "a masonic group" of long-term trusted friends. Whereas with Harry it's different. "Harry has his mates but it's not the masonic brotherhood. That's the interesting thing about Harry. His approach to it is to be so open about who he is. He says, 'Fuck it, let's engage with the world. Yeah, I know who I am but hey, so what, who are you?' kind of thing. He's simply so in-your-face about who he is that everyone quite soon forgets and the awkwardness disappears. He wears his heart so heavily on his sleeve: 'Just take me as I am,' and that seems to work for him. He's the reverse of William in a way. Harry will happily meet up with someone, go out, go to a bar, spend time chatting to the people there until four in the morning. That's why it's so extraordinary that there hasn't been more stuff written about him over the years because he is not remotely guarded in anything he does. And I think that's why people like him so much. Yes, he fucks up quite often, quite hard, but at least he seems like a nice guy. That's what I mean about everyone really loving him. It's really true to say that he has no airs and graces, really true.

"You'd never say that about his father; you'd say his brother had many fewer airs and graces than his father but he's still...The interesting breakdown is how much is nature and position, and how much is nurture and where they found themselves. Is William a lot more cautious and conservative because he has to be, or are they just innately who they are? I don't know what the answer is, but what is clear is that they were both born into the same rather tricky circumstance, they've decided to approach it entirely differently, and Harry is very open."

HACKED OFF

Sandhurst was one place where, behind the heavily fortified gates, this tendency to be open should have posed no danger at all. But stories inexplicably crept out. The *News of the World* headline in December 2005, for example, declared, "Harry's aide helps out on Sandhurst exams." The story alleged that Harry had contacted Jamie Lowther-Pinkerton with a plea for help with an essay on the siege of the Iranian Embassy in 1980, which the SAS successfully brought to an end.

It was not until the phone-hacking trial was underway in 2013 that the source of this and other stories became clear. For some years the *News of the World* had been hacking the voicemails of several members of the Royal Family and their Household.

"Just wondered if you, bizarre question, have you any information at all or you know where to get information from about the siege of the Iranian Embassy because I need to write an essay quite quickly on that," Harry had said. "I just need some information. I have got most of the stuff but if you have got any extra information or websites that you know please, please, please email it to me."

They eventually began to put two and two together, but for years William and Harry had been convinced that someone around them was leaking stories to the tabloids. It seemed to be the only possible explanation for the constant trickle of stories, some of them trivial, some more substantial, but all of them private. It created a corrosive atmosphere of paranoia and mistrust within the Household and their circle of friends. They became suspicious of everyone; the constant refrain was: "Did you tell him? Is he trustworthy?"

The penny finally dropped in November 2005, when a short piece appeared in the *News of the World* about Tom Bradby, who was by this time ITN's political editor. When he had been making *The Forgotten Kingdom*, about Harry's trip to Lesotho, he had used some bits of film that Harry had shot himself with his own camera during his gap year. Harry had simply handed over all the film he'd taken and, finding a lot of the material very funny, Tom had offered to edit it into a video for Harry. William had seen it and thought it was great, so Tom had offered to do the same for him. And they had been trying to find a time when they were both free to meet up.

"If ITN do a stocktake on their portable editing suites this week," said the piece in Clive Goodman's "Blackadder" column, "they might notice they're one down. That's because their pin-up political editor Tom Bradby has lent it to close pal Prince William so he can edit together all his gap-year videos and DVDs into one very posh home movie."

Tom and William had had a phone conversation on the Saturday—the very day before the piece appeared—and agreed to meet on the Monday; Tom would come to Clarence House with some equipment.

When he arrived on the Monday, he and William just looked at each other and said, "How the hell did the *News of the World* get that?" William then said that he'd been equally puzzled by a story about a knee injury he'd had that had appeared in the same column the previous week.

"William pulled a tendon in his knee after last week's kids' kickabout with Premiership club Charlton Athletic," wrote Goodman. "Now medics have put him on the sick list. He has seen Prince Charles's personal doc and is now having physiotherapy at Cirencester hospital, near his country home Highgrove."

William had been thinking the surgeon, or his secretary, must have spoken to the *News of the World*, but he knew, and Tom agreed, it was unthinkable. Then they started going through all the alternatives. Tom knew from his years as a royal correspondent that during Diana's lifetime tabloid reporters had listened to one another's voicemail messages to get stories. If they were doing it then, why not now? Slowly it dawned. After they had spoken on the Saturday, William had phoned Helen Asprey and left a message on her voicemail asking her to leave Tom's name with security at the gate. After he had seen the doctor, he had left a message on Helen's voicemail asking her to fix physiotherapy in Cirencester.

"The other one," says a member of the Household, "was William leaving a jokey message on Harry's voicemail pretending to be Chelsy and giving him a bollocking in a South African accent—there'd been a story about him visiting a lap-dancing club. This story ran in the *News of the World*. How did they know William had left a message on Harry's voicemail?

"At the same time, three of us noticed in conversation that all of our voicemail was playing up. We were discovering messages that had been listened to but not by us. They were being saved as having been listened to, as in 'You have four new messages and six saved messages,' and I would always listen to a message then delete it and I think the others did too. Initially we thought it was a fault with the phones but we had different phones and one was on a different network, so we thought how does that work? I remember sitting in Helen's room and it dawned on us that there might be more to this, that the *News of the World* stories and the funny voicemail situation might be connected, so we called in Royalty Protection, who are always the first port of call."

Because of the security implications, in that their messages were often about the Princes' flights and movements, the police brought in the anti-terrorism squad, who very quickly confirmed that their messages were being hacked and discovered who was doing it. Although, as one of them says, "It wasn't rocket science.

"We decided very quickly to prosecute—William and Harry were very angry and very keen to get something done about it. We told the police, and off we went. There was quite a long period when we carried on as normal while they gathered the evidence, knowing that they were listening to our voicemails. It was evil stuff. I never believed it was just us—as it all subsequently unraveled."

Clive Goodman was one of two men arrested in August 2006 and imprisoned in January 2007 for four months for intercepting mobile phone messages, but they were just the tip of the iceberg—as Lord Justice Leveson discovered, and the criminal cases involving News International journalists and executives attest.

"I remember once dealing with Clive Goodman over a story about Harry," says a former member of his team. "It was a weekend, when Harry was in the papers a lot, and he obviously had a personal animosity against him; he didn't like what he saw in Harry. He unleashed this vicious diatribe down the phone to me with lots of swear words about what a terrible man he was."

"The phone-hacking thing was a complete liberation to them," says a friend, "because all those stories just stopped; they don't appear anymore. With those arrests, they realized that their friends weren't talking and don't talk and that has helped them relax about things."

But both Princes, he believes, are still very angry about it; and angry about what happened to their mother and father. During his twenty-first birthday interview, Harry talked about his compulsion to read the newspapers even though they upset him, and only half jokingly said that he made a note of who the writers and photographers were "for use later."

The friend confirms. "They will never get over that anger; I think it burns as strongly in them now as it ever did. They hate the press; they always have and they always will. Everyone who works with them will tell you, 'Oh no it's not like that, they've come to terms with it, they're fine with it. Bollocks. In a way they've got good reason; somewhere in the last thirty years journalism became very corrupted as a profession and that's the reality. That Diana period was one of the most exciting in the history of the popular press.

"What an unbelievable period; a story that the public cared passionately about. They come through this toxic, spectacular divorce, the two sides get down and play dirty with the media in their own separate ways; that whole business of the gay rape tape and the recording, George Smith's testimony in the Priory. If you were writing fiction no one would believe it. The whole business of phone hacking, that was in the foothills: how did those Tampax and Squidgygate tapes get out there? A radio ham by accident. That's the most ridiculous explanation I've heard for anything. At some point in that period, journalism lost its moral compass on a whole bunch of things. So William and Harry grew up in a world where anything they did, anything they said, any friendship they had, any relationship they had was considered fair game by any means possible and they've got a lifetime's disillusionment with journalists and their morals and their motives as a result of it and, fine, that isn't happening anymore, but they still wake up and read shit."

THWARTED

"The best thing that ever happened to Prince Harry in a military sense," says one of his team, "was his commanding officer of the Household Cavalry at Windsor, Lieutenant Colonel Edward Smyth-Osbourne, a Lifeguards officer and former member of the SAS. Ed would kill me because he's a very self-effacing bloke, but he was brilliant, and he was turning the Household Cavalry into something really quite exciting. He was one of those paragons who got Harry and Harry got him—and William as well—and he really took Harry under his wing. His regiment was one of the few in the Army that was permanently deployed in Afghanistan or Iraq throughout his two-and-a-half-year tour as Harry's boss; he had two Princes dropped in on him and he didn't even break step. He dealt with them in a brilliant way and is still a father figure to them; an amazing man."

The set-up of the regiment is quite unusual, as the team member explains. "The Household Cavalry is a combination of Blues and Royals and Lifeguards, which is based permanently at Windsor, and they have their offshoot which is the Mounted Regiment at Knightsbridge. It sort of falls between infantry soldiering—down and dirty in the hills—and being an armored regiment with tanks and things. They're a reconnaissance regiment so they do a bit of sneaking around and checking out where the enemy lines are. I was always quite surprised that Harry chose to go into that rather than a down-and-dirty infantry regiment which would have tested his stalker skills, but it was quite a good choice because he got the best of both worlds: he could play his polo, which the Household

Cavalry are the best in the Army at, and he could also do the tough bit."

Shaun Pickford was the Regimental Corporal Major, which is the senior soldier of the other ranks, the conduit between them and the officers. It was his task to keep new young officers in check. "Some come in cocky and some don't. Harry didn't. He was a down-to-earth and a soldiers' officer from day one. He was interested in the guys, in what they'd done, what they wanted to do. He wanted to lead them, that's what really stood out with him from when he first joined the regiment. From day one Harry wanted to go to the front line."

Harry was commissioned at the famous Passing Out ceremony, in April 2006, as a Second Lieutenant in the Household Cavalry (Blues and Royals). His grandmother took the Sovereign's Parade in person for the first time in fifteen years, and whatever she said to him when she inspected the rows of newly commissioned officers made his face light up in a broad grin. His brother—a mere cadet for the time being—his father, stepmother, Tiggy Pettifer and Jamie Lowther-Pinkerton were all there to celebrate his success. Chelsy stayed away from the formal part of the day but joined him for the Sandhurst Ball in the evening, as did William's girlfriend, Kate Middleton, when at midnight the pips on the shoulders of the newly commissioned officers, signifying their rank, are traditionally uncovered.

After a short break, Harry arrived at the barracks in Windsor in May and almost immediately went off to Bovington Camp in Dorset for five months of specialist training to qualify as an Armoured Reconnaissance Troop Leader. He had joined A Squadron, which was due to deploy to Iraq the following year, so most of the remainder of that year and the first three months of 2007 were spent training for operations with his men, team building and team bonding (evenings in the pub), as well as the more obvious physical fitness training, planning exercises, maintaining the vehicles—four light tanks—and getting them and the whole troop of eleven men, three to a tank, ready for combat. As Shaun Pickford says,

"You're going to serve with these individuals so you need to know them outside of work as well as inside. It's knowing your blokes on every level." That Christmas, while his brother and the rest of the Royal Family gathered at Sandringham, Harry was on duty. "He was in the cookhouse at brunch when I walked in and there he was behind the counter cooking his own breakfast. He wasn't expecting anything any different than the blokes and was just accepting he was on duty and you just got on with it.

"His time at night was his own like anyone in the military. It is an eight-to-five job unless you're on exercises. He would work hard and also play hard—so there was a good balance of doing what he should and what he shouldn't. He was a young guy, no different from some of the troops going downtown getting in trouble—but they wouldn't hit the front pages of the papers whereas he would. What he did was nothing to do with us unless the papers reported they'd seen him."

If so, there would be a flurry of phone calls—usually on a Sunday morning, to Harry's PPOs, to establish where he had been the night before and whether there was any truth in any story that had appeared. The punishment would be "extras"—inspecting the guns, being in at six o'clock, staying in camp overnight and being on call as point of command for any security incident or trouble—in a sense, he was grounded.

In April 2007, it looked as though all the training and hard work had paid off. The Ministry of Defence (MoD) and Clarence House issued a joint statement confirming that Cornet Harry, his regimental title, would be deploying to Iraq in May or June.

General Sir Richard Dannatt, then Chief of General Staff (now Lord Dannatt), had inherited an agreement made by his predecessor, whereby if the Army decided to deploy either of the two Princes, the decision would be entirely his, as Chief of General Staff, in consultation with the Queen and the Prince of Wales. Dannatt had identified a remote desert area in Maysan Province, on the border between Iraq and Iran, a very inhospitable place, which saw a lot of cross-border smuggling and illegal activity.

A reconnaissance regiment like Harry's had been there the year before and Dannatt thought it the perfect place for Harry to be able to command his troop effectively without putting him or his men in excessive danger. The Queen and the Prince of Wales had accepted it was a reasonable risk; it was in Harry's interests to deploy with his regiment and it was a good thing for the Royal Family.

As soon as his deployment was made public, the media began to speculate, "and their speculation added up, eventually, to being absolutely right," says Dannatt. "The practice at the time was for the Secretary of State for Defence to announce in Parliament that the next deployment of troops to Iraq would be x brigade made up of these units and deploying in November or March or whenever. So it was a matter of public knowledge that the Household Cavalry regiment would be deploying, and you only had to look up what sort of vehicles they operated in and do your own homework to know that that kind of regiment would be taking over from a similar kind of regiment and that regiment was deployed in Maysan. So it was quite possible to join the dots and they pretty much worked out what he'd be wearing, what his vehicle would look like, what he'd be doing. At about the same time the security in that part of Iraq deteriorated; so we came to the conclusion we couldn't send him."

It was the Chief of Defence Staff, Air Chief Marshal Sir Jock Stirrup, who pulled the plug—just three days before the regiment was due to deploy—and, according to Jamie Lowther-Pinkerton, "Harry went boiling mad." Having trained and prepared so intensively with his men, after all the exercises and nights spent sleeping in ditches in the rain, he had to stand back and watch them go off to Iraq and the dangers of war without him. "He went wild, let off steam in a major way, and my God, I understood that. Any soldier who's been on operations would have understood that; your boys are going off and you're not going with them. One of the really dark times for him." He even contemplated leaving the Army, as he later confessed. "I did very much feel like, well if I'm going to cause this much chaos to a lot of people then maybe I should just, well, bow out and not just for my own sake, for everyone else's sake."

"The man who picked him up out of the gutter," says Jamie, "was Ed Smyth-Osbourne. He said to Harry, 'You're coming to Afghanistan with me'—before he even had the basis for saying it. He would have gone the whole way and probably resigned, he's that sort of chap. He said, 'I know you haven't been able to go to Iraq but I'm going to make damn sure that you get to Afghanistan, so hang in there,' and he took him under his wing and really looked after him.

Richard Dannatt gave Harry an undertaking that he would try and create another opportunity to get him to the front line, but says that was only half of the problem. The other was coming to some sort of accommodation with the media. After much head-scratching at the MoD, he decided to invite the editors into the building, pose the problem and ask for their suggestions about how Harry might get there without the enemy knowing about it. Thirty or forty media executives duly arrived and the conversation went round in circles for fifteen or twenty minutes until Dannatt had an idea.

"I said, 'Look, it seems to me that what you want to do is to be able to report about Prince Harry on operations. What I want to do is get him there. The problem is, if you speculate and get it right as you did last time, I can't get him there, so you don't get your story. So the trick we've got to try and work through is, how *we* get him there so *you* can get your story?' We came up with a suggestion that if we committed to giving them access to him before, during his training, while he was there and afterwards—and that material was made available to the media at large but through a selected team—and none of it was used until he came back, then they would have their stories; but if anyone broke ranks they would get nothing. 'That won't work.' 'Let's give it a try.' A very nice chap who was head of the Society of Editors undertook to draw up an agreement that they all signed up to. He duly deployed."

Jamie Lowther-Pinkerton reflects on Dannatt's skills. "Richard Dannatt was brilliant at stamping his foot and making sure at high levels of power that the logic of why Harry going to Afghanistan was different to the last time," says Jamie. "There was no greater supporter of Harry going operational; he stuck his own neck on the line, he was brave as a lion, completely morally motivated—as you'd expect from him."

Meanwhile another of Harry's advocates and close supporters was also making plans: the Commanding Officer of the Household Cavalry Regiment, Major General Edward Smyth-Osbourne. Smyth-Osbourne's genius was in sending him as close to the front as he could, which meant retraining him and sending him as a Joint Terminal Attack Controller, known as a JTAC.

"A lesser man than Ed would have wrapped him up in cotton wool. As a JTAC you're really doing the business right at the front where there are no journalists, day in day out in the frontline trench. The moral courage of a commanding officer in whose charge the third in line to the throne has been placed, to do that is extraordinary. He and Dannatt both had a huge part to play, but very different parts, and both of them we owe a huge debt to."

"I thought the definition of success was getting him to Afghanistan," says Dannatt. "Complete success was keeping him there for a month so he could get his medal, and anything beyond that was a complete bonus. As we know, he was there for about ten weeks, which was complete bonus category."

The Queen and the Prince of Wales had been consulted and were both very supportive. Other than that, the MoD was very selective about who they told. "We told the Secretary of State for Defence," says Dannatt, "we told the Prime Minister; we didn't tell the Ambassador in Kabul. The Secretary of State, Des Brown, said 'You'll never get away with this'; I said, 'Well let's give it a try.' He didn't think the media agreement would hold. The Queen and Prince Charles thought it was certainly worth giving it a go.

"We always knew the risk with the media was that we had made the agreement with the British media; the foreign media we couldn't control. And of course, when it came to it, it was an Australian magazine first of all and then a blogger in the U.S. [who blew the whistle]. I was in Pakistan when it broke. I got a call to say it's breaking on *Sky News*. I sat up most of the night watching it in my hotel trying to work out whether we could ride the storm, as it were, or whether Harry had to come out. Although technically it was my decision, Jock Stirrup, Chief of Defence Staff was in London and monitoring it as well, and it was quite clear to both of us that he had to come out, so word was passed that he had to be extracted at the first convenient moment. And he came back."

Had the plan not worked, or had two lesser, more cautious people been involved, Harry might have been a very different Prince today. Jamie has always felt that the most important part of his job was to enable both William and Harry to achieve their personal goals in life—"to get it right in here," he's prone to say, passionately thumping his chest—before knuckling down to decades of royal duties. "They both needed to have 'Known the days,' as the Irish say, and they have."

If Harry had been thwarted from serving on the front line, he would have left the Army. "We'd have had a really shattered, disgruntled, sapped—morale-wise—individual on our hands who can kick up and be dangerous if he wants to be. A really, really desperate situation, I think for him psychologically and in actuality—and for the monarchy too. He wouldn't have been the great asset he has been; he'd have been completely the opposite. I'm not saying he wouldn't have come out of it because he's a robust type of character, but I think the last four or five years would have been a disaster. It was a high-octane, high-risk situation, but with people like Richard Dannatt and Ed Smyth-Osbourne there that risk was mitigated because they've got courage."

TEN YEARS ON

As the tenth anniversary of their mother's death loomed, William and Harry began planning some kind of memorial, which they hoped might be, as well as a spectacular celebration of Diana's life and achievements, a means too of drawing a line under her death and finally persuading people to move on. They had first implored people to move on after the first anniversary, but there had been little let-up. Scarcely a week went by without some excuse for the media to mention Diana and reproduce her photograph. They had grown used to it but it can't have been easy.

The year before there had been an official inquiry led by Lord Stevens, former Commissioner of the Metropolitan Police. After three years, four hundred witnesses and several million pounds, it had concluded, in December 2006, that the Princess had died in "a tragic accident." She hadn't been pregnant, she hadn't been about to marry Dodi Fayed and "there was no conspiracy to murder any of the occupants of that car."

Clarence House issued a statement saying that both Princes hoped the "conclusive findings" would be the end of the speculation about her death, but their hopes were premature. There was still an inquest led by Lord Justice Scott Baker to come. That opened at the Royal Courts of Justice in October 2007 and gave the media another six months' worth of stories as the evidence was presented. Sir Max Hastings, writing in the *Guardian* at the time, summed it up to perfection.

"The inquest into the death of Princess Diana is providing a circus for the prurient, a dirty-raincoat show for the world, of a kind that makes many of us reach for a waxed bag.

"Day after day for almost three months, a procession of charlatans, spivs, fantasists, retired policemen, royal hangers-on and servants who make Iago [Shakespeare's scheming character in *Othello*] seem a model of loyalty has occupied the witness box at the law courts in the Strand. They have itemized the Princess's alleged lovers, her supposed opinions of the Royal Family (and vice versa), her contraceptive practices and her menstrual cycle.

"The business of an inquest is to examine the cause of a death. In the case of the Princess, we might assume that this would focus exclusively upon what did, or did not, happen in a Paris tunnel more than a decade ago. It should not have been difficult to conclude such an inquiry in a matter of days. Every police officer, French and British, who has examined the case since 1997 has reported that the Princess's death was the result of a tragic accident."

When it finally came to an end in April 2008, the jury returned a majority verdict that Diana and Dodi had been unlawfully killed by the "grossly negligent driving of the following vehicles and of the Mercedes," adding that additional factors were "the impairment of the judgment of the driver of the Mercedes through alcohol"; and the deaths were caused or contributed to by the fact that the deceased were not wearing seat belts, also "the fact that the Mercedes struck the pillar in the Alma Tunnel, rather than colliding with something else."

It had not been a comfortable period for William and Harry, but it was something that had to be endured if their mother's memory was ever to be allowed to rest in peace. When it was over, they released a statement thanking the jurors:

"We agree with their verdicts and are both hugely grateful to each and every one of them for the forbearance they have shown in accepting such significant disruption to their lives over the past six months." They also thanked the coroner, Lord Justice Scott Baker, for his "unfailing courtesy" and to former bodyguard Trevor Rees-Jones—the only survivor—who gave evidence. "Finally, the two of us would like to express our most profound gratitude to all those who fought so desperately to save our mother's life on that tragic night."

One of their team, who spent many hours at the inquest, had nothing but praise for Scott Baker. "He was a genius. He was completely even-handed, he didn't stand any nonsense; he was tough, considerate, straight as a die, analytical. There were a lot of pressures coming in from left and right and he was just very cool. We owe quite a lot to him.

"It would be presumptuous to suggest it was cathartic for the Princes. It was probably cathartic for the country, but she wasn't the country's mum; she was their mum."

Their plans to commemorate their mother were twofold; and although they had help with the organization, the thinking that went into what transpired was entirely theirs. For seven months they oversaw every last detail. The only time either brother had ever before been so demonstrative or adamant about anything was when they chose which regiment they wanted to join. William had successfully passed out of Sandhurst, coincidentally, on the day the inquiry into Diana's death was published. He followed Harry into the Blues and Royals where, because he was a university graduate, he immediately outranked his little brother—despite being the new boy in the regiment.

They wanted a huge, extended pop concert of music and dance, incorporating all the artists their mother loved most—a kind of people's concert that would also raise money for charity. It was to be held in the new Wembley Stadium on 1 July 2007, what would have been her forty-sixth birthday. They also wanted a private memorial service to be held on the actual anniversary of her death with, again, her favorite music. Everyone involved remembers those seven months as being a very exciting, buzzy time, including some memorably funny meetings at which the older members of the team would be teased by the brothers for their ignorance of pop and the tables turning when it came to identifying classical music.

In the run-up to the concert they agreed to do two television interviews: one with America's NBC *Today* program, the other with Fearne Cotton for the BBC. It seemed they were ready to talk a little bit about their mother and their loss.

"We were left in no doubt that we were the most important thing in her life," said William, "and then after that there was everyone else, there were all her charities and everything like that and, to me, that's a really good philosophy—she just loved caring for people and she loved helping.

"We were so lucky to have her as our mother and there's not a day that goes past when we don't think about her and miss her influence because she was a massive example to both of us.

"It's one of those things that is very sad but you learn to deal with it and there are plenty of other people out there who have got the same or worse problems than we've had."

Harry added, "She was a happy, fun, bubbly person who cared for so many people. She's very much missed by not only us, but by a lot of people and I think that's all that needs to be said, really."

"Anything to do with their mother is really tricky," says a friend. "Any event, like the memorial interview they gave, their sensitivity about being seen to say anything about their mother is very noticeable. 'Talk about our mother? Oh God, we don't talk enough about our dad.' There is no doubt that they love their father, but from everything I've seen he is a complex man and difficult to be the son of sometimes, and his reactions to things aren't always as elevated as we might want them to be. They are very careful of his sensitivities and dance around them a lot."

Twenty-two thousand five hundred tickets to the concert made available in December 2006 sold out within seventeen minutes. In all, the stadium was filled with 63,000 people when William and Harry went out on to the stage, dressed casually in jeans, jackets and open-necked shirts. Harry started the proceedings. He simply said, "Hello, Wembley!" and the place erupted. People leapt to their feet and stamped and clapped and cheered—as heartily as if he had been one of the rock stars that followed. "This evening is about all that our mother loved in life," he said. "Her music, her dance, her charities and her family and friends." And mindful of his troops in Iraq who had just been deployed without him, he added, "I wish I was there with you. I'm sorry I can't be. To you and everyone on operations we'd both like to say, 'stay safe.'"

It was an evening the like of which had never been staged before. Sir Elton John, who had performed a specially adapted version of "Candle in the Wind" at Diana's funeral, opened the concert with "Your Song," followed by Duran Duran, her favorite band, and stars like James Morrison, Lily Allen, Status Quo, Sir Tom Jones, Rod Stewart, Kanye West, P. Diddy and Take That. It was an eclectic mix that lasted six glorious hours. There was music, dance from the English National Ballet, songs from Andrew Lloyd Webber musicals, and a comedy sketch from Ricky Gervais—who was left bravely improvising when the next act failed to appear. There were speakers including Sienna Miller and Dennis Hopper, Kiefer Sutherland, Jamie Oliver and David Beckham, who introduced acts and artists, and pre-recorded video tributes from Nelson Mandela, Bill Clinton and Tony Blair. And, all the while, iconic black-and-white images of Diana, taken by Mario Testino, looked down on the proceedings from a giant screen at the back of the stage.

After Sir Elton's closing song, William and Harry returned to the stage for the final word. They had watched the concert from the royal box, surrounded by their cousins and friends—including Chelsy, whose relationship with Harry had been a bit on-off of late, and Kate Middleton, who was back in the fold after a temporary split from William—but no senior members of the Royal Family. They had been banned. William thanked everyone for coming and praised the artists for an "incredible evening. Thank you to all of you who have come here tonight to celebrate our mother's life. For us this has been the most perfect way to remember her, and this is how she would want to be remembered."

The concert was broadcast in 140 countries to an audience of around 500 million people and raised a total of £1 million for the Diana Memorial Fund and her five main charities, including Centrepoint, where she had taken both boys as children to meet the homeless, and Sentebale, which William said were "both charities that continue on from our mother's legacy."

The memorial service, held on 31 August 2007, was relayed on screens and loudspeakers to those lining the streets, but it was a much more intimate affair, held purposefully at the Guards' Chapel in St. James's, which could only take 450 people. This was for family and close friends of their mother's, plus her godchildren, the bridesmaids and pages from her wedding, a few celebrities, representatives from her charities and a few others who had some personal connection. It was designed as much as anything to bring together their father and his side of the family with the Spencer family—"her blood family"—who had been so divided by Diana's death. And although it was the time of year when the Royal Family are traditionally all in Scotland, they all came. But the question of where everyone should be seated was extremely sensitive.

"It became hugely complicated," says a friend, "and William got very fed up even just thinking about it and finally said to his office, 'Right, that's it. I'm off. You sort it out.' They were left trying to deal with Charles via Michael Peat, which was not easy, and at the end of the day it was Harry who sorted it out. He just said, 'Fuck that,' picked up the phone, said, 'I want to speak to my father, put him through.' And he just said, 'Right Dad, you're sitting here, someone else is sitting there, and the reason we've done it is blah and blah. All right? Are you happy?' 'Oh yes,' said Charles, 'I suppose so.' Problem solved.

"William gets quite buttoned up inside and angry about things and often it's his brother who makes it happen. He's the sort of 'Can do, fuck that, let's just sort it out' kind of guy. William's quite complicated and Harry's not at all complicated. He's one of the most straightforward people I've ever met. Everyone adores him."

William sat on one side of the altar next to the Queen and with his father and senior members of the Royal Family, and Harry sat on the other side of the altar with the Spencers—Diana's brother Charles, sisters Sarah and Jane and all their spouses and children.

One person conspicuously absent from the day was Camilla.

The Princes had invited her and she had accepted but, just days before the event, Rosa Monckton, one of Diana's closest friends, and the mother of one of her godchildren, wrote an inflammatory article in the press in which she said Camilla should stay away. "I know such occasions should be an occasion for forgiveness, but I can't help feeling Camilla's attendance is deeply inappropriate," she wrote. Diana would be "astonished" at the presence of the "third person" in the marriage. It had the desired effect and Camilla stayed away. She had intended to go to support Princes William and Harry, she said in a statement, but decided that her attendance "could divert attention from the purpose of the occasion which is to focus on the life and service of Diana."

The music was central to the day—as it had been central to her life—and it was sublime. They had the chapel's own choir as well as the choirs from Eton and the Chapel Royal all singing together, and the orchestra from the Royal Academy of Music, of which Diana had been the President. They played Elgar, Mozart, Bach, and Handel, among others, and the first anthem was from *The Vespers* by Rachmaninov, which Diana used to play to the boys on car journeys. And the choirs sang all Diana's favorite hymns including "I Vow To Thee My Country," which she had chosen for her wedding.

William read from St. Paul's letter to the Ephesians; Diana's sister, Sarah, read from JS Hoyland's poem "The Bridge Is Love"; and Harry, unable to find anything already written that said what he wanted to say, wrote—with his brother's help—his own intensely moving tribute.

"William and I can separate life into two parts," he said. "There were those years when we were blessed with the physical presence beside us of both our mother and father.

"And then there are the ten years since our mother's death. When she was alive we completely took for granted her unrivaled love of life, laughter, fun and folly. She was our guardian, friend and protector.

"She never once allowed her unfaltering love for us to go unspoken or undemonstrated.

"She will always be remembered for her amazing public work. But behind the media glare, to us, just two loving children, she was quite simply the best mother in the world.

"We would say that, wouldn't we? But we miss her.

"She kissed us last thing at night. Her beaming smile greeted us from school. She laughed hysterically and uncontrollably when sharing something silly she might have said or done that day. She encouraged us when we were nervous or unsure.

"She—like our father—was determined to provide us with a stable and secure childhood.

"To lose a parent so suddenly at such a young age—as others have experienced—is indescribably shocking and sad. It was an event which changed our lives forever, as it must have done for everyone who lost someone that night. [Dodi's sister, Camilla Fayed was sitting in the congregation.]

"But what is far more important to us now, and into the future, is that we remember our mother as she would have wished to be remembered, as she was—fun-loving, generous, down-to-earth, entirely genuine.

"We both think of her every day. We speak about her and laugh together at all the memories.

"Put simply, she made us, and so many other people, happy. May this be the way that she is remembered."

It was left to their father's friend, Richard Chartres, Bishop of London, to give the eulogy in which he articulated the message that William and Harry had hoped both events—the concert and the memorial service—would finally achieve closure. "It's easy," he said, "to lose the real person in the image, to insist that all is darkness or all is light. Still, ten years after her tragic death, there are regular reports of 'fury' at this or that incident, and the Princess's memory is used for scoring points.

"Let it end here.

"Let this service mark the point at which we let her rest in peace and dwell on her memory with thanksgiving and compassion."

A former member of the team remembers the occasion. "People

are very protective of Harry for all the obvious reasons, I think, but his bravery and courage in that memorial service when he got up and spoke for him and his brother—it was word perfect, emotionally pitch perfect, and emotionally he held it together. For the younger of the two in front of, genuinely, the watching world. I remember being completely knocked out by it but also thinking that's Harry, very brave—not just in skiing, combat, rugby, but in being able to take on these challenges.

"I like him enormously. He's made mistakes, haven't we all? But they've always been very honest mistakes because there's no calculation and cynicism in him. It's just his energy and emotion that get him into scrapes sometimes. And those battles with the media were deeply rooted in his experiences after the death of his mother, that's a reality that will never change, photographers and paparazzi; he and his brother have a very negative view of what they do and that will never change—and, above them, the newspapers who pay them."

SENTEBALE

The Prince of Wales had made it very clear to both his sons and to everyone in his Household, of which they were still a part, that neither Prince was to start their own charity until they had finished either university, in William's case, or the military, in Harry's. There would be patronages to take over from their mother and other members of the family, so establishing their own charity was simply not going to happen.

When nineteen-year-old Harry arrived back from Lesotho, he went head to head with his father. He was adamant that he was going to set up a charity for the forgotten children of that magical kingdom where, according to the local Department of Social Welfare, "Children have to become caretakers of their own relatives. They have to become parents to siblings. They are dropping out of school, exposed to abuse and vulnerable to exploitation, violence, physical, emotional and sexual abuse. People take advantage of their situation. Child labor is on the increase."

This wasn't just some fad, and Harry wasn't planning to start a charity for the sake of it. He had recognized a serious flaw in the charitable system that was allowing these orphans to slip through the net. As Damian West, who'd helped plan the trip, explains, "If you're a very large organization you have crystal clear rules and regulations about what you can and cannot do and your modus operandi has to be clearly defined, and transparency in accounting, in funding, has to be paramount. So if you have an organization that doesn't have a bank account, doesn't have any accounting methods, it doesn't have the capacity to submit an application for funding because—tick boxes: where is your bank account? who's going to be managing the fund?—you can't touch it." As a result thousands of the children in Lesotho are being cared for by nothing more than the goodwill of their grandparents; and because the grandparents do not have a certificate declaring their care is up to international child-care standards, the large organizations can't touch them—it's too much of a reputational risk.

"There is amazing work being done in Lesotho by some of the big organizations, don't get me wrong, but I think what we identified as a target were the group of children at grassroots level that no one else was able to touch. And when you are dealing with orphaned children, most of whom aren't even registered, and don't have a birth certificate ... Children are a very sensitive area; it's a whole new concept to get in and try and assist at this level.

"Harry went to his father and said, 'I want to start a charity.' And of course it went right against the rules the Prince of Wales had laid down. He was prepared to stand up to his father. He said, 'I'm going to do this come hell or high water and nothing's going to get in the way, even though everyone's trying to stop me for obvious reasons.' Harry knew he could help those children and he wanted to help them—he wanted to give something back. He was very aware of his own ability. He's stood up to his father on various issues but I think this would have been one of the first big challenges. His father adores him so if he delivers a reasonable argument he will be allowed to do what he wants. So the Prince of Wales asked Tom Shebbeare [then Director of the Prince's Charities] to sort it out. It was Harry, Seeiso, Mark Dyer and me driving this thing; we had no experience of charities, and I think that flustered a few people. Tom was hugely experienced so he held our hand for a lot of it and when the British Red Cross Lesotho Fund was set up he was on the board of that so he could report back progress to the Prince of Wales. Tom was a great ally and always very supportive.

"Harry's a born leader, absolutely no question, because of the way he handles himself, because of the way he leads by example. He would never ask anyone to do anything he would not do himself first—and that's why people get behind him and support what he wants to do. He's not going to be fobbed off, or be told you can't do this or that. He's a man on a mission, very driven; he's got many ideas of what he wants to do and how his influence can help change things and make those things happen. He's not going to be sitting down with his days; he's got a lot to do in a short space of time. I saw it in Lesotho; he perhaps should have been concentrating on having fun and enjoying his gap year and taking it easy like most people of his age but he wasn't. When we got back he said I want to go and do this, instead of, 'Well that was fun, what a good time,' it was 'Let's get on with it.' The fun bit was fun, but this was a project. He's a man who enjoys a project and a challenge. If anyone gets in the way, they have to provide a well-reasoned argument for doing so."

And he means anyone. Soon after the Red Cross agreed to administer the funds raised by the television documentary, they all went to a board meeting with the charity's bigwigs at their head office in the City. "I walked in," says Damian, "and there were twelve people sitting there, all of them at the top of their game, this is what they do, and I was very impressed. Seeiso gave the background to Lesotho and to what he and Harry were hoping to do, but Harry was very, very clear to define what areas he wanted this money to be spent on and it wasn't necessarily what the people in the room wanted to hear. It was outside of their capacity for working and I think for a nineteen-year-old to stand up in that room... He was very eloquent and clear on what the objectives were and what he was trying to achieve; he was very impressive. And when he heard something he didn't agree with he required an answer; 'Why are we doing it that way?' It ruffled feathers, I think, but there were people in the room who were keen to support us. The International Director for the Red Cross got it straightaway; he saw this was an area that wasn't being addressed, we'd found a gap in the market and he said, 'You're right on the button, you've got to go for it.' He was a wonderful ally with huge credibility and really helped us drive it forward."

What was compelling to Harry about Lesotho was that it was small; small enough for him to be able to make a difference, and a place that has been forgotten about. "He's known all along there is a big problem, there's the question of who's going to inherit all the patronages of the Duke of Edinburgh, Her Majesty, his mother and father—and the truth of the matter is there are too many to be shared. He knew there was so much work being done in the UK, which he will inevitably become a part of, but there is nothing in Lesotho, and he knew that the only way there would be, was by establishing something himself.

"He would say, 'It's very easy to find a reason not to do something, it's much more difficult sometimes to take something head on and challenge it, address it and make it happen,' and he is very, very happy to do that. 'Why shouldn't I set up a charity because I'm too young? It's not a good enough reason.' He'd traveled with his mother from a very early age seeing the work of charities, he's been seeing this from day one, listening to the experts in their fields talk about what they do, absorbing it.

"It was very interesting, those that said, 'This is right on cue here,' and those that said, 'Hang on a minute, be very, very careful.' The under-riding fact was, 'Is this just a passing fad? You've raised some money, which is great, let's therefore put it into an established organization with no reputational risk. Let them manage it and we can all move on.' But this thing started to gather momentum and we ended up in the position where the money was not going where we wanted it to go, which was to the grassroots level.

"Harry's line was, 'It's all very well people bringing clothes and organizing dormitories and braille, etc., but at the end of the day these children need feeding, and clothes don't feed children. To survive they have to have food and the food has to come from a supermarket across the border [in South Africa]. How can we get this money to these people but also control how that money is spent to make sure it's not abused and that it goes to the children where it's needed?' Those are grown-up thoughts for a nineteen-year-old."

After a lot of discussion about names, it was Prince Seeiso who came up with Sentebale, in memory of both of their mothers, two exceptional women who had died before their time, and who had inspired their sons by their work with HIV/AIDS. It has been widely translated from the Sesotho to mean "forget-me-not," but in truth the meaning is more subtle. According to Damian the precise meaning is " 'Farewell, see you soon.' It's not the flower but as a logo it works very well. It's 'don't forget the children'—we'll see you later, we're not disappearing."

Both Princes were in Lesotho the day the charity was officially launched in April 2006 at the Mants'ase Children's Home where Harry had first met Mutsu, the little boy with the blue wellies who had been his shadow on his first visit. He hadn't seen the child for two years and was delighted to see him again. "He's been waiting for you," said one of the helpers reassuringly. And for the rest of the day, Mutsu, by then six years old, was never far from his side. Harry was asked what impact the orphanage and coming to Lesotho had had on him. "Here especially, it really hits you hard and makes you wake up and think, Jesus, I'm really very, very lucky." And Harry confessed that he got "slightly grumpy" with friends who failed to be thankful for what they have. "It sort of changes your temper with other people who don't appreciate it."

GROWING PAINS

On that sunny day in the mountains, surrounded by colorfully dressed, cheerful children, Harry was filled with optimism. He had taken on his father, and all his father's cautious advisors and many of the biggest guns in the charity world and, through sheer bloody-minded determination, had done what he set out to do. Sentebale was up and running. It would fund and support small community-based projects that were too small or too new to qualify for funding elsewhere, and help the herd boys and all the other vulnerable children. He would put food into the mouths of these children and ensure that they had blankets to keep them warm, and offer them education and hope. "Come back to this place in twenty-five years, you'll see a massive difference," he said. " As far as I'm concerned, I'm committed for the rest of my life."

Today Sentebale is thriving. It is turning over millions of pounds and on the verge of expanding into other AIDS-ravaged African countries. It is a highly respected and effective charity, expertly run; Harry and Seeiso and everyone involved can feel very proud of what they've achieved.

But it wasn't plain sailing from the start. Three years in, the charity had major problems. Large set-up and operating costs had not been accompanied by the necessary fundraising program. The Country Director, employed to identify credible partners, was on a generous salary and benefits package. He spent two years finding the best partners, which, once signed up, had a reasonable expectation that they would soon benefit from Sentebale's coffers. But with little cash left in the bank, Sentebale was unable to meet those commitments, nor pay its day-to-day bills. The very existence of the charity was on a knife-edge. In 2008 the Chief Executive Geoffrey Matthews—who had been part of the Household and had helped organize the Wembley Concert—resigned, and a year later his replacement, Charles Denton, the former Molton Brown entrepreneur, who had come in as Executive Chairman, also resigned.

As Damian says, "There have been lots of ups and downs over the years. Whilst we've always said that lack of capacity would never be a barrier to support, when we do support an organization it is a partnership in the truest sense. Both parties have their responsibilities to each other and they must adhere to these responsibilities accordingly. If we're providing funds and expertise to an organization, a partner, then there are rules that need to be adhered to—proper accounting, transparency—and, if they are not, then obviously we have to let them go. We do have a microscope on our backs, the press, looking for any cracks—because of Harry. It is a total irritation; there's one event they keep referring back to six years later—on the money we hadn't spent. I never thought we were going to be castigated for not spending people's money. Instead we were carefully carrying out our due diligence on potential partners before parting with funds. That was the responsible thing to do. We are just trying to help; trying to help some of the most vulnerable children on earth, and by knocking Harry and what he does, the charities he's involved with, at the end of the day the people that suffer are the children on the ground, or the organization they represent, just for the sake of selling newspapers. But Harry's always said, 'If you make a mistake you must own up to it.' And we must; too many charities hide if anything goes wrong. If something's not working you must say so, and both you and others can learn from it."

Denton was to restructure the governance of Sentebale, but knew that he might not have time to achieve that. The charity was in danger of going bust. Hoping for a quick injection of funds, he approached the former Conservative Party treasurer, billionaire Lord Ashcroft, and asked for a seven-figure sum. Ashcroft was a great supporter of Harry's mother, and his initial response to the request was encouraging. One of Britain's most successful businessmen ever, the value of possible assistance from Ashcroft went well beyond any check he might have written. It all looked very good indeed. Sadly, though, the negotiations were mishandled horribly, and Ashcroft eventually walked away leaving Sentebale with a check for £250,000 rather than the million pounds friends say he would much prefer to have given.

Ashcroft is a man who does not mince words. When a meeting was arranged between him and Prince Harry, no doubt with his tongue firmly in his cheek, Ashcroft said, "Well you've fucked up, haven't you?" Harry laughed.

Kedge Martin was parachuted in as Chief Executive in the summer of 2009, and Denton left in December. "There is a point of view held by some," she says, "that working for a member of the Royal Family leads to manna from heaven and gold falling through the door and it doesn't, because there are all sorts of restrictions, quite rightly. It's not a brand you can go out there and sell, although, of course, it is a very valuable brand in itself. My predecessor had probably brought with him a commercial view as to the value of the brand and wanted to exploit that for the benefit of the children in Lesotho." The current Chairman, Philip Green, who runs a charity of his own in South Africa, says that having a royal patron presents unique problems. "The difference is the media focus and the scrutiny. You could argue you've got to be whiter than white wherever you are, but if you're not whiter than white when you have a royal patron, it will be exposed much faster and much more aggressively than if you haven't. In some ways that's no bad thing, it drives even better behavior, but the focus that Sentebale gets is very much down to the patron rather than what we do or the revenue we have. But equally we couldn't do what we do if we didn't have the patron we have."

Harry and Jamie Lowther-Pinkerton already knew Kedge Martin. She had persuaded Harry two years previously to become patron of a small charity she was running called WellChild—it was his first children's patronage. Kedge is blonde, pretty, gutsy, fortyish and very good fun; also very bright and empathetic with an impressive track record in setting up and turning round organizations in both the commercial and charitable sector. Among other things, she ran the London end of the NSPCC "Full Stop" appeal aimed at ending child cruelty.

WellChild had previously been known as Children Nationwide and was a small pediatric research charity based in Cheltenham. By the time Kedge arrived in 2000, the need for research had diminished; what was needed was nursing for the large number of children with long-term illnesses, so the name was changed. Having heard that Harry had an affinity with children, she wrote to Jamie to see whether the Prince might consider becoming the charity's patron. She was told that he was not yet taking on patronages, but she refused to take no for an answer. Eventually, in March 2007, after a meeting at St. James's, Harry agreed to become patron for a limited period. But Jamie had made it clear that Harry would want to be more than a token figurehead; he would only do it if he could add value—and that was his constant refrain, "Am I adding value?"

There was a brief moment when the newly appointed Chairman of WellChild evidently thought not. Harry hit the headlines with a story that on exercise in Cyprus during his Sandhurst training, he had referred to a fellow cadet as, "Our Paki friend." A video clip was posted on YouTube, in which it was clear that Harry was referring affectionately to a mate. But he was condemned as a racist, causing untold offence to Pakistanis everywhere.

"The Chairman of WellChild wrote a letter to Jamie," says Kedge, "saying the board will have to consider whether we still want Harry." The press had said, 'What do you think of your patron's behavior?' All the staff were told you never talk to the press, but the Chairman gave his opinion and I think it included the fact that WellChild would have to consider the position of Prince Harry as patron. That was a bad moment. So I then had to write a groveling letter, which caused some furor. I think it would be inappropriate for a Chairman who had any member of the Royal Family as patron to have that kind of attitude and speak to the press about it. You might have that opinion but you don't speak openly about it. I remember driving up to London with a letter of profuse apology for my Chairman's behavior in the formal way. There was so much other stuff going on but at the time it was huge. I spoke to Harry about it a long time later. He wasn't angry. I think he's got a more humorous view of the world than that; but, no, the Chairman didn't survive!"

Harry's first encounter with the children—who are all chronically sick and disabled—was on the day of the Concert for Diana at Wembley. He invited some of them with their families. "The families were quite scared but Harry was brilliant with the children," says Kedge. "There is something extraordinary about Harry with children. He has said, many times, it's because he's a child himself—part of him still is and I hope always will be. He's got that level of engagement, he's on the same wavelength and they respond accordingly, which is totally genuine and totally spontaneous. And it's been fabulous for the families who've met him. It's a great fillip if you're having a shite time in life because you've got a sick child. But I also think we were the right charity for him at the time because we were growing."

The charity is small but ambitious. It aims to provide specialist nursing and other practical support for the 100,000 plus children living in Britain with long-term conditions. Some were born with them, others have been damaged by trauma, and many of those children are left languishing in hospital because there is no specialized nursing care in the community. The impact on the families and stresses involved in a child with complex care needs is huge. The divorce rate is way above the national average and siblings become carers themselves. "Not only is there benefit to the NHS in freeing up that resource and saving money," says Colin Dyer, who took over from Kedge as Chief Executive, "there's benefit to the child. Every piece of research will tell you children do better at home. Yet no one had identified that gap in care."

"There is a lot of role-playing in what the Royal Family have to do," says Kedge, "and there are times when there has to be the polite interest and Harry's very good at that, but with children there's a genuine interest as well. He really cares about these children as individuals and what they are going through and learning from them, as well as from the parents, but more from the children. I think he's interested in children having a voice rather than adults speaking for them. He probably understands the vulnerability of children and the loneliness of children more because of what he experienced as a child. If you're talking to a child who's sick and having all sorts of ghastly things happen [like Lachlan who by the age of ten had had fifty-four brain operations], it's a different variant on losing your mother. If you've had a very comfortable childhood that's always been happy and healthy and you're bounced off to school then bounced into work and you've not had many tragedies, you probably don't have that much empathy with people who did. He understands their vulnerability. And possibly, genetically, his heart is so big because his mother's heart was so big. He's such a thoroughly, thoroughly, thoroughly nice, nice man. It's difficult to articulate."

Her role at Sentebale was to save it from oblivion, restructure it and make it viable. "Things had gone wrong and were going wrong and one of the first decisions I had to make was to withdraw funding from one of our partners because they weren't being transparent in their accounting—essentially they were frauds. One of the early projects was a center dealing with children who had been abused. It's a hard decision because you've got to have your principles that Sentebale will only partner organizations that are transparent and accountable and will do what you want them to do. When I first came on board we went through all kinds of processes and meetings, and eventually withdrew the funding, but we made sure there were other donors coming in so the children had food and all their emergency needs catered for, but the salary costs we stopped. And then of course you make a decision like that and they go running to the press and the next thing is 'Harry's Orphans Left Starving,' and they weren't. It's times like that when you think, it's so wrong, so morally wrong, so incorrect, it's so dishonest and it's unhelpful. It's bordering on the wicked, actually, when there is such dishonesty and such misinterpretation."

HELPING HEROES

Having a royal patron may bring unique problems but it also brings unique advantages: media exposure and, from that, profile and revenues of which most other charities can only dream. Not surprisingly, when cartoonist and former Royal Green Jacket Bryn Parry and his wife Emma launched Help for Heroes in October 2007, they hoped that they might persuade William and Harry, as serving officers, to become patrons.

Their son was in the Army so they knew what it was like for families to have their loved ones on the front line, and Bryn had friends who had been wounded, but it was not until they went to visit Selly Oak, the critical military hospital in Birmingham to which casualties from Afghanistan used to be sent (they now go to the Queen Elizabeth Hospital in the same NHS Trust), that they were inspired to found a charity to help those soldiers adjust to life after injury. Those men they saw that day—which was "shocking and moving and the defining moment," according to Bryn—are now immortalized on the home page of the charity's website. "It's about the 'blokes,' our men and women of the Armed Forces. It's about Derek, a rugby player who has lost both his legs; it's about Carl, whose jaw is wired up so he had been drinking through a straw. It's about Richard, who was handed a mobile phone as he lay on the stretcher so he could say goodbye to his wife. It's about Ben, it's about Steven and Andy and Mark; it's about them all. They are just blokes but they are our blokes; they are our heroes. We want to help our heroes."

They had a simple message. "It's not about the rights and wrongs of war, we just want to support those who serve our country and are injured in doing so." It caught the public imagination. The *Sun* got behind it; they launched a massive campaign called HELP OUR HEROES, encouraging readers to wear the distinctive tri-colored wristbands. And then William and Harry put on those same wristbands and were photographed in them.

Bryn had telephoned Jamie and asked whether he might send some wristbands over to Clarence House for the Princes. "William and Harry wearing our wristband gave us fantastic credibility and their support was hugely appreciated," says Bryn. "They wore the wristbands," says Jamie, "and it just kind of went whoosh. That wasn't down to them but they were a catalyst." Soon they were a common sight on celebrity wrists and Help for Heroes took off. Within six months the *Sun* had helped raise over £4 million for the charity.

The original objective had been to raise money for a swimming pool at Headley Court, the military rehabilitation center near Leatherhead in Surrey, where wounded servicemen and -women were sent once they had been discharged from Selly Oak. By the time the swimming pool was officially opened by Prince William in June 2010, Help for Heroes had raised a staggering £57 million. As Colonel Jerry Tuck, who was Commanding Officer there at the time, says, "You don't get a flavor for Headley Court until you see the prosthetics department, because it is that which delivers the feel-good headlines. It's a strength and a weakness of this place. As a strength, we can demonstrate to the nation that we are doing the best we possibly can for our patients; the weakness is that that might be interpreted by the nation as Happy Ever After, and for our complex trauma survivors, we don't do Happy Ever After. We do maximum functional capacity that your injuries will allow you to do, but if you are a triple amputee, at the end of every day before you go to bed, you take off your very expensive componentry and you see, surgically, what is left of three previously fully functional limbs. I don't believe that's happy ever after. I don't know what's going to happen in ten, twenty or twenty-five years, thirty years, forty years—we've still got veterans from World War Two with prosthetics. What are the mental health implications down range? I'm not necessarily talking about post-traumatic stress disorder, but I am talking about reactive depression. It's going to be very difficult if you are depressed because of the way your body looks, because your body's going to look like that until the day you die."

William and Harry had both visited Headley Court in April 2008. As William said in his speech of that day. "We expected to find a place of suffering with, perhaps, a pervading atmosphere of desolation. Nothing could be further from the truth. Here reigns courage, humor, compassion and, above all, hope for the future. How can this be? Well, part of it—it seems to me—is down to the extraordinary spirit and indomitable nature of the British soldier, sailor and airman. However, it is also about individual courage, the refusal to give up—even in those darkest moments that each and every one of you must have gone through. But if courage is the foundation stone of recovery, the unconditional love and support of friends and family, and the unstinting dedication and selfless care of the staff here, and at Selly Oak, are the tools by which this stone is levered into place. And that unconditional love is exemplified by that of Help for Heroes for this place, Headley Court. This great day—the opening of this state-of-the art complex behind me—has been brought about by this unique charity and the millions who support it.

"Very occasionally—perhaps once or twice in a generation—something or someone pops up to change the entire landscape. Help for Heroes, under the magnificent and brilliantly quirky leadership of the mad cartoonist, Bryn, and his equally inspirational wife, Emma, is one such phenomenon. What it has achieved here at Headley Court is, in truth, but the tip of the iceberg. Help for Heroes has galvanized the entire British people. Always supportive of its men and women in uniform, this country has been elevated by Help for Heroes to a state of realization and proactive support for our military that has made me personally, very, very proud to be British, and a member of our Armed Forces."

The brothers had also made several secret visits to Selly Oak. On one such visit, Harry met the families of two soldiers who had been unconscious for five days while their families sat at their bedside and waited. It was a common sight in Selly Oak. These boys were in a very bad way, but it seemed probable that they would pull through. The staff had put diaries at the end of their beds, in which the nurses and families and other visitors were encouraged to write something. These diaries had been shown to be helpful for patients when they came round and are usually wholly disoriented and think they are still on the battlefield under attack. According to the critical care manager, soldiers read the diaries over and over again and it helps to put their experience into perspective. Harry wrote, "For God's sake, mate. Came to see you and what were you doing? You were kipping." The families were delighted.

Bryn had asked whether the Princes might become patrons of Help for Heroes but was told they preferred not to be patron of any service charity but that they would be supporters. And when they were asked to the premiere of the James Bond film *Quantum of Solace* at Leicester Square, wary of being seen as celebrities, they accepted on two conditions: that the proceeds were split between Help for Heroes and the Royal British Legion; and that both sides of the red carpet should be lined with veterans from Headley Court.

It was a cold night, but both Princes spent a full hour outside chatting to the wounded and their families. They then met the stars of the film, Daniel Craig and Dame Judi Dench. "Harry arrived in the foyer of the cinema laughing," remembers Bryn, "and said to me, 'I've made a terrible boob. I've just told Daniel Craig that Sean Connery was the best James Bond!'"

Bryn Parry is passionate about what he does—and with good reason. "When we started we thought we were going to raise half a million pounds and give it to some other charity that would help build a swimming pool," he says. "Then we started meeting the guys. Rory Mackenzie, for example, is a very high leg amputee; he'd been a Para but had then gone to the Medics and been blown up in Iraq. He told us that he'd been to the Priory [a mental health hospital in Roehampton] because he thought he had post-traumatic stress disorder (PTSD); he'd been asked not to talk about his military experience because it might upset everybody else in the group, and he was roomed next to a lady who was having bereavement counseling for losing her cat He didn't stay there very long. He didn t have PTSD; he had stress because he'd lost his leg, his life had been turned upside down, he could no longer do the job he wanted, and his mum was miles away. Very early on, Emma and I started realizing we were in this for the longer haul."

There are some extraordinary personalities who have done remarkable feats post-injury, like the Paralympians but, as Bryn says, they are not representative of the wounded population.

BY HOOK OR BY CROOK

Harry arrived back from Afghanistan in March 2008 to a hero's welcome. General Dannatt had pulled him out four weeks ahead of schedule, after news of his deployment broke, and as he touched down at RAF Brize Norton in Oxfordshire, the media were waiting for the promised interview. He had shared the flight with two injured soldiers; both were comatose for the entire trip. One of them, Ben McBean, a twenty-one-year-old Marine, had lost his right leg and left arm. The other had taken shrapnel in the neck. One can only imagine how Harry must have felt that morning as he stood in front of the cameras with all his limbs intact, having been on that aeroplane for no better reason than because he was third in line to the throne.

It was a Saturday morning and Prince Charles and Prince William were both waiting at the airfield to welcome him home. Like every father and every brother of every soldier in Afghanistan, they had been extremely anxious about him and were greatly relieved to see him safe.

The interview began and Harry was very swift to point out who "the real heroes" were, and to dismiss any suggestion that he was one of them. After about twenty minutes of questions, Harry was asked what was next for him. As he started to answer, William, who had been sitting to one side during the press conference, turned to Miguel Head, Chief Press Officer at the MoD, who was in charge of the proceedings, and ran his finger across his throat, indicating it was time to end the interview.

Aware that he was supposed to be the one in charge (and that there were still supposed to be another ten minutes to run), but loath to ignore the heir to the throne, Miguel got to his feet, stood in front of the camera and said, "Thank you, the interview's over." Everyone was very surprised, not least Harry, who chucked his bags into the back of the car and sped off with his father and brother to Clarence House. The Princes later sent a message saying how impressed they'd been that they had asked a press officer to end an interview and he'd actually done it. Never having met Harry before, Miguel had not known his comfort levels; one can only assume that William recognized his brother had done enough.

A few months later Miguel, who is not much older than both Princes, had a call from Clarence House, which culminated in an interview with them. They had decided they wanted their own spokesperson and had talked to their father who had agreed. Paddy Harverson's principal focus was inevitably Charles and Camilla and, because of William and Harry's historically rocky relationship with the media, they wanted someone whose focus would be on them alone.

"Harry had gone through a period when he'd been spotted falling in and out of nightclubs a lot," says Paddy. "Compared to most other lads of his age, he was almost monk-like. What was happening again and again was, he would go out on a Friday night and admittedly he would have a big night and be up until 6.00 in the morning—but those pictures taken that night would be repeated for about three weeks, often as different stories, so you were left with the impression, as a reader, that he was out every night. He wasn't at all and he got very fed up with it. They felt they needed someone to put the record straight on things like that and they wanted someone to help take them through their career, help ensure that the coverage about them was balanced, nothing more than that. I remember them saying this in the interview—it didn't have to be positive, they just wanted it to be fair and balanced."

Miguel joined the team as Assistant Press Secretary in September 2008 (and left to become William's Private Secretary at the end of 2012), but in all that time says the only instruction he ever had from either of them was, "Please, please, always, always tell the truth."

Frustrated by being pulled out of Afghanistan, Harry was immediately very keen to get back to the front line. "Of course, having gone once," says Richard Dannatt, "he got a real appetite for it. Quite soon after he came back, he and Jamie Lowther-Pinkerton came to Kensington Palace, where I was living at the time as the Chief of General Staff, and we had a long talk about it, and with Pippa, my wife—the four of us had lunch together—talking about what really was the next stage in his military career to fulfill his ambition of getting back to Afghanistan. I was Colonel Commandant of the Army Air Corps at the time as well as everything else, and I said to him, 'Why not think about flying—because you're pretty anonymous in a helicopter? We've got attack helicopters, communications helicopters—Apache, Lynx—you can fly either of those.' 'How long will that take?' 'Well, it will take quite a long time, the best part of two years.' 'That's far too long.' 'Yup, but actually it's a really good skill to have; I think you'd enjoy it and there's a very high probability that we'll still be in Afghanistan and you can get back there.' Of course at that stage one didn't know whether he had a natural aptitude for helicopter flying. I suspected that being a whiz kid of the younger generation he probably did, because they all grow up with buttons and switches and joy sticks and things."

The Army Air Corps training base is at Middle Wallop in Hampshire and the Chief Flying Officer was Lieutenant Colonel David Meyer. "When I first heard that Harry was going to come flying I had two thoughts: first, very simply, that's fine; second was, but we don't drop the standards because this is too serious. We all knew he was going to have to go on to Afghanistan; whether on an Apache or Lynx, he was going to have to be an operational pilot and the risks are too high. That message needed to be conveyed and I spoke to Jamie and he completely got it. There was a standard to be met and we weren't going to cut corners. So he had a series of meetings along the lines of what if we did this, how would it look in terms of course length, opportunities, challenges, etc.? Then it was, okay, let's give it a go and see what happens—how does he get on with his medical, his aptitude test, his interviews? He had to pass them; there wasn't a bye at any stage.

"I first met him when I was on the interview panel. He came in, I thought, remarkably under-confident and very reserved. I was expecting somebody to fill the room more than he did, to be quite cocky and self-assured, and I was pleasantly surprised. He came across as a young subaltern, just another young subaltern, and I thought, that's interesting, so you're like anybody else because those interviews are not easy and I don't think he thought he was going to get through it without problems."

Having the right motivation was crucial, but so too was understanding just how long and relentlessly tough the course was. "It wasn't so much are you quick-witted, have you got good hand–eye coordination? Those were going to be found out very quickly. It was: can you see it through to the end? Every day you are going to be criticized; every day you are going to have to perform and it's a long course. The motivation has to be there to get up every morning and perform to the best of your ability and then do it again the next day and the next day and the next day, despite the fact that somebody's saying you're not good enough. You've got to be really determined to do it. It's one of the longest professional qualification courses in the Army—and nobody sails through it. I used to say, 'You want to fly? Great, but we're not talking about flying from one airport to another; we're talking about doing this at night in some pretty hostile environments. Flying's one thing; operating is a completely different thing, and in eighteen months we've got to invest a lot of money and time and we've got to get the right result at the end of it.' It's a pretty tough course and the quality coming in is pretty good. They get weeded out. There's a lot of competition so it takes quite a lot of courage just to put your head above the parapet and give it a go."

There are three distinct phases to the course. Students start at Barkston Heath in Lincolnshire on light fixed-wing aircraft to learn the basic skills of flying. From there they move to RAF Shawbury in Shropshire, a tri-service school, where they learn the specific skills needed to fly a helicopter. The third stage, known as the Operational Training phase, is at Middle Wallop in Hampshire, which is Army specific, and involves training in flying in formation, flying at night, in bad weather, controlling other aircraft, controlling artillery. After four months of that, the pilots are awarded their wings, and told which aircraft they are most suited to fly—the workhorse Lynx or the Apache.

"One of the great strengths on any course is that if it's well bonded and well integrated, the students will invariably do better, because they drag each other through it. If someone's having a problem and they're in isolation, that's an issue. Harry's course—and I do genuinely believe it had a lot to do with his influence—was incredibly well galvanized and they tended to galvanize around him. That was one of his key strengths, because he wasn't better than anyone else at flying or anything like that, but he just understood the whole team ethic, how to win together, as opposed to be individuals going forward; and that was very refreshing. The problem with flying training is it can go wrong very quickly. If you have a bad trip, that's fine, everybody has bad trips. If you have two or three bad trips, you're suddenly on a very slippery slope, and by the end of the week you can be off, finished. You lose confidence, the course is marching on...It's pretty ruthless, you can't afford to carry people.

"I think he has innate leadership. There's a big debate about what leadership is, but he just had the ability to be in the right place at the right time, interface with the instructors correctly, look after the junior members of the course, not be standoffish—all those things. He could have found himself in a situation where he was isolated because he was Prince Harry and everybody was tiptoeing around him but, not a bit of it, he's right in the middle of it and everybody comes to him, and I think that's innate leadership. And I think you see it in spades when he does trips down to the South Atlantic; he's just very easy to get on with and everybody warms to him. I didn't find anybody who had a bad word to say about him; it was always good to be in his company."

For six months, Harry and William overlapped at Shawbury. Like Harry, William had signed up for a short-term commission with the Army and had felt as strongly as his brother about serving on the front line, but because of the way the squadrons were rotating within the Blues and Royals, there was no chance he would get to Afghanistan during the length of his commission. There would also have been the same concerns about sending him as thwarted Harry. He had therefore decided, since he will one day, as King, be Colonel-in-Chief of the Armed Forces, to spend some time in the other services, to give him an understanding of all three at ground level. The job he finally settled on was search and rescue with the RAF, based at RAF Valley in Anglesey, which was the perfect solution and confounded any worries that he would be putting others in danger. On the contrary, it put no one but himself in danger, but allowed him to rescue others.

At Shawbury, they shared a tiny cottage off the base, living together properly for the first time since childhood.

"The first time and the *last* time, I can assure you of that," said Harry in a joint interview in June 2009 that was peppered with jokey banter. Both were studying hard and putting in dozens of flying hours, but they clearly had very good fun together. William claimed he did all the cooking and clearing up after his messy brother (who snored a lot), and said, tongue-in-cheek, that living together had been "an emotional experience. Harry does do the washing up," said William, "but then he leaves it in the sink and then it comes back in the morning and I have to wash it up." "Oh the lies, the lies," said Harry. Harry said William definitely had more brains than he did, but pointed out that William was losing his hair. "That's pretty rich coming from a ginger." William said he had been helping his brother out quite a bit. "It's the RAF way," he said, "you have to help the Army out."

William was three months ahead of Harry at Shawbury and, just having gone through the same module, he was very helpful to his little brother when they were doing their prep in the evenings. There was a lot of prep. The first four to five weeks were spent on the ground taking exams, which had never been Harry's forte, as he was the first to admit. "It was very funny," says one of their team, "because he's a really bright boy in an instinctive way, he gets it before other people, he has a brilliant turn of phrase, thinks completely outside the box, comes at things from a very, very innovative and novel way, but he ain't an academic by any stretch of the imagination. When he started his helicopter training, a lot of the early days, learning about charts and oil pressures and this sort of stuff, a massive technical tsunami hits you and people were thinking, hang on, are we seriously going to risk the reputation if he completely nosedives in the first two weeks of this thing? It was a real credit to him. He didn't find that sort of stuff at all easy, but he ploughed through it, and his brother was really helpful to him as well; they kind of did it together and they shared that cottage at Shawbury. It was really great. That was the time when they were doing the really technical stuff. In the air, suddenly there was this revelation where the guy flies...God, everyone I've ever spoken to says, he's very, very rare, he's an absolutely fantastic instinctive flyer."

An aide jokes that "if Harry isn't dyslexic, he bloody well ought to be, because he's got this instinctive wisdom and is charismatic and delightful with it." And curiously, dyslexics often make the best pilots. "It's an interesting fact," says David Meyer, "but there are a lot of dyslexics flying and it's to do with spatial awareness and ability to visualize things in 3D which is a strength of dyslexics apparently. Couple that with good strong hand–eye coordination. I, for one, was rubbish at school but I was quite a good sportsman— as is Harry—and so when people said to me, he's not very bright, 'No, but he's a bloody good polo player, he's a good shot, he makes a decision pretty quickly; actually he's a really good pilot.' That's good enough for me. Lots of people have said, 'Oh you got him through, didn't you?' Absolutely not. He got himself through and I think a lot of it is that innate quick-wittedness and basic skills. I think he thought he struggled more than he did over the textbook stuff, but my belief is yes, it's important to know your aircraft and know the ins-and-outs of it, but that really doesn't impact your ability to deliver the effect that the Army wants from you. I know he found some of the academics challenging and I know he was concerned about some of it, but to my mind that was absolutely not as important as, could he do the job at the other end?

"I don't think doing the job comes easily to anybody, but he had all the skill sets there that he just needed to tap into. He was a good soldier, a good officer in the Household Cavalry; he could talk on a radio, he could control fast jets in Afghanistan; and all you've done is lifted him up and put him in a cockpit and said, 'Right, talk on a radio, control fast jets in Afghanistan and at the same time understand what's going on in this new dimension that we've given you.' He could do that, and he got better and better and better as the course went on because he was getting more and more into ground that was familiar to him."

At the end of the course, the Chief Flying Officer calls everyone in one by one, congratulates them on passing the final exercise, and recommends which type of helicopter they should go on to fly. The decision is based on three things: their ability, their aspirations and what the Army needs at the time. The assumption from the beginning had been that Harry would fly the Lynx which, although less glamorous, requires more piloting than the Apache, but fewer operating skills.

"I sat Harry down," says David. "'Congratulations, you've done amazingly well [he was number two on the course in quality]. As you know, you're going to go Lynx, but under any other circumstances you would have got an Apache recommendation, but that's the way it is.' And there was a big, big broad smile and he said, 'That's all I wanted to hear, that I was capable of doing Apache, but I've got to go Lynx.' And I said, 'Sorry to give you that news but that's what I would have recommended,' and he said, 'That's fine.' He then left the room and his Squadron Commander came up to me and said, 'You know, I think you need to go and have a chat with him again, you need to reinforce that message that he was good enough to go Apache.' After I'd interviewed everyone else I went to Harry and said, 'Listen, I wasn't just blowing smoke, you really were absolutely good enough to go Apache,' and we had this little conversation that went along the lines of: do you think it's completely impossible? Can we persuade the Household that this would be a good idea? We agreed he would go back to his Household and ask the question and I would ask the question up the military chain of command. I think it was a Bank Holiday and we were coming back from this exercise and a decision had to be made because the following week they were going to get their wings, so there was only a week before the end of the course. I rang up the Army Air Corps chain of command and said, 'Prince Harry has passed the course and I think he ought to go Apache,' and there was lots of, 'Really? Are you sure?' I said, 'Absolutely, I'd stand by that, definitely he should go Apache, and I rang up Jamie and said this is what I think and he said, 'Right, let's see what we can do about that.'"

"I'd got this great, marvelous plan stretching out," says Jamie, "where he'd be a Lynx pilot and bounce onto aircraft carriers and fly with the Navy...It would be wonderful; tri-service and ticking all sorts of boxes. But the best-laid plans...I got a call from the boss [David Meyer], who was a very cool guy, who I'd shared my plans with, and he said, 'If this was anybody else we'd be sending him straight to Apache.' Half an hour later Harry rang. They were all having their end of that bit of the course night and there was jollity in the background, and he said, 'Listen, I'm in a real pickle here. What do you reckon?' We'd talked about the Lynx and it was just one of those moments when you think, okay, there are going to be massive potential issues with you flying the most lethal machine on the battlefield. Imagine some of the commentary; but at the same time, my view is, if you find, if there's one moment in your life when you're really first-class at something and can be right in the top tier by your own efforts, absolutely top of the pile, then you've got to go for it."

"Harry came back to me a couple of hours later," says David, "and said, 'Listen, I need to speak to my father. I need to speak to the Queen, I really want to speak to my brother.' I said, 'Okay, fine. Tuesday morning, please come and see me in my office, we need to make a decision and I'll let you know what the Army chain of command thinks. He came into my office on the Tuesday and he said, 'I've been thinking about it.' I thought: what now? He said, 'I want to go and sit in a cockpit.' You're trained on a single-engine Squirrel helicopter, then you covert to type. So I sent him off to the Apache squadron [at Middle Wallop] and spoke to the Squadron Commander and said 'Prince Harry is on his way down to see you. By the way, he just wants to know he's capable of passing the course; tell him he's capable.' Harry came back a couple of hours later and he'd sat in an Apache, and he was up for it. Great, that's what we'll do then, the Army's content, the Household appears to be content, let's go for this."

"And sure enough," says Jamie, "he is a seriously brilliant pilot and co-pilot gunner. Ever since that point he's been right at the top of the class, he just suddenly realized, I'm brilliant at this. I can't take exams, I can't do this, can't do that. But the people that know, *they* know he's always been exceptional. He went out to Afghanistan, and by all accounts out there he was absolutely superb. His commanding officer came back and said, 'He was really, really, really twenty-four carat out there.' Without going into operational details, that's pretty cool and this is the guy who never greatly enjoyed exams and he's flying a £45 million helicopter better than almost everybody else."

The Prince of Wales, as Army Air Corps Colonel in Chief, presented a grinning Lieutenant Harry Wales, and eight of his fellow trainees, with their provisional wings and their distinctive pale blue berets. There was a short ceremony at Middle Wallop in May 2010 and, sitting in the audience, cheering heartily, was a delighted Chelsy Davy—giving fuel to the rumor that their on-off relationship was back on course. Lady Jane Fellowes and Lady Sarah McCorquodale, his mother's two sisters, as well as Camilla were also there to see his great moment.

"It is a huge honor to have the chance to train on the Apache, which is an awesome helicopter," he said. "There is still a huge mountain for me to climb if I am to pass the Apache training course. To be honest, I think it will be one of the biggest challenges in my life so far. I am very determined, though, as I do not want to let down people who have shown faith in my ability to fly this aircraft on operations. It is a seriously daunting prospect, but I can't wait."

FIRM FOUNDATIONS

About seven years ago, William and Harry were both with the van Straubenzees. The family was thinking of starting a charity in memory of Harry's friend, Henry, who had been killed so tragically that night at Ludgrove. William asked Henry's brother Thomas whether he could be patron. Harry, who happened to be in earshot, said, "Oi, I want to be patron too. Henry was my friend!" So it was that, in January 2009, the Henry van Straubenzee Memorial Fund was launched at the Troubadour in Old Brompton Road, with, uniquely, not one but two royal patrons.

The collection at Henry's memorial service at Harrow School in 2003 had raised an astonishing £6,000, which Henry's parents, Alex and Claire, had decided should go to the school in Uganda, Bupadhengo Primary, where Henry had been due to work during his gap year. Peter Gate, the boy who had taken Henry's place that year, had maintained an interest, and set up the Ugandan Rural Schools Initiative; via him, the money went directly to the headmaster, who built a classroom block for sixty children. But that was not the end of it. Henry's young friends kept ringing Mrs. Van, wanting to do something in his memory—they ran marathons, went on bike rides and canoe races and the money kept rolling in. So the van Straubenzees decided to join forces with Peter Gate. The money the fund raised went directly to the schools he identified. The charity is currently helping over 25,000 children in thirty-five schools in Uganda and making a very real difference. Out of tragedy has come good.

William spoke first at the launch: he said he was "delighted" to be involved, and to be so was one of the "easiest decisions" he had ever made. "Having lost someone so close in similar circumstances, Harry and I understand how important it is to keep their memory alive. There's no finer way than that Alex and Claire have chosen. This is the first charity of which we have both become patron and it couldn't have been a better one, as Henry was such a very close friend of ours and because we believe so strongly in the need to alleviate poverty and assist development in African countries."

Harry, like his brother, reading falteringly from prompt cards, said, "As some of you know, Henry was one of my greatest friends, and his death was truly shocking, to many people. Henry would be so proud of his family for what they are doing in his name. Everything that's going on in Uganda and the way they are carrying his memory on is remarkable."

Their confidence at public speaking has developed in leaps and bounds since then, and at the charity's annual Christmas carol service at St. Luke's Church in Sydney Street in 2011, which is always a sell-out, Harry delivered a touching, charming and very funny tribute to Henry. He wasn't mentioned in the program, he slipped in quietly, sat halfway down the aisle next to Henry's brothers, Thomas and Charlie, and took the congregation by surprise when he spoke. The combination of him and Pippa Middleton, Kate's younger sister, handing round the sausage rolls and collection box afterwards, did no harm to the funds at all.

In January 2009, just a few months after Miguel Head had settled into the press office at Clarence House, it was announced that the Queen had "graciously agreed to the creation of a joint Household for Prince William and Prince Harry." It was to be funded, as before, by the Prince of Wales, and have offices in St. James's Palace, but would remain close to their father's Household in Clarence House (the two buildings are in the same complex), and although they had Miguel as their own dedicated Press Secretary, they still came under the umbrella of their father's press office—and continued to share other back-room offices like personnel, IT and finance.

Today, as then, the Prince of Wales, with his income from the Duchy of Cornwall, funds his sons in their royal lives and takes a keen interest in how they are spending his money. They have to seek his approval for all their initiatives—their Private Secretaries are in constant touch and, according to a friend, "Their father gives them stick about every penny. There are constant arguments about money." He had been in no rush to set them up on their own. It was his view that the process should evolve, slowly and naturally, and he had allowed their office to grow up within his Household until it reached the stage where their team were doing most things autonomously. At that point the Queen—in whose gift the creation of a Royal Household is—agreed they should have their own.

With it came the announcement that, "Sir David Manning, the former British Ambassador to the United States of America, has been appointed by the Queen to a part-time, advisory role with The Princes and The Household."

It was felt that William, as he moved into the next phase of his life in early 2009, would benefit from the guidance of the sort of wise old man that she had had as a young Princess. Hers had been Lieutenant General Sir Frederick Browning, known as "Boy" Browning, who had given her advice on how to survive in the world that she would one day rule over. For William, she had identified Sir David, then in his late fifties; the Queen had met him on her last state visit to America in 2007. He was just back from Washington and was invited to see the Queen; she personally gave him the job.

As he says, "The idea was to have the old, gray-haired guy who had a bit of experience of government and international relations as William moves on to the national and international stage."

The small team were at first a little taken aback; things had seemed to be going rather well. Was this some form of criticism; were they failing to give the Princes the right advice? They were assured it was not. They were also nervous, as the Princes were too, about the idea of a British Ambassador coming into their little Household of three. They were afraid things would change.

Now, as Jamie Lowther-Pinkerton says, "We don't know how we survived before David came into our office. He knows everybody, he's politically very astute, he has been there and done everything and been through some of the most controversial political decisions of the twentieth century—Iraq and all the rest of it. His advice is incredibly wise and he knows how to advise, and the questions to ask. He's a phenomenal guy, very understated as well and very modest. He's there as a sounding board.

"Things were hotting up and the Princes were beginning to step on to the national stage and do foreign trips, and it hasn't changed things. It's just added a whole new skill to the support we can give them."

Sir David immediately became an important part of serious deliberations about the future. Jamie had worked hard to help William and Harry hit their own personal goals in life, for them to get their hearts and minds in the right place during their twenties before knuckling down to royal duties. "It's ticking that operational bit which gives self-confidence and self-belief and means that you can go, twenty years down the line, and say, 'I've been there; I did it.'" For many years that was his mantra—and he succeeded. By the end of 2009, William was on his way to becoming a search and rescue pilot with the RAF—flying out into the middle of the Atlantic in gale-force winds, rescuing people—and Harry was flying Apaches and would be going back to Afghanistan. It was time to look ahead.

They had been prompted by a question from the Duke of Edinburgh's office three or four years before. His ninetieth birthday was looming and there was an assumption—erroneous as it turned out—that he might want to slow down. Were any other members of the Family interested in taking on some of his patronages?

There followed much soul-searching and lengthy discussions about how the royal landscape might look in twenty or thirty years' time, which led to two conclusions. One was that it wasn't necessary to become patron of a charity in order to help it—as their support for Help for Heroes had convincingly demonstrated. They could dip in and out, lend support for specific projects perhaps, and move on to the next cause, thereby sprinkling the stardust more widely.

Charity work is now one of the monarchy's main and most important functions. It began with George III at the end of the eighteenth century, but it was the present Queen who made it an integral part of her family's daily work. And as the historian Frank Prochaska wrote in *Royal Bounty: The Making of a Welfare Monarchy*, "Barring cataclysm or self-destruction, the monarchy is only likely to be in real danger when the begging letters cease to arrive at Buckingham Palace." As the monarchy's constitutional importance declined, it forged a new role for itself as patron, promoter and fundraiser for the underprivileged and deserving.

There are currently over 160,000 registered charities and other organizations in the UK, and about 3,000 of them have a royal patron or president. The Queen has more than 600 patronages, the Duke of Edinburgh more than 700, the Prince of Wales more than 600, the Princess Royal nearly 300. The Duke of York and the Duke and Countess of Wessex have fewer but still significant numbers, as do the Queen's cousins, the Gloucesters and the Kents. William and Harry's cousins have chosen to lead normal lives and, apart from Princesses Beatrice and Eugenie, the Duke of York's daughters, they do not have royal titles. As the older generation starts falling by the wayside, the number of royal patrons left to go round—currently eighteen—will be drastically reduced. Even if William and Harry had four children each in quick succession, it wouldn't be possible for them to share even half of that number of patronages between them. The existing model of charitable patronage has to change.

The second conclusion they came to was that they needed some funds of their own to be able to distribute from time to time. Initially it was a very human response—going to the scene of a human tragedy and wanting to be able to help. The Queen and the Prince of Wales have their own funds, which they occasionally dip into when they visit an earthquake zone or other catastrophe. However, because of the way their finances are set up, the two Princes have never been able to do that. They wanted to be able to put their hands in their pockets, as seed corn, and encourage others to give.

The solution they came up with was to start a royal charitable foundation—something that had not been done in living memory, possibly ever. And the person they found to set it up was Nick Booth, who for ten years had run the NSPCC's Full Stop campaign against child abuse. He had recently moved his young family to Philadelphia to become Vice President of Big Brothers Big Sisters, the world's largest mentoring organization. "After all those years of royal patronage, for them to say, 'Let's try something different, let's build a foundation that finds really exciting projects, put in some money, some leverage and awareness into those, scale them, but not necessarily stay with them for ever,' is very interesting," he says.

Speaking of its creation in September 2009, William said, "We are incredibly excited about our new Foundation. We believe that it will provide a unique opportunity for us to use our privileged position to make a real difference in the future to many areas of charitable work. We feel passionately that, working closely together with those who contribute to our Foundation, we can help to make a long-lasting and tangible difference."

"The Princes were the first people to put money into it," says Nick, "which is good philanthropy—'I'll give and I'd like others to support, and we're busy fundraising.'" The Royal Foundation has no big endowment; it has to raise all the money it distributes, which in the first year was about £3 million. Within weeks of Nick arriving, three private donors paid all of its administration and staff costs for the first three years. So every donation went straight into the projects being supported.

"Before I arrived they chose three areas of interest. We are not constrained by those, but currently those are: disadvantaged children and young people, veterans and military families, and sustainable development conservation. They may change over time, but these are first baby steps. We are working out within those broad areas what our first priorities are going to be. Also, what the DNA that runs across them is—and that's an interesting thought process because they feel quite disparate. I think they are linked by two things.

"One, because the Princes are passionate about them, and that's a perfectly valid reason to have three disparate areas. It's a personal foundation of two, now three, living principals, as opposed to an endowed historic institution.

"The second link is that in each of those areas you have a group of people who cannot fulfill their potential because of the circumstances they find themselves in. We are tiny, but can we use our convening power and our leverage and our resources to either remove the blocks to those people fulfilling their potential or put in place accelerators that will help that process? What is it in each of those areas that will allow us to help those people really go on and be all they could be in their lives? For two young Princes and now a young Duchess that's a very compelling alignment of values and vision."

Five years on, there has been a name change and many remarkable projects are underway. "The Foundation is a work in progress," he says. "We're not in any sense getting everything right, I'm sure we're not, and we're far from knowing what our future will look like, but that's the interesting thing about building something that's never happened before; there's never been an organization like this in however many years of royal history; there's no book on how one does it, so we're learning as we go."

It was set up as The Foundation of Prince William and Prince Harry; after William's marriage to Kate Middleton in 2011, it became quite an unwieldy name with the addition of "the Duchess of Cambridge." "So, after some discussions," says Nick, "we became The Royal Foundation of the Duke and Duchess of Cambridge and Prince Harry, and the use of the words Royal Foundation [which is how it is generally referred to] needed the permission of Her Majesty. She was very supportive of that process."

The Princes' Charities Forum completes the picture. Every six months the Chief Executives of all the charities of which both Princes are patrons, and a few of which they are not, get together with them both—and now Kate too. It started out when they had just three charities between them: Tusk Trust and Centrepoint, of which William was patron, and Sentebale. Jamie came up with the idea of getting them all together round a table as a way of demonstrating to each charity wanting their patron's time that there was no favoritism, and of seeing where they could double-up on engagements to maximize its use. They used to meet more frequently and less formally, with no fancy name, but there are now so many charities involved—forty-three at the last count—that it would be impossible to arrange. But what no one could have foreseen was that the Forum would take on such a life of its own. Everyone involved agrees it has been brilliant.

"I don't think anyone envisaged it—at the beginning—going beyond that initial remit," says one of the Household, "but what happened was that these charities got into a room and found that they could help each other out with all sorts of things that had nothing to do with the Princes."

As Charlie Mayhew of Tusk says, "The first time we met, there didn't seem to be any synergy between us, but we quickly did see there were opportunities to share ideas." Julia Samuel from the Child Bereavement Charity, which is now working with the Armed Forces, WellChild and Centrepoint, providing training and resources to each, agrees. "The Princes' Forum extends our reach into areas that we would never have been in otherwise. It means we don't compete because we all feel so pleased with ourselves to be sitting round the table. There's a real generosity of spirit; we are all very lucky and want to help each other and learn from each other."

NOT JUST A BIMBLE

William and Harry's trip to southern Africa in June 2010, the year South Africa hosted the FIFA World Cup, was their first official overseas tour together and a gratifying example of everything the Princes' Charities Forum had come to embody. In six days they visited three countries and gave a massive fillip to four of their charities, which because of the Forum, they both knew and cared about.

Their travels began in Botswana with Tusk, which was celebrating its twentieth anniversary year. Tusk, set up in 1990, is dedicated to halting the destruction of Africa's wildlife. It is not just about elephants, as its name might suggest, and it's not just about wildlife either, but about local communities and teaching them how to appreciate and manage the assets they have and profit from the tourism the wildlife brings. Tusk's Charlie Mayhew admits he had been a bit naive in anticipating quite how much interest there would be in this tour—and was astonished to discover just what William and Harry have to endure. "On the first engagement we had something like eighty overseas media in addition to local Botswanan and South African press. It was a huge. We had two TV crews from the U.S, a German crew, five UK TV crews plus the newspapers. The logistics of just trying to get them around was not easy." That first engagement was just twenty minutes outside the capital, Gaborone, at an environmental education center in the Mokolodi Nature Reserve. It is one of Tusk's flagship projects in southern Africa, teaching 12,000 children a year, in short residential courses, about conservation and the wildlife that sustains the country through tourism. "Many of them," as Charlie points out, "are growing up in a part of the country where there's no contact with that world, no connection with the environment, and yet they are the future leaders of the country."

Four young people from Centrepoint, who had once been homeless in London, were working at the center for six weeks. Had it not been for the Forum, they might never have discovered Africa. Pat Randall, one of two support workers with the group, says, "The effect on the guys was incredible to see. They were really shy and anxious at the start, with arguments between everyone, and people wanting to come home because they missed their friends and didn't like the conditions they were living in; it was very hard work. By the end, none of them wanted to come home; they were all so proud of what they'd achieved and the friends they'd made in the local community and between themselves. It is really going to help them through their lives; they've all gone on to do good things. Two have gone to university, one is doing a course in dental nursing and the other is at college."

After the press had gone, both Princes stayed for a barbecue at the center and immediately had the young people in fits of laughter. Nineteen-year-old Iesha from Peckham says, "They were really cool. I asked William for his fleece, and he said, 'As a souvenir or to keep you warm?' I said, 'Both,' and he said, "You can have a picture instead.' And Harry said, 'Back off Iesha.' He was cheeky, a really cool person. I would love to chill out with him and have a normal conversation. I thought they'd be stuck up but they were really friendly and the best part was they remembered our names and used them."

There followed a private meeting with the country's President, Ian Khama, who is a keen conservationist, then the Princes parted company. William went on to do another couple of engagements for Tusk, and Harry flew to Lesotho, where they caught up a day later. In Botswana, William had taken the lead; Lesotho was Harry's patch. Although William had helped his brother raise money for Sentebale on many occasions, this was the first time he had seen for himself what all the fuss had been about.

Most of their joint fundraising has been done on the polo field, where they have raised millions of pounds for charity over the years, but in 2008 they had swapped horses for motorbikes and taken part in a 1 000-mile cross-country adventure in the Eastern Cape of South Africa. The Enduro Africa Motorcycle Ride was an endurance test: eight days in sweltering temperatures, over mountains, gorges, scrubland, rivers, dry river beds and coastline—hostile terrain in the country's poorest province. "It's not just a bimble across the countryside, that's for sure," Harry had said before they left. "We're expecting to fall off many a time." Making light of the river crossings, William said, "We've got our armbands in our pack. We're ready to go." Alas, one of their fellow riders was less well equipped; when he fell into water up to his waist, Harry was the one who swam to the rescue, thereby earning himself the "spirit of the day" award. Eighty riders took part and between them raised over £300,000 for Sentebale, Nelson Mandela's Children's Fund and UNICEF. Simon Smith, who had organized the ride was impressed by the Princes. "They were both fantastic riders and didn't run from anything. They asked us to treat them as one of the group and that's what we did. They mucked in with chores and shared a beer and food round the barbecue. They were outstanding companions."

Miguel Head, their new Press Secretary, flew out to join them in South Africa. It was the first time he had seen the Princes since his job interview in London, and since he was organizing a press conference about the ride, he was surrounded by journalists and photographers. Spotting William and Harry coming out of a hut in the camp where they'd been staying, he went across to say hello and give them the line of questions he thought the press conference might follow. William was immediately friendly, Harry less so. "I'm really sorry," Harry suddenly said. "But who are you?" He had thought I was from the BBC and I looked at him and William looked at him and said, 'Harry, it's Miguel,' and he said, 'Of course; you look completely different out of context here.'

"Coming from the MoD you were trained always to take bullet

points to hand to a minister before an interview to remind them—
or teach them. I went down to South Africa with a bunch of bullet points about the charity they were working for and I went to
hand it to them and I can't remember which one it was, but he
looked at it and said, 'What's this?' And I said, 'It's a load of lines to
take.' And he looked at me, totally baffled, and said, 'I think we're
okay actually.' I was taken aback and thought, how can you do an
interview without lines to take? And that was when the penny
dropped for me that, of course, for them this isn't a job, this is their
life. They have to talk candidly and naturally. They can't for their
entire lives use a set of lines that are not theirs and don't come from
their own heart because they'll soon be found out. And I thought,
gosh this is different to what I expected but also far more interesting and rewarding."

Charlie Mayhew traveled with William from Botswana to Lesotho. "It was extremely interesting to see how much regard Harry
is held in within Lesotho, from government level to the little children, in the projects on the ground, in very remote mountain villages. They absolutely adore him there, there's no doubt about it.
Harry's really good with little kids—babies and kids he's brilliant.
And it was very interesting to see Harry take the lead because he
was effectively then hosting us and showing William his work, and
that was part of the idea: for William to show Harry his charity's
work and Harry show William his, and the two CEOs would tag
along." He says there was a very definite shift between the brothers
in the two countries.

Charlie had been invited to Lesotho, in the spirit of the Forum,
to see whether Tusk might be able to get involved in the country.
"I hadn't been aware of the deforestation in the country," he says,
"or the extreme poverty, so I had a really interesting couple of days
there, looking at what Sentebale was doing and how we might
potentially work with them. I'm sure that will evolve.

"Sometimes, through the Forum, you get a sense that although
Harry's not our patron, he is almost as interested in Tusk as William is and that he is happy to be an ambassador for Tusk if he gets

the opportunity and it's appropriate. It's not an exclusive patronage. They both wore the logos. I rather nervously asked, 'Do you think William would be prepared to wear branded clothing during the tour?' 'Yes, no problem, he's there to promote the charity,' was the reply. 'Great; then can we have his size?' At which point Miguel said, 'What about Harry, he's going to be there too?' I hadn't presumed I could ask both. Harry was so enthusiastic about wearing it, he lived in our fleece, even in Lesotho. It was freezing cold because it was winter there, and at one point Kedge [Martin] who is Sentebale's CEO, said, 'Harry, no disrespect to Tusk, but we're on a Sentebale engagement now, would you mind taking the Tusk fleece off?' 'Drat,' said Harry. 'Well you'd better get some Sentebale ones.'"

One evening Kedge had organized a Gala Dinner for them with the King and Queen at the Maseru Sun Hotel. "It was all marvelous," she says, "and we'd done the seating plan and you know for these events you need to get the guest list done and cleared and all the rest of it. In Africa it depends on how anyone's feeling at the time as to who they bring to dinner, so I didn't tell the two PPOs that the guest list was a complete make-up of names because that was all one could do. It was a night of terrible, terrible storms because it was June or July, and halfway through dinner the lights went out. We had checked there was a generator but inevitably it didn't work and I did start to seriously worry that the people in the room were quite vulnerable and this could all go amazingly wrong. And it was all on my watch. That night aged me about fifteen years. Then Prince Harry wanted to go and have a wee and he was gone rather a long time and it was after the lights had gone out and I thought. Should I have told the PPO or not? And time went on and on and on, so then I did tell the PPO and he went and found him and Harry was chatting to someone, but the nerves! I told him later. He wasn't alarmed by the lights going out at all—this was Africa."

The tour was a huge boost to both charities but in publicity alone, Charlie discovered that Tusk had been mentioned in 391 articles in publications all over the world. In addition there were hundreds of photographs, two of which appeared ubiquitously. One was of William and Harry with an eight-foot rock python rapped around their necks, the other William attempting to blow a vuvuzela (the sound of the 2010 World Cup) for a child. In both photographs they were wearing fleeces emblazoned with the Tusk logo. "It was a fantastic demonstration of the power of the Windsor brand," says Charlie. "A good example of how William and Harry can come together and make a big impact."

From Lesotho, they flew to Cape Town for the football, but combined it with a visit to the Red Cross War Memorial Children's Hospital, the only dedicated children's hospital in sub-Saharan Africa. Some of the children were asked if they would like a visit from one of the Princes. A young boy with muscular dystrophy, who was undergoing treatment for lung problems, said through his breathing mask, "I want the naughty one." His day was made when Harry sat on his bed for a happy chat, his face just inches from the little boy's.

England's 0–0 draw against Algeria was, according to Simon Johnson, Chief Operating Officer of England's 2018 bid, "One of the worst games of football any of us have ever seen. England played terribly and at the end of it were booed off—and we didn't know it at the time, but Wayne Rooney, on his way off, spoke into the lens of one of the TV cameras and insulted the people booing." Simon was sitting with William and Harry throughout the match, after which, William, as President of the FA, wanted to go down to speak to the team. "The drill we'd arranged was I would phone the team's administrator to check if it was all right for William to come down," said Simon. "He said, 'Oh, I don't know, it's a very bad dressing room down there.' So I said to William, 'Do you want to go?' 'Only if it's okay with Fabio [Capello, England's coach].' 'Well, I think they're having a bit of an inquest at the moment.' 'Well then, no, no, no, I don't want to go; I don't want to interfere, they've got another game to play.' I'm not sure Harry was of the same view. He said, 'Come on, we should go down.' I thought people were being a little bit protective of the team so I phoned the administrator and said, 'They're coming down, you've got five seconds to tell me if it's not okay.'

"William and Harry already had a rapport with David Beckham, and he introduced them to everybody. When they came out after about twenty minutes, I asked William how he thought it had gone and he said, 'They were fairly upset with how they played, but we tried to raise their spirits... I used some of my analogies from the military: they've got more to go, they're strong players. I did my best to gee them up.' To which Prince Harry said, 'Oh, they'll have really enjoyed that—being told how to play better by a posh soldier!'"

A GENUINE PASSION

It is often said that Harry is an Arsenal supporter but football is not really his game. He much prefers rugby and can often be spotted among the crowds at Twickenham, with a baseball cap pulled down over his eyes, enjoying an afternoon with his mates. During his gap year, he took official RFU coaching qualifications and helped coach in five different state schools dotted about the country— during which he further injured his already damaged left knee. So when he was approached by the English Rugby Football Union to become vice patron, there was not much to mull over before accepting; his grandmother is patron.

"The great thing about Harry's involvement with rugby," says Ian Ritchie, CEO, "is clearly he loves it. When you talk to him about it you know he's a fan, you know he's interested and understands it. It's a genuine passion. When he was out in Afghanistan he was talking about sitting watching the England rugby team play; when you're in the middle of Camp Bastion I can imagine it is quite an emotional thing, it's fantastic. The good thing about it is there are all sorts of obvious areas of connection. The services all play a lot of rugby. We had the Army-Navy game playing here last year; 74,000 people came to watch. There are connections into Harry's charitable activities: like everybody else, we do things for Help for Heroes or the various services organizations as well which, again, is a happy symbiosis and that's what we're all looking for."

Rugby is a team sport just like football, but because it has only been professional since 1995, most of the players earn in a year about as much as the top footballers earn in a week. Bad behavior is not tolerated. "The current England head coach has made it very clear," says Ian. "When we were going to South Africa in 2012, he was asked, 'What if any of the players are off-message?' And he said, 'They're off the tour.' They all know that, you can't have that sort of thing." He believes that what distinguishes rugby as a game is a combination of the camaraderie that attaches to it, and the core values it espouses of teamwork, respect, enjoyment, discipline and sportsmanship.

"I went up to Chesterfield to a club when I was just two weeks into the job," says Ian, "and a man comes up to me and he says, 'Are you from the RFU?' and I thought, this is not going to be a happy conversation. 'Yes.' 'What do you do at the RFU?' 'I'm the Chief Executive.' So he says, 'Come down this corridor with me' and he points to the 'Core Values' on the dressing room wall and he says, 'See these? That's why my eight-year-old son is playing rugby,' and I said, "Wow.' And I came back and said to everyone here, 'Those should not just be for playing rugby, these should be the core values that we—as an organization—espouse. That sort of culture—the way in which you deal with people, in which you act with each other, the teamwork, the respect, the enjoyment—apply in a business as well.'

"Harry fits very well into all of those sort of feelings, those core values, all the resonance around rugby; I think he genuinely feels very comfortable within that and therefore comfortable encouraging people to be involved and to play."

In October 2013, he became patron of the RFU's All Schools Program, which is trying to introduce rugby into state secondary schools that don't currently play it, and took part in a coaching session for a group of school children, declaring he was already "past it." Red-faced, out of breath and dripping with sweat, he was tackled by the former England captain, Jason Robinson, who joked that Harry could make it into the England team for the World Cup in 2015. "We're looking for a winger or a full-back," he said.

Headmasters ring up Ian after Prince Harry has done something like this or been to visit a school and they say, "You can't begin to understand the impact this has had on the children." "Sometimes we're all a bit cynical about these things," he says, "but I think he is an inspirational figure."

The physical nature of rugby means that there are occasionally casualties, so in 2008 the RFU set up a charity specifically designed to care for those few players, at any level of the game, whose lives have been catastrophically changed—most commonly by a broken neck, paralysis or brain damage. It is called the Injured Players' Foundation; the Director is Mike England, a former soldier, a rugby player and a physician, and Harry was asked to be patron.

"One of the fortunate things about rugby," says Mike, "is you can go anywhere round the world, bump into someone who knows something about rugby and you can start a conversation. So he has that natural affinity with our clients and gosh, does that help."

The charity is small, it gets on average four new clients a year; within hours of someone being injured and hospitalized, the Foundation is on the case, visiting in hospital, supporting the family, paying any costs if needed, and later sorting out mobility, housing and so on. "We try to make things better in what can be a very distressing and challenging situation," says Mike.

"We had a player two years ago who was in the Army, came back from six months in Afghanistan, first weekend home, went and played at his local club, suffered a spinal injury, ended up in Stoke Mandeville. They did their bit, got him to the stage where he was in a wheelchair and able to transfer to his bed or into a chair. Over a period of six months we put him through some very intensive specialist neuro-rehab and have got him to the stage now where he can walk with a frame, and stand unsupported. He can now stand at the bar again. It's a small thing, but for a young man that's a massive step; not physically but in terms of quality of life and his perception of himself, that's a massive step."

The Foundation is largely funded by the RFU, which also provides a corporate box at Twickenham that has been specially adapted for wheelchairs. "When the injured players come here they feel that rugby still cares about them, and at the end of the game the England players often come up to visit the box. And if Harry comes and watches a game he usually comes to the box to meet clients. He spends more time with us than I would expect— he was there for just under an hour after the New Zealand game last season, which I wasn't prepared for.

"There are very few who look genuinely relaxed with people with disabilities, but with him there's an instant connection. Part of it is that he loves rugby and these are rugby people whose lives have been changed by the game. I love watching him, he's so relaxed in the same way he is when meeting children. Usually he comes down to their level, which is a good thing to do on the whole; he'll get down on one knee and he's quite comfortable making physical contact. If you touch someone's hand and the hand doesn't move it can be quite disconcerting. He doesn't flinch and he'll just leave his hand there sometimes, which is fascinating to watch.

"People know Harry loves rugby. When he comes to the box, he will go out on to the balcony so people can see, and all the crowd turn round and start clapping. That's a very powerful thing for any charity to have. He's had functions he's invited some of our clients to, and he makes time to go and talk to the families and that engagement is very personal. We talk about the number of grants we give out, but that's the sort of thing money can't buy. That genuine personal engagement from someone in that position to a family which has gone through a whole change in life is priceless."

GAINING A SISTER

Asked who is the more robust of the brothers, one of their team who knows them both well finds it impossible to say. "It's very difficult to compare William and Harry because they are so different—emotionally and in their approach to life," he says. "That's why they're such a great team, but the one remarkable thing about them is how they completely complement one another. William's a steady bloke, unemotional and unflappable. His way of approaching life is considered. Harry's an adventurer. You just have to look at the helicopters they chose to fly; they sum them up. William was flying a huge mountain of a helicopter that would go through storms and get battered left and right and just keep going; and it was all about working out fuel loads to take him into the Atlantic and how much time they had over the target and every option taken into account, which is exactly how he deals with me and the work we do. Every avenue is considered and, interestingly, he comes in with stuff I haven't even thought of. Whereas Harry was: turn off the computer, fly the thing at 150 knots over the treetops. It's an Apache, that's what it's all about, it's completely instinctive. His brain engages in an instinctive way. He will go, 'Yep, yep, yep, what are you doing here? Ah, okay, yep, yep, yep, done,' and you can get on and talk about other things. It doesn't mean he hasn't thought about it, but he's got very good instinctive judgment and he's right 99 percent of the time. And actually, thank God that it's that way round with the brothers, and we haven't got to invade France or anything, otherwise it would be quite handy to have Prince Harry in the saddle."

The brother's relationship with women could be similarly defined. Harry has been an adventurer. A friend says, "There's definitely been a period when he's lived what you can politely call a rock-star lifestyle; and what's so extraordinary is none of them sold their stories. My impression is, in the years when he was single, he wasn't spending his time at home twiddling his thumbs. Images that slightly spilled into the public in Las Vegas were not that unusual—only unusual in that they were in that format. Harry is a guy who likes a good time, but you never get women talking about it and I think that's because he's very nice; they like him. He's charming and, even if it was short-lived, they don't want to dob him in; he's got something about him that makes people want to do the right thing by him."

His relationship with Chelsy Davy was different. It was not a short-lived fling and she was not a minor celebrity or a girl on the make. It was his first serious love affair, with someone who had no interest in his royal status and who loved him despite—rather than because of—it.

And Harry was clearly confident enough of what they had together to talk about her briefly in his twenty-first birthday interview, albeit in the context of the media.

"There is truth and there is lies," he said, "and unfortunately I cannot get the truth across because I don't have a newspaper column—although I'm thinking of getting one . . .

"It does irritate me because obviously I get to see how upset she gets and I know the real her but that's something we deal with on our own time and unfortunately it's not something I can turn round to people, to the press, and say, 'She's not like that, she's like this.' That is my private life. I would love to tell everyone how amazing she is, but once I start talking about that, I have left myself open."

By 2004, Chelsy was in her first year at Cape Town University, studying Philosophy, Politics and Economics, and living with her younger brother, Shaun. For the next couple of years, while she studied and Harry was at Sandhurst, they conducted a long-range relationship, both flying to see the other as and when possible. But it can't have been easy to keep things on an even keel, particularly with the tabloids in the mix. "The press has got it so wrong so many times," says Damian West. "If Harry had been linked to every girl they say, he'd have done nothing else."

Meanwhile, in Cape Town, Chelsy's life became intolerable. "It was still, anything goes, pre- the hacking inquiry," says a friend of Harry's. "Photographers were putting tracking devices on her car and following her everywhere she went. There was serious intrusion into her life. The escape and evasion that was required when they got together was substantial and she hated all of that. Why wouldn't you?"

Their relationship lasted on and off for about six years—for three of them she was doing a second degree at Leeds University, in Law—and while it's obviously impossible to speculate whether it could have lasted longer, there is no doubt that Chelsy hated everything that came with the HRH aspect of Harry. And that would inescapably have been part of any future they might have contemplated together.

Paddy Harverson says, "Some of the stuff poor old Chelsy had to put up with were horrendous. Endless harassment and pursuit by paparazzi and reporters who followed her everywhere she went. She was a student in Cape Town on her own; luckily she had her brother Shaun with her, but they were followed and photographed everywhere. She was a young woman, quite vulnerable, as any young girl would be, and she was followed by burly men in cars and on motorbikes. It's very intimidating and they never, ever let up. Their tactic is to scream obscenities and abuse at people to force a reaction that produces a better picture. It is a sad reality that people in public life have to cope with that. Harry feels it very deeply, particularly for his friends and family, who get sucked into it by virtue of being his friend."

William's relationship with Kate (officially known as Catherine) had also been a bit on and off, but by the time he asked her to marry him, they had known one another for eight years. They had met at St. Andrews; because the PCC Code of Conduct was still loosely in place, they were left alone to get to know one another without the need for subterfuge.

Once they left university and came to London, however, it was a different story. Kate was followed and photographed, criticized, baited and bullied. Not long before the engagement, she was walking through an airport on her own when a couple of paparazzi spotted her. "Bitch!" "Whore!" "Slag, look this way!" they shouted, hoping to provoke some kind of violent reaction. "Ideally they'd love her to slap them," says Paddy. "It would be a gift to them. Of course, the press never reports that side of pap activity, so you never, ever see it, but that's how they operate at the rough end. They would have called Chelsy a bitch and whore too—just as they did to Kate."

Kate was from a solidly decent and happy middle-class family who lived in the pretty Berkshire village of Bucklebury. William loved them. He loved the normality, loved the lack of butlers and footmen, loved sitting around a table with the family over Sunday lunch or walking the dog across the fields for a pint in the village pub. As an old friend of Diana's says, after the chaos of his childhood: "It's safe, and that regularity and consistency, which for someone not in his position might find boring or too ordinary, is balm to his soul. You go there and you know what you're going to expect, you can predict it. Most of his experiences are unpredictable, uncertain and disturbing." William could relax with the Middletons, be himself, and the feelings were entirely reciprocated. Michael and Carole immediately welcomed him into the family and there is a very genuine friendship between them all. Kate wasn't flashy; she wasn't after the high life, or the fame, or the idea of being a princess in a grand palace—she was as fiercely private as he was. She had fallen in love with the man—a man who during those years at St. Andrews had been through some emotionally tough times—and she had been there for him; she was someone he felt safe enough with to confide in. And through all the ups and downs, including a very public split, and all the provocation from the tabloids, which called her "Waity Katie"; through all the harassment and jokes about her middle-class origins, even the offers of money to talk about him, she never rose to any of it. She kept her counsel and spoke to no one but her family, and they too spoke to no one. She and they proved to be 100 percent trustworthy.

They announced their engagement on 16 November and Harry could not have been more delighted for his brother. He said he "was enormously pleased that William finally popped the question. I've known Kate for years and it's great that she is now becoming a part of the family. I always wished for a sister and now I have one." He was genuine. William's friends had at first been a little ambivalent—as with any man who shows signs of settling down before the rest of the herd, he had started to be less fun for the remainder. And the herd blamed the woman, as always happens. They felt she was too clingy, too much of a killjoy, even though all that was happening was that William was growing up.

Tom Bradby was asked to conduct the engagement interview, in which the public heard their future Queen speak for the first time. Wearing royal blue, as Diana had on the day of her engagement to Charles in 1981, and wearing the very same diamond and sapphire engagement ring that Diana had worn, comparisons were inevitable. It was a tricky assignment for Tom. As a respected political editor he couldn't afford to be asinine, but neither could he be rude and aggressive. The three of them chatted it through for half an hour before they began. "My main aim is not to fuck up your happy day," he told them, and William said, "That would be really helpful, Tom, thank you. Do try not to."

William had chosen his mother's ring, he said, because: "I thought it was quite nice because obviously she's not going to be around to share any of the fun and excitement of it all—this was my way of keeping her sort of close to it all."

But there the similarity ended. When Charles had been asked whether he and Diana were in love he had said, "Yes, whatever love is." There was no need to even ask the question of William and Kate. Nervous though they were, their body language spoke for itself.

The wedding on Friday 29 April was everything William and Kate wanted it to be—given that they couldn't be married quietly in Bucklebury Church. "What we want," William told his team, "is a personal day that's going to be special to us. We want a day that is as enjoyable as possible, for as many people as possible." Those exact words drove the entire event. The task was to create a day that was intimate for them and their families, but which would give the British people a suitably royal and memorable celebration. And they succeeded. "What made it an intimate day was nothing that we did. It was the two of them, the smiles they gave one another, the comments: 'You look beautiful, babe' and to Michael [Middleton], 'Just a quiet family wedding...' The perfect choice of words to a man, unaccustomed to the limelight, who had just walked his daughter for three long minutes up the aisle in Westminster Abbey to give her away to the second in line to the throne, in front of forty television cameras, thirty journalists, scores of clergy and swathes of guests that neither of them knew.

Harry, as best man, helped to keep the mood light and informal in the midst of all the formality. He arrived with his brother, the pair of them looking immaculate in their full military get-up—Harry's with pockets specially sewn into it to keep the rings safe. His grin and his relaxed manner immediately put everyone at their ease. There was an audible chuckle from the congregation when Kate and her father arrived to Hubert Parry's soaring anthem, "I Was Glad," and Harry had a quick peek over his shoulder, before turning to his brother, and playfully whispering in his ear. Whatever he said, Kate looked glorious and beamed when she saw William. Her dress, which had miraculously remained a secret until the day, was close-fitting satin and lace with a nine-foot train, and a veil of ivory silk tulle, held in place by a tiara loaned to her by the Queen. She had four little bridesmaids and two page boys, and her sister Pippa (whose bottom became an overnight sensation) was maid of honor.

The two brothers had spent the night at Clarence House, and at 8:30 in the evening had surprised and thrilled the hundreds of well-wishers camped in the streets outside, by suddenly appearing among them. For ten minutes the Princes wandered up and down, joking, laughing and shaking hands, thanking people for being there. The press called it a PR masterstroke, but it had nothing to do with the Household. It was the Princes' idea entirely, and William told the police they were going to do it just five minutes before they left the house. Afterwards, the groom had sensibly had an early night; Harry hadn't. He had been at the Goring Hotel round the corner, which the Middletons had taken over in its entirety, and hadn't left until the early hours.

After the marriage ceremony, the carriage procession and all the magical pomp that the British monarchy does so well, and not one but two kisses on the balcony, the Queen hosted a lunch for 650 people. Afterwards there were speeches, the cake was cut, the champagne was drunk and everyone was ushered into the garden at the back of the Palace to see the couple off. And there, waiting for them, was the Prince of Wales's dark blue Aston Martin DB6 Mk II, with the roof down, tastefully decorated by the best man. Harry had been out and bought a whole lot of stuff, some of which he wisely vetoed at the last minute. What survived the cull were heart-shaped balloons and colored streamers and rosettes, a learner's L plate on the front and a specialized number plate on the back— JU5T WED. To the delight of the crowds outside, who had not expected to see the couple again, the car emerged from the gates of Buckingham Palace, with William at the wheel and Kate beside him—the newly created Duke and Duchess of Cambridge. As it made its way slowly down the Mall and into Clarence House, a yellow RAF Sea King helicopter appeared and hovered noisily over their heads—the groom's colleagues had come to wish them well.

The evening party, hosted by Prince Charles, was a far more intimate affair, with 300 of their closest friends and family—with the exception of the Queen and the Duke of Edinburgh. They had excused themselves to give their grandson and his friends "the run of the place." Prince Charles had made a touching speech at the lunch in which he'd reminisced about William as a teenager, sitting in his room, playing his music loudly and refusing to come down for hours on end; and giving him advice about what he was wearing or telling him not to slouch and getting a two-fingered response. "He is a completely loving and close father," says one of their team, who was there that day and who has watched the relationship between father and both sons over many years. "He has had a unique relationship with them in some respects—and went through a hell of a period with them—but it's very close. They are very straightforward with one another and loving and supportive as well."

After a magnificent dinner and fine wines in the ballroom, Harry took over. Acting as compère, those there say he stole the show with flawless comic timing and hysterical one-liners. Guests were crying with laughter as he recounted tales from their childhood. His brother had beaten him up, he declared, and shot him with air rifles. Now it was his turn and he teased William about everything from his romantic style to his receding hairline. But alongside the jokes, there were emotional moments too—and a moving tribute to their mother. He introduced the other speakers: Kate's father, then William, giving his second speech of the day, and finally a double-act from Thomas van Straubenzee and James Meade, William's closest friends, who delivered a series of quick gags about the groom, which again had the audience in fits of laughter.

Jamie Lowther-Pinkerton, whose son, Billy, was a pageboy, felt sorry for the other speakers. "Talking to three hundred people without a note—and there were some people in that room who slightly believed the press about Harry before; well, they certainly didn't afterwards. He was absolutely brilliant, cryingly funny, and held everybody and built everybody up with his speech but still made everybody howl with laughter."

After dancing until three o'clock in the morning, the bride and groom made their second and final departure of the day, in David

Linley's bright yellow Fiat 500, which William had secretly borrowed. Their guests then noisily saw them off, as they stood with their heads through the sunshine roof for the drive round two corners of the building to be delivered to another door. The Queen had given them the Belgian Suite for the night, which President Obama and his wife had stayed in.

Harry led those who were still up for more onto a waiting coach, which took them to the Goring Hotel. He and William had discussed how best to organize things. The last thing they wanted was to have their friends, full of good wine, spilling out of the Palace into their usual Mayfair haunts, which would be crawling with journalists. So, much to the disappointment of the media, it was some days before even halfway accurate stories began to appear about the party. The after-party went on until just before first light, at about 5:00, when Harry slipped out unobserved and made his way home.

Harry had outwitted the press over the stag weekend too—nothing gave him greater pleasure. He, Thomas van Straubenzee and Guy Pelly had organized it between them, and the tabloids had repeatedly got it wrong. The *Sun* did eventually get the right location, but by then the party was over. A group of about twelve of William's closest friends had driven down to north Devon a month before the wedding, and stayed at Hartland Abbey, which was the setting for the BBC's adaptation of Jane Austen's *Sense and Sensibility*. It is a secluded twelfth-century former monastery, owned by William's friend George Stucley and his family, and surrounded by magnificent gardens and parkland leading down to the Atlantic coast. They were spotted surfing at Spekes Mill, a beach along the coast, but otherwise how much they drank and how they spent their time remains between the twelve of them.

Hello, Wembley! Ten years after Diana's death, a star-studded concert in her memory.

With Kanye West and P. Diddy— just two of the stars who helped raise £1 million that night for charity.

Showing solidarity at the Australian High Commission in London after devastating bushfires killed more than 200 people in Victoria in February 2009.

At the WellChild Awards in 2009. His rapport with children is second to none.

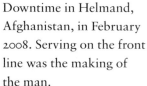

Girlfriend Chelsy Davy in May 2010, delighting in his success as a pilot the day he was awarded his wings and distinctive blue beret.

Downtime in Helmand, Afghanistan, in February 2008. Serving on the front line was the making of the man.

Echoes of his mother Harry in a minefield in Mozambique highlighting the work of the HALO Trust

Jamie Lowther-Pinkerton, a key figure in Harry's transition from boy to man.

Bonded by an eight-foot African rock python on a joint tour in 2010. "A fantastic demonstration of the Windsor brand."

He is determined to help the AIDS orphans of Lesotho.

To them he's just Harry, their friend.

Three generations, all freezing
cold, during the Diamond
Jubilee River Pageant.
"Look warm, wave and smile,"
instructed the Queen.

Portia Simpson Miller, the
republican Prime Minister
of Jamaica, hugging Harry
on his Jubilee tour of
the Caribbean. "She was
completely starstruck."

Triumphant after "beating"
Usain Bolt. The *Daily Mail*
called Harry "The Royal
Family's secret weapon."

Harry, William and Kate, the three patrons
of the Royal Foundation, at the launch
of Coach Core, July 2012.

Two genuine sports lovers caught up
in the excitement of the 2012 Olympic
Games in London.

The Apache's display
monocle to his eye feeds
him all the information
he needs to fly the
aircraft and fight.

Camp Bastion, Afghanistan,
2012–2013. Running for real
this time—to give Apache
assistance to coalition forces
in trouble on the ground.

Sitting volleyball with the British Warrior Games team in Colorado Springs in March 2013. He determined then and there to bring the games to London in 2014.

There but for the grace of God goes every soldier who comes home from battle. The Arlington National Cemetery, where 400,000 military casualties are buried.

Giving it his all at a rugby coaching session with children at Twickenham. At 29, red-faced and out of breath he said he was "past it."

"Are you all right in there?" Moments before Harry takes a pitch from New York Yankees baseball star Mark Teixeira in Harlem.

Harry with Simon Daglish, co-founder of Walking with the Wounded. "If things go wrong in the South Pole, no one's coming to get you."

13 days and 200 miles later, a triumphant Harry jumps for joy at the South Pole.

Cressida Bonas with Princess Eugenie, who introduced her to Harry in 2012.

Together at the We Day event in March 2014. The press forecast an engagement, but less than two months later it was said to be over.

Launching the Invictus Games. "It was such a good idea by the Americans, that it had to be stolen, it's as simple as that."

Unannounced, William and Harry joined Army colleagues to help defend the town of Datchet during the floods of 2014.

Three Princes ("two heirs and a spare") united in their passion for conservation, marching off to the London Conference on the Illegal Wildlife Trade.

FOUR DAYS ON THE ICE

In July 2009 Edward Parker's twenty-six-year-old nephew, Harry Parker, a Captain in The Rifles, lost both his legs in Afghanistan. He had stepped on an improvised explosive device (IED). One of his legs was blown off in the explosion; the other had to be amputated after it became infected. Ed had been a soldier in the same regiment for ten years and served in Northern Ireland. Edward's brother and Harry's father was General Sir Nick Parker, then Commander of Regional Forces—a very senior figure in the military.

"Having been a soldier myself and having seen men who were wounded before, I thought it would be something I would very much take in my stride," says Ed, "but of all my family, I think I was the one who was most affected by it. I remember going to the hospital [Selly Oak] with my wife and saying, 'Just go in and grin and try not to look at the injuries; just be there for the boys and girls who are in there.' It was the first time Harriet had ever seen anything like that and she was brilliant. I went in there, and my nephew, who used to be six feet, had suddenly become four feet. He looked awful and I remember thinking, this isn't very good. It had more of an effect on me than I would ever have guessed, and that was the trigger."

What it triggered, ultimately, was Walking With The Wounded (WWTW), a hugely successful charity that has taken amputees to both Poles and three-quarters of the way up Everest, to prove there is a life beyond injury. Ed and a friend, Simon Daglish (known as Dags), whom he'd known at Sandhurst, had been planning a trip to the North Pole; Ed was by then in the wine business and Simon was commercial head of ITV. "Subsequent to Harry being wounded," says Ed, "Dags turned round to me and said, 'Well, why don't we do this with wounded servicemen instead of a group of middle-aged old idiots and try and make it worthwhile?' He always maintains it was after the first bottle of red wine. I think it was after the second! And so the seed was sown. And if Harry Parker hadn't been wounded, none of this would ever have happened."

First they found a guide, Inge Solheim, a Norwegian who had worked with disabilities in the Arctic. Next, Ed phoned Jamie Lowther-Pinkerton, who's a friend. "I fished and said 'Do you think one of the principals might be interested?' and, to give Jamie his credit—he's a very dear friend—half an hour later he phoned back and said, 'I think Harry might be interested.' This would have been September 2009 and, as soon as that happened, it suddenly had momentum. Simon and I could see that with royal patronage we could go and talk to people." Among those people they spoke to were filmmakers. They envisaged a documentary to raise money and profile, and the production company they chose was Twofour, based in Plymouth, and specifically Alexis Girardet, who had made a number of adventure films and had recently been to the South Pole with Ben Fogle. Alexis works with a sound man, but is effectively producer, director and cameraman. Next they looked for wounded servicemen or -women to take part in the expedition. To their surprise, they had 120 applicants, which they narrowed down to twenty, then four: Guy Disney, a Captain with the Light Dragoons, who was hit by a rocket-propelled grenade (RPG) and lost a leg below the knee; Steve Young, a Welsh Guardsman, who broke his spine when his vehicle was blown up by a roadside bomb; Martin Hewitt, a Captain in the Parachute Regiment, who was shot in the chest in the midst of a firefight and has one paralyzed arm; and Private Jaco van Gass, another Para, a South African whose arm was ripped off by a direct hit from an RPG.

Jaco's injuries went way beyond the straightforward loss of a limb, and he was still at Headley Court and very ill when he first met Ed, Simon and Inge. He was hoping to be one of the team.

Jaco remembers the conversation. "They said 'Can we see your injuries?' and when they'd seen them they looked at me and said, 'Are you serious? You want to take on one of the toughest challenges in the world with those injuries you've sustained?' 'Yes, why not?' They said: 'We'll get back to you.'" Their decision was disappointing but, as Ed told Jaco: "'Yours were the worst injuries we've ever seen. We admire you for even thinking of coming but, sorry, it's too big a risk.'"

When Jaco had woken up in Selly Oak, after seven days in an induced coma, he was on morphine and having vivid dreams. He was convinced he was still in a firefight in Afghanistan and was angry that his family had been allowed to visit. His mother, who had flown from South Africa with his father and sister, asked how he felt, terrified that he didn't know about his injury. "I feel like a guy who's lost an arm," he said, and they all burst out laughing. He had known very soon after the explosion and had tried to tie a tourniquet around the bleeding stump. "The first guy on the scene to help me said, 'Shit, Jaco, you've lost your arm,' and I remember so clearly, I just went calm and collected. 'No shit, Sherlock!'" What he didn't realize was that the blast had also ripped a third of the muscle and tissue from his leg, shrapnel had ripped through his body and punctured a number of internal organs, he had a fractured knee and an ankle broken in several places. And for the first seven months he had to wear a colostomy bag. He was twenty-three years old and all he wanted was to get back to his mates in Afghanistan. Gradually the reality dawned on him that it wasn't going to happen any time soon.

During his stay in Selly Oak, Prince William and Prince Harry both happened to visit the hospital. "They went to every patient and sat for ten or fifteen minutes with each guy, which was fantastic. I've got the photo still of me with my leg in this massive cast and this machine that moved my leg so I didn't lose all my muscle, and he's sitting next to my bed and I'm there with my hair shaven off. I was extremely excited, I didn't really know what to say and I thought: no one at home will believe I've met Prince Harry and

Prince William. Both of them were so sweet. I think we spoke a little bit about the Army and about what happened to me, which regiment I was in, there's a bit of banter between the Paras and any other regiment. We call the rest of the Army 'Hats' or 'Crap Hats.' It doesn't matter whether you're in the Household Cavalry or The Rifles or the Artillery or the Air Force, if you're not a Para, you're a Hat."

Jaco's recovery was helped by seeing on TV—while he was lying in his hospital bed—an Australian woman who had been paralyzed. "She said, 'Life is 10 percent what happens to you, and 90 percent how you respond to it.' And I thought, that's very true. Once you make peace with something, it's amazing how everything in your body changes, your spirit, your will to do something else, your health, your wanting to get better. If I'm still fighting to be a frontline soldier and I keep getting disappointed, I am just holding myself back, but the moment I knew, right, I'm not going to have my arm back, this is probably the end of my career as an infanteer, but there must be other stuff I can do; I'll find out what it is..."

At Headley Court his fitness increased by leaps and bounds. He learned to ski, to play golf, and when the opportunity to run a marathon in Kenya arose, he leapt at it. Just before the race, he saw Martin Hewitt, who had been selected for the Pole and told him two spaces remained. "He said, 'Are you still interested?'" Ed and Simon were so impressed by Jaco's progress that they gave him a place. Then, in February 2010, it was announced that Prince Harry was to be patron of the expedition.

"The next thing we knew we were doing this press conference at the Rifles Club in Davies Street, which Prince Harry had agreed to come to," says Ed. "Four huge news satellite trucks were parked outside, and as soon as it was over, the phone started ringing. On the drive back to Norfolk it rang and rang, with corporates saying they'd like to be involved, and production teams saying they'd like to make documentaries, and newspapers saying, 'Go exclusive with us—we'll give you the real thing.' I got home to Norfolk and it was completely beyond anything that I understood. I remember talking to Simon the next day and saying, 'We do one of two things. We either pretend it never happened and we crawl back under our stone and people will forget us quite quickly, or we really go for it.'"

Alexis started working straight away; for him it was an eighteen-month project, with all the soldiers' back stories to be filmed, as well as the group as they prepared and trained—most of which was in Norway—and occasionally working with Harry. Trust was an initial hurdle to be overcome. "Harry was obviously cautious; he didn't know who I was or who Rob, my colleague, was, but as we've done more and more we've built a relationship that, fingers crossed, so far has worked." Along the way was a photo-shoot with David Bailey for GQ magazine. The great man, famous as much for his combative nature and rich vocabulary as his iconic photographs, had charitably waived his fee, and Harry had agreed to take part, so a studio was rigged up at a hangar in Chilbolton, near Middle Wallop in Hampshire.

"Harry turned up and—to be honest—David Bailey was more scary than Harry and all of his team. I said, 'Can I film, is that all right?' And he said, 'You point that fucking camera in my fucking face and I'll bite your fucking nose off, you fucking c★★★!' Okay sir! I thought, who gets David Bailey saying that to them?"

It was the first time Harry had met the boys. "We were all prim and proper," says Jaco, "and Harry just said, 'Guys, relax; relax around me,' and he started telling jokes and we laughed and he just made us feel easy. David was, 'Come on boys, have fun, tickle him on the ear, or grab his bum, and all of us were standing there thinking, what's this guy on about?' Harry's face in black and white on the cover of the May issue was the bestselling copy of GQ in 2011, even outselling the boy band, One Direction. As the editor Dylan Jones, whose idea it had been to use Bailey, said, "I think it's fair to say that Harry is his own one-man boy band. According to music industry lore, in order to succeed in the marketplace, a boy band needs a cute one, a funny one, a huggable one and a difficult one."

At a second press conference in January, it was announced that Harry was going to join the expedition for part of the way. "His brother's wedding was the elephant in the room," says Ed. "They wanted him back at least two weeks before, so we had to lift him off the ice after four days. He was disappointed. I think he would have given his eyeteeth to have walked with us to the Pole, but he has so many lives he has to live. But the one thing he said to me was he had always been worried that if he walked to the Pole the story would have been about him and not the wounded, and he felt that the story was about the four guys getting there."

The party flew into the Russian base, Svalbard, where they were held up for three days by bad weather, and were then helicoptered to their starting place. From there they skied 160 miles across difficult and dangerous terrain, dragging pulks—or sledges—packed with tents, food, cooking equipment, and everything else they needed for five weeks on the ice. There are pressure ridges that can be three or four meters high, and treacherous narrow linear cracks in the ice known as leads, where polar bears often hunt. "You come across leads, which are steaming and jet black because no light gets down there," says Alexis, "so you're looking at this fathomless, bottomless ocean which is at least four miles deep, and you have to work out ways to get across that, either ski a long way round it or swim across it, so at least that's something that breaks up the monotony. Or you get pressure ridges where, instead of it being pulled apart, two plates get pushed together; it's like a mini mountain range formed in a day, and the only way over that is to climb over and to drag all your stuff with you. It can be very boring when you wake up in the morning and look out and you've got a day's worth of this rubble to get through, and frustrating if you're a wounded serviceman with one leg and you fall over for the tenth time on ice that's as hard as concrete, that's no fun at all. And a couple of the guys, how they didn't come back more damaged than they were when they set out is incredible."

"On the ice, Harry was bloody good; he worked hard," says Ed. "He is no more and no less than one of the team. There isn't time for airs and graces from anyone—not that there would ever be any from Harry. If you need something doing quickly you do it quickly and you say it to him how you'd say it to anyone else. You could point and F and blind [swear], and he reacted brilliantly to that. There wasn't even a heartbeat missed. There could be a threat of the ice opening up and you've got to do things quickly and soldiers being soldiers, the language gets quite blue. He was the eighth team member; the fact that he was at that time third in line to the throne was completely irrelevant—because then we were doing our job.

"When we're back in front of the media, the fact that he's third in line to the throne is key and he was patron of the expedition, but out there we had the job to do which was getting from A to B safely and he fitted into that like a hand into a glove. He used to slightly, not take the piss, but he used to call me 'Boss' when I was saying we've got to do this. These sledges weighed eighty, ninety or a hundred kilos, they were bloody heavy, and when you're getting them over broken rubble you take your skis off and it takes two of you to carry them over, and if a bloke with one leg is stuck there, I turn round to Harry and say, 'H, you nip back and help him, and I'll go and do this,' and he's off, he's doing it. We only had him for four days on the ice and we had no close protection; they were sitting at the helicopter base but we had telephones—and guns in case polar bears come and had a munch—and if it had all gone tits-up they were on the helicopter.

"There's a very clear hierarchy on the ice with the guide as number one, and what he says goes, and there were one or two occasions when Inge turned round and was firm because things were getting a little bit hairy, as they do. We went through some very soft ice and there was water and Harry started sinking down a little bit, the back of his skis started going down, and there isn't the time for the niceties—'Oooh look, you're beginning to slide down into the Arctic Ocean which is four kilometers deep and quite cold and if you go in there you'll die.' Things start happening pretty bloody quickly and Harry appreciated that they needed to happen pretty quickly so he took and takes orders very well because he got it. There's not much different about him when you take out the Prince.

"We missed him a lot when he left, not just as a teammate and as a friend but as a capable pair of hands too," says Martin Hewitt, who had thirteen major operations in two years, the first of which saved his life. "When two of your team members are missing arms, that extra pair of hands comes in handy crossing a lot of the obstacles, the pressure ridges, and he'd get stuck in, he didn't need any prompting. He was just one of the boys, one of the team, which was difficult for him because we'd been training as a team together for almost a year before he came in. So he had to insert himself into a group at fairly short notice, but it was a seamless transition because he's very down to earth, very likable, easy to get on with— and he gets it. He's a military officer, he's spent time on tour, he's spent plenty of time with the soldiers and with the officer core, so there's a lot of common ground there, despite coming from very different backgrounds, very different lives."

"He loves being with those guys," says Alexis. "Away from the cameras, they can be a bunch of guys together, soldiers who have trained and worked together. Bringing the publicity is obviously important, but being with the guys means more to him. You can just see it. It's not 'Sir,' it's not 'Prince,' or anything like that. It's 'H' or "Hazza,' or whatever nicknames they've got for each other and they all take the piss out of each other genuinely, and I know that several of them text with Harry regularly, send each other pictures that shouldn't be sent; they get on, they have phone calls and all the rest of it."

"Prince Harry was never, ever shy of helping," says Jaco. "If we were struggling over a ridge he would ski up and try to pull the pulk over. If you fell down he would reach up and hold your hand. There's not a lazy hair on his body. He was such a great asset." He was much loved by everyone—not least for surprising them all with a giant ice-cream cake that he had secretly bought in Svalbard and dragged across the ice hidden in his pulk. "It was about forty or fifty centimeters across and every night he would come around and give us a slice of cake for dessert."

They reached the Pole three days ahead of schedule, and *Harry's Arctic Heroes*, a two-part documentary shown on BBC 1, did them proud. "I'm absolutely thrilled that the guys have made it—what an awesome achievement," said Harry, who phoned them via satellite with his congratulations. "They should be incredibly proud of making this world record, as we are proud of them. I took part in only a small section of the trek, but know full well how physically demanding it was. The spirit and determination of these lads is second to none. They are true role models." Then joked that they were "showing off" by arriving early.

Bryn Parry remembers some of the team coming to talk to wounded colleagues at the Help for Heroes recovery center at Tedworth. "It was inspirational stuff," he says. "I was sitting behind Toby. Toby is tetraplegic, shot through the neck, can't move anything below his chin, so he's on a breathing tube, twelve breaths a minute, he has two full-time carers, he comes to us periodically to get away from just being cared for the whole time, and a bit of banter, and to be part of a wider community. He's in his early thirties, an amazing man, absolutely amazing. And we've funded him, we've helped him buy a house, got him a computer that he works from a mouse on his head. The WWTW boys said, 'We've walked to the North Pole and next year we're going to climb up Everest,' and I was sitting behind Toby thinking, I wonder how this sounds to someone who can't even brush his teeth on his own to hear other people talking about climbing Everest, that's quite tough. And what saved the evening was one of them said, 'We understand that not everybody can climb Everest; but everybody has an Everest to climb.'

"That was fantastic and I have quoted it so many times because there are some people who find it very hard to get through the day, let alone find a reason to live. There are other levels of success. We've got a girl called Charmaine who's got crushed hips but *her* Everest has been in writing a poem, despite being profoundly dyspraxic and dyslexic. For her, seeing that poem describing her emotions, mounted on a canvas, was her achievement, and that was the first stage on her road to recovery."

TOP GUN

During Harry's time at Army Air Corps Middle Wallop, learning to fly Apaches, he made a lot of unexpected friends. Someone who knows the base well says that when he first arrived, the locals were quite belligerent. They were resentful that "a bloody royal" was being sent to them "and the mood was, sod this for a game of soldiers, there's no way we're giving him special treatment. By the time he had gone through the system two years later, there was not a single person that I heard or encountered who had anything to say about him that was less than bordering on worship. They said he was one of the best people they had ever taught in terms of his dedication and application and determination to get through, which is not something you would necessarily have associated with Harry up to that point in his life.

"It's a big deal to qualify as an Apache pilot; that is the best of the best, like the old *Top Gun* cliché; it's the most sophisticated piece of kit the Army has. You don't get to fly one unless you really can do the business and Harry really, really impressed them. But, more than that, all the cleaning staff loved him, all the waiters in the mess loved him. He was really startlingly universally popular and the Commander, as well as thinking he was a very good pilot, said to me many times that actually, he was the natural leader in the pack and people really deferred to him and it had nothing to do with his being a royal."

Much the same could be said of the impression he made at Wattisham Airfield, where he went at the beginning of 2011. Having spent eight months learning to fly the aircraft, a lot of it in a simulator, he moved to the largest operational Army Air Corps base in the UK, where he began to learn how to use the Apache in battle. He joined 662 Squadron of 3 Regiment, under the command of Lieutenant Colonel Tom de la Rue, and Wattisham, an unprepossessing military base in the middle of the Suffolk countryside, became home, on and off, for the next two years.

The Apache is a lethal machine. It has three different weapons systems: a thirty-millimeter cannon, which, according to Tom de la Rue, is "the workhorse in Afghanistan," which fires 625 rounds a minute; two sorts of rockets—one with a small explosive payload and charge, the other firing tungsten steel darts which, usefully, don't make a bang; and Hellfire air-to-surface missiles, which home in on a laser beam that is directed onto the target and has to remain on target until the missile impacts. The missiles and the rockets can both be used out to about eight kilometers, which is also the approximate radar range of the aircraft's Longbow Fire Control Radar. The cannon is usually used at much closer range. Learning to use those weapons and, crucially, learning the rules about *when* to use them in combat, takes another eight months of intensive training.

"The really important thing about this aircraft and what we do with it," he says, "is that, although it is a tremendous weapons platform and has incredible capability, we use it as an absolute last resort and so our aircrews are trained to exercise restraint over and above anything else."

There are two cockpits in an Apache, one in front of the other, with a blast shield between them, which means, unusually for an aircraft, that the two-man crew can't see each other. They rely entirely on voice to communicate; they are in constant radio contact with several other voices too during a mission. The pilot sits in the back, the co-pilot gunner, who is usually the more experienced of the two, sits in the front and is in control of the weapons, but can also fly the aircraft if necessary. Harry was trained for the front seat. It's a cramped cockpit, which he would sit in for up to ten hours a day, with three computer screens feeding him information, and countless switches—each with a different texture so the operator can tell them apart by touch in the dark. On either side of the central screen are two optical relay tube (ORT) grips, and most of the real business is done with very quick thumb movements and two triggers—one to fire the laser, the other to fire the weapons.

"Pilots and co-pilot gunners both wear helmet-mounted display monocles," explains Tom, "which project all the information they need to fly or fight the aircraft, directly into their right eyes, in the form of digital information with an infra-red or television video underlay from the sights. It's effectively a monocular black-and-white display with no depth perception and, importantly, the infra-red display isn't a picture per se, it's a dynamic image reflecting a scene's heat differential. So the weather and external environmental conditions have a significant impact upon what can or cannot be seen." In addition, the sights and weapons can be linked to the gunner's helmet, so whichever way he turns his head, the sights and weapons can follow. "The most useful weapon to link to your helmet is the cannon, which traverses allowing the gunner to literally look at a target and shoot."

"You've got to get the right person," says David Meyer, who chose Harry. "But once you've done that, it's a very intuitive aircraft, in that you're part of that computer generation who's not afraid to press buttons and go backwards and all that sort of stuff and can assimilate information quickly. It's absolutely purpose-built from the wheels up to the cockpit seat to the fact that everything's at your fingertips, you don't have to lean back or look behind you or down between your toes, it's all in front of you."

"There are some things that can be done in a pretty automated fashion, but actually we take great pride in having the human mind in the loop to make sure that the right judgments are being made," says Tom de la Rue. "We are paying our pilots to lead in battle but also to display the ability to make very, very fine judgments very quickly, which is tremendously important, particularly in a counter-insurgency campaign [like Afghanistan], where the enemy is unknown and is mixed in with the population. If soldiers on the ground in Helmand Province, for example, are in a tricky situation and require Apache support, you have to very quickly work out where the friendly forces are, where the enemy forces are, what the threats look like, what you think you can and can't do about it, taking into consideration the rules of engagement, the law of armed conflict, the ground commander's intent and the various munitions that might be available to you. Sometimes these judgments, particularly at night, when you can't see anything apart from what is seen through the sights, are having to be made very, very quickly, in tremendously difficult circumstances, but you've got to get them right every time. And it's invariably the co-pilot gunner who makes those critical decisions.

"When it comes to inter-cockpit crew management, the Apache is uniquely all about voice, which is something that pilots in training sometimes find tremendously difficult. So you really have to understand each other, the two of you, so that when things start to go a bit wrong or somebody starts to experience capacity problems, you tune into it straight away. For example, you might have quite a talkative rear-seat pilot and suddenly he's not talking very much. Why? Is he capacity saturated? You could fly a sortie by day and find that the aircrew have lots of capacity because they can see what they're doing, it's a simple sortie and they therefore just get on and do it. By contrast you can be flying very complicated, demanding, and high-risk operations in Afghanistan at night with fifteen other aircraft with all sorts of mixed military and civilian activity on the ground, and four radios transmitting in your ear simultaneously. Then add the fact that what you're seeing is a black-and-white infra-red picture with no depth perception—all in all, a very challenging set of dynamic circumstances. So it's critical to understand where each other's limits are, particularly at the most demanding end of the operational spectrum."

In November Harry finished off his training with two months in America, known as Exercise Crimson Eagle. As Tom explains, "We need to do that bit in Arizona just to hone the skills and do the slightly more dynamic stuff that we need to do. It's not lost on a lot of people, particularly the ground forces, that some of this stuff is really quite challenging. You have a moving aircraft, a moving supersonic munition and maybe a moving target; three things moving simultaneously, which requires real skill in the aircraft if the desired outcome is to be achieved. The Americans have some wonderful ranges, the Barry M. Goldwater bombing range in Arizona is something like 2.7 million acres. It looks very similar to Afghanistan so it's an excellent place to conduct Apache live fire training."

In February 2012, Harry became a fully operational Apache attack helicopter pilot, and went almost straight into pre-deployment training. By late summer he was back in Afghanistan. During a dinner to mark the end of the course, he was awarded the best co-pilot gunner trophy out of about twenty others on his course. Tom de la Rue has great admiration for him. "This is an incredible achievement, as most people are never remotely capable of even getting into the back seat and flying this aircraft, let alone doing what's required in the front seat. He's got a tremendous aptitude for this but, like his fellow Apache contemporaries, he also has tremendous empathy for those on the ground. The Apache capability resides in the Army for very good reason—we are all Army officers and soldiers and intimately understand what is happening on the ground. We are not in the business of bombing from 25,000 feet; we are part of the ground battle and employ the aircraft accordingly. Harry fits into this environment perfectly, he has talent in spades and is a master attack aviator—an amazing and most commendable achievement."

Sir David Manning believes the whole experience has had a huge impact on Harry. "Nobody expected at the beginning of this venture that he would turn out to be one of the few who is asked to do Apache training, so he wasn't expecting it, and I'm not sure how welcome it was when it came really [within the Household], but he did it and turned out to be very, very good at flying Apaches, and that experience turned him into a very serious professional officer. He took his flying very seriously, had very high standards.

I think it changed him a lot. If you suddenly discover you are very good at something it changes the way you feel about yourself and the world, and certainly Harry was very good at something—and this was a surprise, I suspect, to him and to a lot of other people, but it was for real. You cannot get in an Apache helicopter and fly just because you're wearing the uniform. Either you can do this stuff or you can't, and since the Army think these things are the Crown Jewels, they're not going to put them in the hands of someone who's going to make a mess of it.

"I think there was a general perception that he was in his brother's shadow and that his brother was more able, more talented and more academic than he was, and I think the discovery that he's one of the very best of his generation, at something that is very difficult that he does very well, is a big watershed, and I suspect will condition what he feels about himself and what he can do for the rest of his life. It has also proved to him—this period—that he can give real leadership. One of the other things that's very clear is that people relate to him very easily and they really like him and this isn't just because he's a sex symbol—there are many more layers than that. He finds a way of talking to people and motivating people and he has this great gift; he's funny, he's direct, he's very quick to respond and that leadership skill, that ability to mobilize people to make a difference is something that if it's deployed intelligently, will make a big difference."

SECRET WEAPON

The year 2012 was a very good one for Harry, and not just wearing his Army hat. He excelled in his royal role too. And after he and Chelsy had broken up for the last time, he found a new girlfriend in Cressida Bonas. He triumphed in the Caribbean representing the Queen in her Diamond Jubilee Year; then at home, along with his brother and sister-in-law, as ambassadors for Team GB at the Olympic Games. It was a good year for his grandmother, too, with huge outpourings of affection and gratitude for her sixty years on the throne; which served as great affirmation for the monarchy. It was a good year for Britain as a whole, despite the continuing economic hardship. The Jubilee celebrations brought hundreds of thousands of well-wishers on to the streets, undeterred by the terrible weather, and once again there were street parties where strangers greeted strangers and communities pulled together, buoyed up by a sense of national pride.

The Queen and Duke of Edinburgh confined their travels to the British Isles, leaving the younger members of the family to visit the Commonwealth on her behalf. It was the first time Harry had represented his grandmother, and there was necessarily a fair amount of formality in the program, but he managed to blend it with his inimitable sense of fun, and in two weeks he charmed his way round four countries, winning fans everywhere he went. In a Diamond Jubilee street party in Belize, he drank rum and wowed the locals with his snazzy suits and snappy dance moves. In the Bahamas he attended a service of thanksgiving and delighted 11,000 school children at a youth rally, and in Jamaica he "beat" the fastest man in the world, the Olympic sprint champion, Usain Bolt, and was hugged by the republican Prime Minister, Portia Simpson Miller. She "was reduced to a blushing, hugging schoolgirl at her first meet-and-greet with the Ginger one," reported the *Daily Mail*, which hailed Harry "the Royal Family's secret weapon." And in Brazil, as an ambassador for British trade and the Olympics, he was mobbed.

As a former diplomat, Sir David Manning was impressed. "He was very conscious he was representing his grandmother and he certainly reminded me that that was what we were doing; I didn't have to remind him. He took it very seriously, worked extremely hard, absolutely not the playboy, early to bed and he handled people very well. There was a lot of press speculation about how on earth we were going to manage Jamaica. The Prime Minister had said just before we came that: 'One of these days we're going to get rid of the Crown.' He managed her very well, he managed the whole tour very well; and he decided he was going to send personal messages to the people who had looked after him in each country we left—I didn't suggest that to him—and I think he genuinely made a big impact. [His note to the Governor General of the Bahamas was typical. "What a fantastic couple of days. I am truly sad to leave and can't thank you enough for such a memorable tour."]

Harry had joked in the interview he gave on his twenty-first birthday that he read everything that was written about him and he took down the names of writers and photographers for later reference. One of the journalists covering the tour for the *Mail on Sunday* discovered that Harry hadn't been joking. He took George Arbuthnott to task for giving readers the impression he had been knocking back excessive quantities of rum and lethal Caribbean cocktails. Harry collared George and confronted him. George protested that it had been the headline writers back home who had twisted his story, and the two parted friends; but the point was made.

Another member of Harry's team, on the tour, says, "With Prince

Harry there is a tendency among people, because his persona is so fun-loving and humorous and quite informal, to underestimate him and assume that he's somehow quite lightweight as an individual. The opposite is true. He's incredibly professional; he expects very high standards of his staff and those around him. He is very demanding about the quality of briefing that he gets and the kind of advice. In my view so much of that stems back to that first successful tour in Afghanistan. I think it did the world for him and made him the person he is today. He's very impressive, and he's got great emotional intelligence. He knows how to read people and judge them and you can see it in the way that he interacts with children and prime ministers."

He had been forewarned that the Prime Minister of Jamaica, for all her republicanism, might go for a hug. "Portia Simpson is, actually, quite well known for it; she has hugged the Prince of Wales before and people [the media] have either chosen to ignore it or not known about it. Father had said to son, 'By the way, when you meet Portia Simpson there's a chance she may hug you.' So I think he was prepared for it, but he read the situation incredibly well and knew how to respond there and it won him a lot of plaudits, deservedly so. The same day that he was running on that track with Usain Bolt, and again reading that situation brilliantly well, generating not just a lot of humor but a real warmth and respect for the people he was meeting. He'd said, 'On your marks,' I thought what's he doing? The idea was they would race one another but jumping the gun was completely off-the-cuff. He hadn't told any of us he was going to do it. He and his brother are never fake; they are very honest themselves and that enthusiasm you see when they meet people is genuine. I don't think you can fake that."

Even the formal moments had a masterful lightness. Speaking at a State banquet on his last night in Jamaica, he wove a line into his speech from the famous Jamaican singer Bob Marley. "I count it a great privilege to be standing here tonight, representing the Queen in Jamaica on her Diamond Jubilee. Her Majesty has asked me to extend her great good wishes to you all, and is sorry that she can't be here—so you're stuck with me...but don't worry, cos every liddle ting gonna be aright!"

His grandmother's lifetime of service had been "an inspiration," he said, adding, "She combines all her virtues as a leader and as a Head of State, with those of being a wonderful, caring grandmother—to whom we, her grandchildren, are utterly devoted.

"As for me, I haven't been here for long, but—wow—if I had, I'm not sure my grandmother would get me back."

He had spoken at length to his grandmother and other members of the family beforehand about what a successful Jubilee tour should look like. And he was in regular touch with William throughout the two weeks, both by text and phone. "Both brothers always say," says an aide, "they are never directed by their father or the Queen. People above them always give advice but never directions. They are very keen for them to find their own way in life and make their own mistakes and find the things that they are good at themselves. There is no sense in which this is the only model and the one you have to follow and if you don't do this, it's wrong. They give them quite a bit of latitude." A former aide concurs. "His father loves both his sons to bits, and takes a paternal interest in everything they do, but he lets them lead their lives."

From Jamaica Harry flew to Brazil where he waved the flag on behalf of the British government and celebrated the sporting links between London 2012 and Rio 2016. Once again he cleverly combined the fun with the serious. One minute he was suited and booted and launching the government's £25 million "GREAT" campaign to promote Britain and encourage Brazilians to visit the UK—the first time he had ever been used in this capacity. He opened a major exhibition of British culture and business on the top of Sugar Loaf Mountain, where he was greeted by screaming girls and samba bands. Introduced by David Beckham via video link, he said, "Everything about Rio makes you want to dance. I'm just so thankful that my brother isn't here because he might actually do it—and that would not be cool." The next minute he was larking about barefoot on the beach playing touch rugby and volleyball. And the next, he was immersed in the less glamorous side of Rio. An afternoon was set aside to visit a favela in one of the city's poorest districts, where he was immediately surrounded by children, while he inspected projects and opened a newly renovated community center.

"Brazil wasn't one of the realms," says Sir David, "but he did a big number there, promoting British trade, and got absolutely mobbed. I think he was a bit shocked at the scale of it—quite uncomfortable. Neither of the Princes wants to be celebrities and I think his worry in Rio is there was a risk of too much celebrity in there and not enough seriousness—although what he was doing in the favelas was incredibly serious. And he did it very well. Like Prince William, he's good on tour; people respond immediately, they like him, he's interested in what he's seeing and doing and it shows; it's not simulated. He's in there trying to find out what it's all about and he's done his mugging up. These are real assets, these two. Send them out into the wider world and it's good for UK Ltd."

The final day in Brazil was polo—the third Sentebale Polo Cup match, sponsored by Royal Salute in the Campinas district of São Paulo. In 2010, he and Prince Seeiso had launched the event in Barbados as a major annual fundraiser, and each year the great and the good get together for a lavish lunch and an afternoon of top-class polo. In São Paolo there were over five hundred VIPs. "The most important thing for me in life is kids," Harry told them. "I don't know whether I got that from my mum and my father. I just have this massive kid inside me. I've always had that connection with kids and I always will hopefully."

Afterwards he summed up how he and his party felt about the tour, saying to journalists: "I tell you what, it's been an emotional trip. I'm absolutely exhausted but the warmth of the reception that we've received from every single country that we've been to— including Brazil—has been utterly amazing. I personally had no idea how much influence the Queen has on all these countries.

And to me that's been very humbling, and I was actually quite choked up at times seeing the way that they've celebrated her sixty years. She's thousands of miles away to some of these countries and yet they celebrated her in the way they did, and made me feel as one of them, so I couldn't thank them more."

He'd spoken to the Queen before he left. "We had a great chat. She wished me luck and she said 'Enjoy it, I hope you do me proud.' It was a typical grandmother-to-grandson chat. I just hope that my grandmother is proud of what we've done."

There was little doubt about that. Jeremy Hunt, the Secretary of State for Culture, Media, the Olympics and Sport, who was also in Rio for the GREAT event said, "Prince Harry has the impact of a thousand politicians. Watching him during his tour of the Caribbean and in Rio de Janeiro, he is becoming an extraordinary phenomenon. He has not been on top of our list before as an ambassador, but seeing the electrifying effect he's had here, his real connection with children and sport, shows just how he has taken to the role."

The Diamond Jubilee celebrations kicked off on Saturday 2 June with a forty-one-gun salute fired at the Tower of London, echoed by gun salutes in Edinburgh, Cardiff and Belfast—and on Epsom Downs in Surrey, with the National Anthem sung by mezzo-soprano Katherine Jenkins; and a startling display from the Red Devils Parachute Team who fell from the sky with a giant Union flag. The Epsom Derby is one of the highlights of the Queen's diary, and was the perfect place for her and the Duke of Edinburgh to begin four days of celebration.

A very cold Sunday saw the largest river pageant ever staged anywhere in the world (according to the *Guinness Book of Records*) and the most spectacular that had been seen on the Thames for 350 years. A thousand boats, from tugs, barges, steamers and pleasure cruisers to dragon boats and kayaks, slowly made their way through driving rain from Albert Bridge to Tower Bridge, a distance of seven miles. Among them was a collection of small ships that were used in the evacuation of stranded troops from the beaches of Dunkirk in 1940, and leading the procession was a ninety-four foot royal row barge, the *Gloriana*, specially commissioned for the Diamond Jubilee, the first to be built in over a century, at the cost of £1 million. It was powered by eighteen oarsmen, including two Olympic gold medalists, Sirs Steve Redgrave and Matthew Pinsent, three ex-servicemen who lost limbs in Afghanistan and Iraq, and the British Paralympic rowing hopeful Pamela Relph.

In the midst of the flotilla, following on from the rowing boats, was the royal barge, the *Spirit of Chartwell*, lavishly and regally decorated in red, gold and purple and adorned with ten thousand flowers from the royal estates. Harry, who since his trip to the Caribbean had been busy with pre-deployment training, joined his grandparents, his father and stepmother and William and Kate on the barge, while other members of the Royal Family and VIPs were accommodated in other boats. The only plan that had to be abandoned because of the weather was a "Diamond Nine" fly-past of Royal Navy helicopters lead by a Swordfish biplane built in 1934, which was to have provided a spectacular grand finale to the pageant. The rain was remorseless, but the crowds were undeterred. Hundreds of thousands of people lined the banks of the river, crowded onto the bridges, and crammed onto balconies and rooftops along the way, cheering, singing and waving flags. And no one looking at the Queen and her party, smiling broadly and enjoying the feast of sights and sounds, would have guessed how cold they all were. At one point the Queen, sensing that her grandchildren were frozen, turned and said, "Look warm! Wave and smile!"

And so they did. They stood out on deck for more than four hours, marveling at everything around them, chatting cheerfully and waving to the crowds. But when the barge pulled up for forty-five minutes to allow the rest of the procession to pass it, everyone dashed below deck to warm up and revive themselves with a stiff drink. Just as they were putting the glasses to their lips, the music from a choir filtered down the stairs, at which the Queen's face lit up and she said, "We've got to hear this," and raced up on deck again. Reluctantly, the younger members of the family, frozen to the bone, abandoned their glasses and followed their grandparents back into the cold.

The following evening was party time. The Queen Victoria Memorial in front of Buckingham Palace was transformed into a stage and the Mall and the parks to either side of it became a vast open-air concert venue that teemed with humanity. Waving Union flags, people laughed, danced and sang along to the greatest collection of superstars spanning sixty years of popular music and entertainment that had ever gathered under one sky—all brought together by Gary Barlow, the singer songwriter from Take That, who—with Andrew Lloyd Webber—wrote the highlight of the evening, the Jubilee song, "Sing," that was performed by the Military Wives Choir and musicians from Kenya and other Commonwealth countries. It included a fourteen-year-old soloist called Lydia, whose voice sent shivers up the spine. Other artists included Robbie Williams, Jessie J, will.i.am, Kylie Minogue, Annie Lennox and a quartet of knights and a dame: Cliff Richard, Tom Jones, Elton John, Paul McCartney and Shirley Bassey. There was an orchestra, the Kenyan Slum Drummers and the African Children's Choir, opera singer Alfie Boe, pianist Lang Lang, and comedians Lenny Henry and Jimmy Carr.

The extravaganza culminated with the Queen, who had arrived halfway through taking to the stage alongside all the performers. Following a heartwarming tribute from the Prince of Wales, she lit the last of more than 4,000 beacons to have been lit across the United Kingdom, the Commonwealth and overseas territories in celebration. Then there were fireworks that could be seen and heard from many miles away.

There was one noticeable absentee that night: the Duke of Edinburgh, who was just a few days short of his ninety-first birthday. He had fallen ill during the afternoon at Windsor Castle and been taken to King Edward VII's Hospital in Central London, suffering from a bladder infection. It was the second time his health had caused concern in recent months and his grandsons were not the only ones to be worried. At Christmas he had spent four nights in

Papworth Hospital in Cambridge where he had surgery to clear a blocked coronary artery.

"Your Majesty...Mummy," began Prince Charles again, to roars of approval from the crowd. "I was three when my grandfather George VI died and suddenly, unexpectedly, your and my father's lives were irrevocably changed when you were only twenty-six. So as a nation this is our opportunity to thank you and my father for always being there for us. For inspiring us with your selfless duty and service and for making us proud to be British." There were once again deafening cheers from the crowd and from members of the Royal Family.

"The only sad thing about this evening is that my father cannot be here with us because unfortunately he's been taken unwell. Ladies and gentlemen, if we shout loud enough, he might just hear us in hospital." At this more than a million people roared their approval, stamped their feet and chanted, "Philip, Philip."

The Duke's absence was felt all the more keenly on the final day of the celebrations, when the Queen and other members of the family attended a national service of thanksgiving at St. Paul's Cathedral, lunch at Westminster Hall and an open-carriage procession back to Buckingham Palace. She struck a very lonely figure as she walked up the aisle of the cathedral on her own, followed by Charles and Camilla, then William and Kate, then Harry. It was a stark reminder that the Queen and the Duke of Edinburgh will not be here forever; but also that there are others who will, in the fullness of time, follow in their footsteps.

That message was strongly reinforced by the traditional appearance on the balcony. As an RAF fly-past and a gun salute from the Queen's Guard brought four days of festivities to a thrilling climax, there were just six people on the balcony. For the first time it was not the familiar picture of the Queen along with generations of her extended family. The Queen was flanked by her son and grandsons, Camilla and Kate. No explanation was offered by Buckingham Palace for this departure from the normal line-up, but the directive had come from the Queen herself, and no one was in any doubt that we were looking at the future: a scaled-down monarchy with a clear and secure line of succession.

"Those of us who have been privileged to work with William and Harry closely for a long time see it as absolutely fundamental to the future of the Royal Family that they remain a working pair," says one of the Household. "Inevitably, as the Royal Family shrinks over time, the focus will shift more and more on to them and their growing families. That was recognized, of course, on the balcony, when it was three generations plus Prince Harry. Goodness knows what the thinking behind that was from the Royal Family's view, but for us looking on that was a very heart-warming moment, with Prince Harry being recognized for the central role he will continue to play in the Royal Family."

LONDON 2012

After eight years of planning (satirized by the BBC television series *Twenty Twelve*), the London 2012 Olympic Games opened on 27 July with one of the most unimaginable stunts. The eyes of the world were on the spectacular, dizzying opening ceremony, three hours of glorious theater and music, devised by the film director Danny Boyle, in the newly built Olympic Stadium at Stratford in east London. In the midst of the show, called Isles of Wonder, which followed the progress of the British Isles from the early nineteenth century through the Industrial Revolution to the present day, the giant screens throughout the stadium suddenly cut to the actor Daniel Craig, as Secret Service agent James Bond, arriving at Buckingham Palace and making his way along the red-carpeted corridors to the Queen's study. Looking up from her desk, she turns to him and says coolly, "Good evening, Mr. Bond," before getting up and leaving the Palace with him, corgis at her heels, and heading towards a waiting helicopter.

Moments later, spectators at the Olympic Stadium heard the roar of a Westland hovering overhead, and a figure, dressed identically to the Queen, jumped out and parachuted into the arena (closely followed by Mr. Bond) to rapturous and incredulous gasps—not least from members of her own family. The thousands of people in the stadium with them, and the billion more estimated to have been watching the event on television around the world, were astonished and delighted. No one knew about it, save the Queen's closest aides; not even the International Olympic Committee.

Doom-mongers had forecast an organizational disaster, but the sceptics were proved wrong. The Olympic Games and the Paralympic Games that followed were a resounding success and generated extraordinary goodwill—much of it, unexpectedly, towards the Royal Family. The Queen's willingness to be part of such an elaborate stunt at the age of eighty-five won her nothing but respect and admiration, not least from her grandchildren. Speaking to the BBC's sports commentator Sue Barker, Harry said that both he and his brother had been slightly surprised by their grandmother's "secret hobby of parachuting." William said, "We were kept completely in the dark, that's how big the secret was. Harry got a sniff of it on the night and the rumor mill was going into overdrive, but in fact she did such a good performance that she's been asked to star in the next Bond film. I'm thrilled for her." Harry called her "an unbelievably good sport" and said, "I can't quite believe it when I see those pictures back."

But the Queen wasn't the only member of the family to win respect. The Princess Royal, President of the British Olympic Association, was hailed by sports minister Hugh Robertson as "one of the great unsung heroes of this whole process"; and Zara Phillips, her daughter, one-time Sports Personality of the Year, winning silver as part of the British equestrian team, became the first member of the Royal Family to win an Olympic medal. But William, Kate and Harry, as ambassadors for Team GB, had a significant part to play, too. They were at the events day after day supporting the athletes, most of the time dressed in the Team GB kit. They encouraged the army of volunteers and the genuine military who were all key to the smooth running of the games. They went up to the lounge where the athletes relaxed either to give them a pat on the back or commiserate with them. They really threw themselves into it, admitting that Zara's event was emotionally the most thrilling for them because of the personal connection. "We as cousins are very, very proud," said Harry. "It now explains why we never get to see her because she is always riding.

"The support from the British public is something else," he said. "We've had the chance to be at quite a few of the events, and just to feel the buzz of the British public getting behind the teams is astonishing." Like William, he had been afraid that they might be seen as freeloaders, taking seats when so many people in the country struggled to get tickets, but the public made it very clear that they were pleased to see all three of them—and they ended up seeing many more events than they anticipated and watched more on television. They didn't look like royals, and that no doubt was part of it; all three looked like genuine sports lovers caught up in the excitement of watching people performing at the peak of their game. But, as always, there was a wider agenda. Harry joked about his money being on Usain Bolt for gold "because obviously I'm not allowed to compete," but then talked about the positive effect the sprinter had had on young people. "There's kids back in Jamaica now who started running or doing track events simply because they look up to him . . . he's a wonderful example for his country, for the nation, for the world." And they both hoped these Olympics—and their own efforts—would encourage and inspire future generations to get involved in sport, "rather than sitting in front of the TV and playing computer games."

Surprisingly, it fell to Harry, as the most senior member of the Royal Family, to preside over the closing ceremony. William had to return to work at RAF Valley and so Harry and Kate took center stage. It was by far the most high-profile engagement of his twenty-seven years, and he carried it off with extraordinary confidence and self-possession. In a stirring written message, he said, the Games would "stay in the hearts and minds of people all over the world for a very long time to come. I congratulate all the athletes who have competed. They have shown us that there are few boundaries to human endeavor." The spirit of the Olympics represented "a magnificent force for positive change." The athletes, he said, had "captured the imagination of the world."

CONDUCT UNBECOMING

Harry was riding the crest of a wave. It hadn't been many years since people at Buckingham Palace had been sidling up to Jamie Lowther-Pinkerton and expressing concern about Harry's wild behavior. "You've really got to find something to keep Harry busy," they were saying; "you've got to find a way of dealing with Harry." Now the more enlightened ones were saying, "How the hell are we going to use Harry? How are we going to capitalize on this guy and all that he's got?"

But hardly had the plaudits been expressed before Harry was making headlines again, with a spectacular fall from grace. A drunken game of strip billiards with a bunch of girls in an expensive Las Vegas hotel room had been captured on one of the girl's mobile phones and sold for a song. Images of the third in line to the throne wearing nothing but an African necklace and bracelets appeared online on a gossipy American website, TMZ. Initially, the British press, post-Leveson, merely reported the story, accompanied by other photos of Harry during his stay in Vegas. "Harry Grabs the Crown Jewels," "Palace Fury at Harry Naked Photos," "Harry Naked Romp." But the *Sun* finally broke rank and put one of the images on the front page alongside the headline "Heir It Is! Pic of naked Harry you've already seen on the Internet."

Harry, it seemed, was back to square one, the loose cannon back to his old antics: no self-control, no judgment, too much money. However, Harry was on the verge of deploying to Afghanistan again. It was the last time he would be able to let his hair down with his friends for the next four months; and if things were to go catastrophically pear-shaped, perhaps for ever. He had completed years of disciplined training and was about to put his life on the line—along with hundreds of other servicemen and -women—and to see and do the things that most of those judging him couldn't begin to do or stomach.

Paddy Harverson feels he was badly wronged. "It was a nasty betrayal by a girl who pretended she was on her phone, took a picture, sent it to her boyfriend and it was in the newspapers. It was nasty, the press were really nasty and the *Sun* was disgraceful. They waited twenty-four hours before taking the brave decision and dressed it up as 'freedom of expression' and 'right to know' but then put a banner across the top, 'Souvenir Edition.' It was rank hypocrisy; a cheap shot. You can make an argument about judgment but he didn't break any laws, he was on holiday. And we knew and the press knew—but of course no one else knew—that he was on his way to Afghanistan, which put it in a different light. He was particularly upset about someone at a party making money out of him. Every time it's private, there's money in it. I hope these individuals sleep at night. These are their lives, it's not some career, they have to live their whole life with this nonsense."

"Perhaps because the conflict's been going on for so long now," says another member of his team, "we've become inured to just how bloody dangerous going to Afghanistan is. Had he been shot down and captured, it would have been unimaginably horrible—I mean unimaginably horrible. As a soldier you don't dwell on these things but it's there and you know it's there, and like every soldier going out to conflict, beforehand it's incredibly important that you have a chance to let off steam. It's not just a by-product of what they do, it's not a tradition that's grown up; it's releasing a part of themselves in order to give themselves over to something which might end their life and may prove utterly catastrophic for them. You can't take that away from any soldier, whether you're Prince Harry or Sergeant Bob Woods."

Jamie Lowther-Pinkerton believes it was not all bad. "If you're trying to hook in to the fifteen- to thirty-five-year-olds—what the media call the lost generation, who these guys down at West-minster simply can't reach—the generation that tweet their feel-ings and don't vote, you've got to be of the age and you've got to be credible.

"There was a scheme we went to in Manchester Moss Side three or four years ago and I had an opportunity to talk to some of the guys who worked with the young gangs. They were really inter-ested in Harry. They said he's a good guy. I said 'Why do you think that?' and they said, 'Well, he comes from a broken family, like us, he gets himself into all sorts of shit and gets all sort of shit poured over him because he's like he is, like us, and he's just come back from Afghanistan so, like us, he understands violence.'

"So looking at Las Vegas with the benefit of twenty/twenty hindsight: how has it affected his image with that fifteen- to thirty-five-year-old bracket? Not at all negatively. How has it affected his image with my mother sitting reading her *Telegraph* in Suffolk? Actually, my mother and others like her probably think he's rather a saucy boy so not that badly. But there is an element, a constitu-ency out there that will have been quite offended by it."

What everyone agrees is that he could get away with this sort of behavior as a single twenty-seven-year-old—particularly given the extenuating circumstances—but that it can't go on for much lon-ger. "Then the lovable-rogue bit turns to the slightly seedier royal and you've got a problem."

"We've all misbehaved in our teens and twenties," says one of the team, "and people will expect that. But I don't think people expect you to be a playboy in your thirties, forties and fifties. I sus-pect that happens because you don't have a hard center to your life. If you're really committed through your profession, through your flying, your Foundation, to things you really care about, I suspect you're much less likely to fall into this trap. It's not foolproof at all but there's nothing like a vacuum for inviting disaster and I don't think either of the Princes is interested in living in a vacuum."

"Las Vegas was an aberration," says Lord Dannatt. "I think he regrets that and I think Jamie and the others regret allowing him to be put in that position or him getting himself into that position. It was a bit of a failure all round, really. At the time I thought, oh my goodness, this is quite unnecessary and, given recent behavior, rather out of character. Disappointing. All of that was in the past but then he went back to square one. Snakes and ladders: he got to ninety-eight, ninety-nine, and hit that long snake that comes down to about three. But I think the public who love him anyway, forgave him, and then he was in Afghanistan and he was flying his helicopters and I think they discounted the behavior."

The Army would have been a little less forgiving. "He would have tapped the boards in front of his commanding officer, I am quite certain. An Army officer, forget Prince or not a Prince, does not appear in public with no clothes on—section 64, conduct unbecoming. Royal Marines can, it's a different issue, but that's by the bye. Royal Marines love taking their clothes off, but soldiers don't and Army officers definitely don't. I am absolutely certain they dealt with it informally; the commanding officer will have given him a good old-fashioned bollocking. Quite right too."

His commanding officer was Tom de la Rue. "Las Vegas was interesting because it came in his final pre-deployment leave period, and all I'll say is that because it was literally two weeks before he deployed, my focus, the focus of his squadron, and of anyone else for that matter, was purely and simply on getting him deployed on the 6th or 7th of September in good order. Las Vegas was not something that I dwelt on. There were all sorts of stories in the press—from left of arc to right of arc—and I do remember that some of them were rather extraordinary. Nevertheless, they were all founded on pure speculation."

RULES OF ENGAGEMENT

"Harry has got the ability to make this thing last a thousand years or bring it crashing down; he really has," says someone who knows him well. "He's the umbilical, the credibility, the connect; and where he has got to be—where he is in kit form at the moment—is globally recognized. What he's got to transform himself into is, not just the most popular man on the planet under thirty, but in his own way a statesman and an ambassador with a capital A for the whole country and the realms. It's the Beckham effect. When Beckham went to China, he opened doors for the British Ambassador that had been closed for two years. The Governor of the province, whom the Ambassador had been trying to get hold of for his whole tour, turned up at the airport to meet them both. Beckham was there on a footballing thing. You could overlay Harry on that. He'll have his wild moments, and his Las Vegas moments, but he ain't going to have them when he's in work mode. He's not going to do it; he's too clever. He's brilliant.

"And I don't think he'd stand a chance of brilliant if he wasn't quite dangerous with it. As long as it's two steps forward and one step back. Las Vegas was a real shock to him—so I think we're moving in the right direction."

Speaking of the Vegas incident, Harry said, "I probably let myself down, I let my family down, I let other people down. But at the end of the day I was in a private area and there should have been a certain amount of privacy that one should expect. It was probably a classic example of me probably being too much Army and not enough Prince. It's a simple case of that."

He was angry about the invasion of privacy and angry with the press, but he felt mortified that after all he had achieved that year this should have happened. "He's got a pretty thick hide, so he's used to the way he is, and bumps along with that. Quite right too. He's not going to beat himself up." He also had Afghanistan to focus on. And as one of his aides said to him, "It's not what I wanted to see but don't get hung up about it because nobody died and it would be far worse if you fell short of expectations in your Apache. Let's keep it in perspective. It's the sort of thing we all did but, fortunately, we don't all have the glare of the world's media on us."

Harry's pre-deployment training had been very intense. "The big issue is about restraint," says Tom de la Rue. "Engagement is the last resort and pre-deployment is all about judgmental training. Week after week after week we put our Apache crews through various demanding exercise scenarios until they are absolutely 100 percent confident that in any circumstance they will come to the correct judgment.

"There are broadly two aspects to what we do. There is deterrence, which works tremendously well. [For example]: there is an engagement happening on the ground, the patrol is being contacted in the Helmand River valley and they need Apache support. The Apaches come into the overhead and the patrol is able to withdraw because the Taliban melts away—that's deterrence. We know anecdotally that these insurgents really do quite revere the Apache capability. They call us mosquitoes because we're everywhere, and have the ability to attack them even at ranges where they can't see or hear us. This interesting dynamic plays deep into the psyche of the insurgents. The Apache is a formidable aircraft and it certainly does deter the enemy. The other very important aspect of our focus is saving life. What I say to my crews is, 'Listen, you are not here to win the campaign outright, you are a squadron of Apaches delivering a single capability as part of a widespread counter-insurgency campaign. You are not politicians, so you don't make a decision about whether you should be here or not.

Essentially, all I am asking you to do is to boil your job down to two things: deterrence—and if deterrence doesn't work, then save coalition lives by attacking and defeating the enemy wherever he presents himself as a legitimate and justifiable target.' If that's the mind-set they launch with, then they are in a very good place.

"But before firing a single weapon the crews have to ask themselves three vital questions—Can I? Should I? Must I? The answers will give the Apache crews their rough engagement parameters."

"The British Army is absolutely scrupulous about rules of engagement and whether or not it is legal to engage the enemy," says David Meyer. "One of the things with the Apache is you can record what people are doing, what is being said in the cockpit and any engagement, however small, however long, is scrutinized to see that it is fair, legal, proportional, etc. The understanding of that is drilled in at the very, very beginning. This is not a game; this is really important stuff and you are legally responsible for your actions. You've got incredibly destructive power at your fingertips; you can't just use it willy-nilly."

On his first deployment, as a JTAC, Harry had been in the middle of nowhere, as close to the front line as it was possible to be, in an American patrol-based unit, away from the media and even away from his close protection, just concentrating on his job. He loved it and still has friends among a unit of Gurkhas he came across. Camp Bastion, where he was based the second time around, for the full four and a half months, was a very different experience. Bastion was roughly the size of Reading and temporary home to 30,000 to 40,000 soldiers as well as locally employed civilians of every nationality. It was a sprawling, ugly, utilitarian mass of military humanity, blast walls, razor wire, tents and converted shipping containers in the middle of the desert in Helmand Province, with a constant turnaround of military personnel.

The runway, the aircraft, the ops rooms and everything else used by the Joint Aviation Group, of which Harry and his squadron were a part, was in a separate area within the compound, fenced off from the rest; and only those who worked there were admitted.

There were about 550 people in all from the three services and, within that area, everyone was used to seeing Captain Wales; to them he was just another Army officer doing his job. But when he left that area to go to his accommodation, to the NAAFI, the gym, or the cookhouse, where several thousand people would be eating at any one sitting, he was suddenly Prince Harry and an object of curiosity, which he hated. "There's this slightly uneasy dislocation at times where one minute you're having to do what the aircraft is designed for," says Tom, "and the next minute you're in this big central cookhouse; you're getting two worlds merged together; whereas in the patrol-based locations you have none of that—there's no media, there are no other units gawping at you, you're simply getting on with your job."

The crews worked through a cycle, switching between very high readiness (VHR) days, when they would hang out in the VHR tent—making brews, watching videos, playing computer games—waiting for the phone to ring, when they would run to the aircraft and could be airborne in six and a half to seven minutes; and deliberate operations days, which were less stressful. Those could be spent on deliberate flying operations, or providing cover for troop movements.

"There's a lot of sitting around doing nothing," says David Meyer, "and then suddenly you're thrown right into the thick of it in what can be very trying circumstances. There's a very strong bond between the aviation community—be they Chinook, Apache or Lynx pilots—because it's been formed in adversity. If the Chinook crews can't trust the Apache crews to ensure that they're safe, that they're providing protection when those crews are on the ground, then that whole thing will break down. It comes back to making the right decision under pressure, often at night in what can be difficult weather and difficult flying conditions, whilst on the radio you're hearing there's a British soldier who's lost two legs or something. So the pressure comes on like that and you've got to react and make the right decisions. You could be drinking a cup of coffee; five minutes later you could be in your aircraft, ten minutes later you could be over a very tricky situation unfolding on the ground and you could be there for two and a bit hours and then you come back and it's like, 'Well, what on earth was all that about?' And then you hear that a British soldier has died. So it's a very difficult environment to operate in."

What had so convinced David that Harry was right for the job was his ability to make decisions. "Make a decision right or wrong, but make a decision. You'd have a scenario in Afghanistan with troops on the ground in contact with the Taliban, in either mortal danger or need of assistance and the last thing you want is somebody to arrive in an Apache—who can make a significant difference to what's going on on the ground—to dither around. You want someone who's going to come in there, read the situation on the ground very quickly, understand what's going on and understand what they can do to effect the right outcome, either in getting the troops out of danger or getting a Chinook helicopter in to pick up an injured soldier or something of that nature. He's got to make all those right decisions and operate a very complex machine as well."

The public didn't know about Harry's deployment until he came back at the end of January 2013, when several interviews he had given during the four months were released along with a full-length documentary. The cameras showed him at work and at play—at Christmas, wearing a Santa hat with pigtails; fixing himself Weetabix for breakfast, just feet from his unmade bed; playing uckers (a board game traditionally played in the Navy—"the loser becomes the brew-bitch for the day") and trashing his mates at the video game FIFA. He was a lad among lads. And they showed him on call, discussing the more serious aspects of the job—and, in one of the most dramatic pieces of television, in mid-sentence he realized there was an emergency going on behind him, ripped the microphone from his shirt and ran off to his aircraft. He wasn't enjoying Bastion. "My choice would have been back out on the ground with my regiment," he said. "That sounds quite spoilt when I'm standing in front of this thing—£45 million worth—but

I think hopefully my friends and family back home know exactly what I'm talking about. I'd much rather be out with the lads in a PB (patrol base). The last job was, for me personally, better. It's a pain in the arse being stuck in Bastion. I go into the cookhouse and everyone has a good old gawp, and that's one thing that I dislike about being here."

He talked about the aircraft and about flying it and the sort of work they did. "There's a lot of pressures, obviously, when we go and support the Americans or when we're escorting the Tricky [mobile hospital]...but essentially I think it's less stressful being up here than it is down there. We don't have to put on all the kit and walk around through the desert, sweating our balls off." And when goaded about whether he had killed anyone, he said, "Yeah, so lots of people have. The squadron's been out here. Everyone's fired a certain amount."

How did he feel knowing that when he fired the aircraft's weapons, that job was essentially killing the enemy? "Take a life to save a life," he said; "that's what we revolve around, I suppose. If there's people doing bad stuff to our guys, we'll take them out of the game. It's not the reason I decided to do this job; I did it to get back out here and carry on with a job." As for his skill as a gunner, he said, "It's a joy for me because I'm one of those people who loves playing PlayStation and Xbox, so with my thumbs I like to think that I'm probably quite useful."

The condemnation was instant. "I'VE KILLED TALIBAN" was a typical tabloid headline, while all the newspapers berated him for casually comparing battle to playing a computer game. Harry had also taken the opportunity to say exactly what he felt about the media.

It wasn't quite the triumphant homecoming it should have been but, as Paddy Harverson says, "It was just him being true to himself. He's not a politician, he doesn't think, Oh, I can't say that or I'd better say that, or I'll dodge that question."

"I don't believe there is any such a thing as private life any more," said Harry. "I'm not going to sit here and whinge. Everybody knows about Twitter and the Internet and stuff like that. Every single mobile phone has got a camera on it now. You can't move an inch without someone judging you, and I suppose that's just the way life goes." He said his father was always telling him not to read the newspapers, but, "Of course I read it. If there's a story and something's been written about me I want to know what's being said, but all it does is just upset me and anger me that people can get away with writing the stuff they do. Not just about me, but about everything and everybody."

He scathingly referred to a typical example, when asked about Kate's pregnancy. "Obviously I'm thrilled for both of them," he said. "It's about time. I can't wait to be an uncle…I had a chat to them. I didn't send a letter of congratulation like most of the papers said." Kate had been forced to announce that she was pregnant in December, earlier than she would have chosen because she was admitted to hospital with severe morning sickness. The *Sun* had run a front-page story that Harry had sent her a letter of congratu- lations from Bastion. "It was just made up," says Paddy. "The *Sun* came to us and said, 'We have this story, is it okay to run it?' You know when they don't know; they want to take the story forward so they just make it up. How could they ever know that? It's indic- ative of how the media treats not just the royals but celebrities. It's creative journalism gone mad. They'll give you a wink and say they're in the entertainment business, but these are these people's lives."

"People who know him can all understand why he was critical of the press and it sums up his character," says his friend Damian West. " 'It's true, it's what I think and I'm not scared to express my opinion, I'm not scared of confrontation' [is what he might say]. Sometimes it has to be reined in for obvious reasons, but if he feels something or someone is being mishandled or misjudged he will try to rectify it. I remember when a group of friends were staying the weekend somewhere and were returning back to the house after a long afternoon walk, a member of the domestic staff said, 'Just leave all your kit here,' and so we left our kit there and went and had tea. Harry then came in and said, 'What the hell do you think you are all doing? Take that stuff and put it in the right place.' Very strict on, 'You don't have someone else tidying up after you.' He feels very strongly about that, about how people are treated in every walk of life and at every level. He would never ask anybody to do something he would not do himself. He's the last person to take a seat in a room. He's very sensitive to people and the difference between right and wrong. What is right should be done. It's a real driver for him."

As for the suggestion that being good at computer games was handy in an Apache, "What he meant by that unfortunate turn of phrase, the Game Boy analogy," says a senior aide, "is that the bloke in the front of the aircraft has got to be of the generation that's able to do thirty-five different functions at once. It's exactly the right analogy. You need five hands and you need your eyes going in different directions and you're controlling three weapons systems for the aircraft. I think you can acquire thirty-six targets at once, which you have to prioritize—which are the threats, which aren't; you've got to tell the pilot in the back to maneuver it this way or that and then you've got to identify the target and then do the radio transmissions back to base to get permission to engage and you're talking to the air people and the guys on the ground. It's a nightmare; that's why it is the key role.

"He was a soldier speaking as a soldier on operations. You can't expect the guy to possibly engage the enemy and not speak as a soldier. The plain fact is unless you are in the logistics chain on operations, to a greater or lesser degree you are going to be there to potentially inflict lethal force, whether you've got a rifle in your hands, or whether, as the last time, you're there to talk in U.S. air power, fast air on to targets. It's what they are about. What weapons you are carrying or operating at the time, philosophically is almost irrelevant. It's a degree of firepower we are talking about.

"Dare I say it, it does no harm for someone with his profile, who's right in among it, to say, 'Guys and girls, this is what it's about. It's statistics on the news, but actually this is what we're doing here.' People are going to be nasty and accusatory, but your intelligent *Sun* reader is going to win through; he's going to say, 'Hang on—what did we expect him to do?' And it hasn't done any damage to his reputation in credibility terms. Ever since those interviews, you don't hear that it's all a con, that he's being protected by the SAS when he's out there. You don't hear any of that anymore.

"Essentially, the whole point about taking life is not something that British soldiers talk about a great deal, I don't suppose any soldiers do, but it's something, in the final analysis, you are paid to do. You do it to help other people who can't look after themselves, who are exposed. I know that's his view. I'm not saying every soldier, including Harry, go out there with some great geopolitical mission statement imprinted on their brain, that they are there to preserve the democracy of Afghanistan; I think it's more localized and personal. It's enabling little girls to go to school, it's making sure some Afghan policeman who's the pillar of the community is not topped by the Taliban. It's the personal in the end that is the motivator."

Harry spoke to Jamie Lowther-Pinkerton when he came back, a couple of times at length. "I've always heard, 'Oh he flies his helicopter frightfully well,' but what came out of these, listening to him talk about the operations he'd been on, not in a showy-offy way but literally downloading, it came across in spades that this guy is a very professional operator. His maintenance of standards and his fury if he felt that he had dropped below at any point, the fact that he had rehearsed and rehearsed and trained and trained to overcome things; and he would not look lightly on other people's standards dropping either. He's a really professional soldier. They're all good guys but you don't see that sort of vehemence that often and it impressed me."

Tom de la Rue, who was with Harry in Afghanistan, is not alone in believing that that second tour of duty was a defining moment in his life. "I think his training for the operational tour and then the tour itself really changed him as a professional officer. He suddenly became very wise overnight—not that he wasn't before, but if you're put in a situation where you're in charge of a capability like that, you've got to be extremely professional, and you've got to get it right every time. Being granted authority to fight in the British Army's most formidable attack capability comes with huge responsibility...Getting it wrong could have devastating consequences. It doesn't get any more serious than that.

"When he came back in January he was quite different—all for the better. Much more mature...But equally I would say that every single officer or senior NCO who has gone through this process has experienced exactly the same thing. They all—to a man or woman—come back from their first operational tour as a changed person because of the unique experience they have just had.

"These guys are just so full of confidence and anything that they thought they were lacking previously...the cobwebs are blown out and they come back really feeling they are on top of their job. In this case he really did pull it out of the bag and consequently came back a completely different person.

"I'm tremendously proud of his achievement but I'm not entirely sure it's been captured in its fullest sense; the difficulty, the complexity, the level of achievement that he's had to reach is just extraordinary and the fact that he deployed to an operational theater, and was able to act as a co-pilot gunner in a counter-insurgency campaign that has all sorts of nuances attached to it is remarkable. It's never black and white, everything is always gray, and the fact that he did that absolutely with faultless distinction is something that I hope is remembered about him for a very, very long time. He did a tremendous job out there for Queen and country."

"Las Vegas was before he went to Afghanistan," says Sir David Manning. "I think there are phases in life and sowing his oats and being a bit of a wild boy was okay, but I think that's over. We have to assume he's moving into a different phase and I do see Afghanistan as a real watershed."

Jamie agrees, and sees Harry's tours of Afghanistan as the "two weigh points" in his development. "Going on operations is like having a fizzer under you in terms of growing up, and particularly for these guys in the last ten years who have been at war. His commanding officer, who was out there with him, said to me in the middle, 'I think you'll be quite surprised, I think you'll meet a quite different man.' And I think that's true. Not that he's lost his sense of fun or ability to kick the traces over, but he has a depth now because of this. It's the old Keith Miller story about the captain of Australian cricket, who went away, fought in the Battle of Britain, came back and, in the first Test after the war, England had them up against the ropes and a journalist asked how he handled pressure on the cricket pitch. 'Pressure,' he said, 'is a Messerschmitt up your arse!' That's Harry... Some of the little things that would have mattered before don't matter anymore. He's come through it. There's an acceptance that he's going to have to ride with the punches of some of the more intrusive things from the media. Before, that would have been one of the defining things of his life but there's a perspective there now, he's able to compartmentalize these things. He still gets steamed up, who wouldn't? But he's able to put it in a box and say, 'Let's get on with it.'"

THE END OF THE BEGINNING

Taking leave after an operational tour is not voluntary and it's not a luxury. Every member of the Armed Forces who has been in combat is expected to go away for four or five weeks for the sake of their sanity. "They take themselves out of that high-octane mind-set and reintegrate into the family or social environment, as it does take some time for the brain to just settle down," says Tom de la Rue. "Mental illness comes in all forms—it just depends on the particular individual and their chemical make-up. Nobody's immune."

Harry went to Verbier with his bohemian new girlfriend, Cressida Bonas, to celebrate her twenty-fifth birthday. They had met in May 2012, introduced by his cousin and good friend Princess Eugenie, who had known Cressida for years. She is the daughter of the 1960s socialite and model Lady Mary Gaye Curzon, whose late father was the 6th Earl Howe and heir to the Curzon banking dynasty. Cressida has a complicated assortment of half-siblings, as well as step-relatives who have come and gone from her life. Her childhood was turbulent, like Harry's.

Despite a colorful, high-profile life (and poor taste in men), MG—as Lady Mary Gaye is known—is good fun, kind and well liked; and in that respect her daughter takes after her. Cressida's father, Jeffrey Bonas, a businessman and entrepreneur who lives in Norfolk, is a less popular, more controversial figure. But, despite the privileges of an aristocratic background, a good education, good looks, brains and talent, life cannot have been easy for Cressida. Her mother was married three times before she married

Jeffrey Bonas; Cressida was her fifth child—which is why, when she's not known as Cressy, she's called Smalls or Smally.

Mary Gaye's first husband was the late Esmond Cooper-Key, whom she married at Penn House, her family seat in Buckinghamshire (which, on her father's death, to her great sadness, went to her uncle's branch of the family, because her father had no male heirs). The wedding photographer was Cecil Beaton. She and Esmond had a daughter, Pandora, but the marriage broke down when Pandora was three. Her second marriage was to John Anstruther-Gough-Calthorpe. They were together for nine years and had three children—Georgiana, Isabella, and Jacobi, who is a good friend of William's. When she fell in love with Jeffrey Bonas, he was married and his divorce was said to have cost him £1.2 million. But their marriage didn't last and she left him when Cressida was very young.

Her fourth husband was financier Christopher Shaw, who had been married twice before and had three children. Said to be reminiscent of the fictional Jay Gatsby in his extravagant lifestyle and lavish entertaining, Shaw wanted the Curzon connection. Mary Gaye finally gave in to his repeated proposals of marriage, but it was never happy, and they divorced when Cressida was eleven. In January 2014 he died suddenly of a suspected overdose and Cressida went to his funeral. The *Daily Telegraph* obituary described the house parties he had thrown at Hinton Ampner, the grand house near Winchester that he leased from the National Trust. "Children," according to the piece, "were invariably accommodated in the stable block, and it is unlikely that he knew their names (newspaper reports that Cressida…was mourning a surrogate father, were wide of the mark)."

Today, Cressida's mother seems to be happy at last. She is with David McDonough, who runs a public relations business. They live in Chelsea.

In many ways, Cressida and Harry are kindred spirits—they have the same confident, relaxed attitude to life; they're sparky; they know how to let their hair down but equally know how to work; and the shared experience of loss and domestic trauma during their childhoods was possibly some of the attraction. They also have interests and friends in common, not only via Eugenie and Beatrice. Cressida's half-sister, Isabella Calthorpe, married Harry's friend Sam Branson (Sir Richard Branson's son) in 2013, and they had all been at Sam's birthday party on Necker Island the week before Harry's fateful trip to Las Vegas. She is a free agent; she dresses in her own style, happy in torn and faded dungarees and hippyish skirts with her hair in a scrunchie or loose and disheveled. She dances tirelessly at parties and festivals, and also shares Harry's love of tennis and skiing. After school—she went to Stowe, like Chelsy—she studied dance at Leeds University and worked as a ski instructor in Verbier and a model for Burberry. But modern dance was her passion, and after Leeds she did a year at the prestigious Trinity Laban Conservatoire in Greenwich. She was said to be planning to make a career of it, but meanwhile took a job in theater marketing. In 2008 *Tatler's Little Black Book* described her as "really pretty, really nice and absolutely obsessed with [jazz singer] Eva Cassidy."

It was on the slopes in Verbier that the world first saw evidence that Harry and Cressida were an item. A photograph appeared on most front pages of the two of them on skis, wearing sunglasses, hats and well wrapped up against the cold; Harry was giving her an affectionate bear hug. "HARRY'S GAL" was one headline. "Prince shows off new love ... as insiders say she's The One"; "Has Prince Harry finally found love?" were others. The photo was one of a series that had clearly been taken by a paparazzo, but they were embracing in full view of other skiers, so were obviously happy to be seen—and they were consistently seen with one another thereafter. When those first shots were taken, they were staying in Verbier with Beatrice and Eugenie, her parents and a party of friends. The Duke and Duchess of York, although divorced, take a chalet every year for Andrew's birthday, which was the day after Cressida's. That year the Duke turned fifty-three. Harry has always been close to the York family. While they are very different characters, he and Prince Andrew are both second sons, were both "spares," and were both helicopter pilots who served on the front line—Andrew in the Falklands War in the 1980s. There was also a connection through Sarah, who had once been good friends with Diana. On the night of Andrew's birthday, twenty of them celebrated with dinner in a local restaurant where, according to reports, late in the evening Cressida had sat on Harry's knee and they had "kissed like love-struck teenagers in the back of a cinema."

After four months in the heat and dust of Afghanistan, the Swiss Alps with friends, family, good food and good wine, and nothing more dangerous than a paparazzo, must have been bliss, but with three distinct lives to lead, and so many charities all wanting a piece of him, Harry was never going to be able to holiday for long. And Sentebale not only had ambitious plans, the charity also had a new Chief Executive.

Cathy Ferrier is short, northern, dynamic, fun, feisty and impressive. In the spring of 2012, she had quite an unusual day ahead. She met two Princes. "It was quite frightening, quite scary. I'd never met a prince before—then two in a day." After seven years at Oxfam, and twenty-five years before that as commercial director of the bookseller, Borders, she had been earmarked for the job by the new Chairman, Philip Green. She met Prince Harry at St. James's Palace, then Prince Seeiso at the Lesotho High Commission, where he then worked as High Commissioner.

The first meeting was in Jamie Lowther-Pinkerton's office. "Harry asked me lots of questions about what I'd done before and then told me what his ambitions were for the charity and why he'd set up Sentebale and why he was passionate about it; asked me a lot about what I thought I could do for it and what difference I could make, etc. But in the middle of the interview...we were on the first floor with a net curtain on the window, and just outside on the street was a tour bus going by with some chap talking to a group of tourists and they were just below the window. We could hear them talking and I think Philip [Green] said, 'If you pulled the curtain back and just smiled, can you imagine how shocked all those tourists would be to realize just how close they were to you?' Harry said, 'Yes, I think it might create a diversion. Probably best not.'"

Cathy got the job. And in the time she has been running Sentebale she has struck up a good, friendly, easy relationship with Harry and has taken the charity forward in leaps and bounds. "He's great and he's always been incredibly easy to work with," she says; "very friendly and very informal. I do regular one-to-ones and give him an update on the charity and send him documents and he'll text back and say, 'I like this. I would like a bit more of that, and have you thought about x?' The moment I realized we had gone through any kind of formal barrier was when he came in late for a meeting. I was at St. James's Palace waiting for him and he'd been down to the Olympics—I think the rowers had just won a gold and he was late. He came hurtling in, and I was in the kitchen making a cup of tea. 'Cathy, I'm so late,' and gave me two big kisses on the cheek and then carried on and I made him a cup of tea. And you think, Okay, this is not a formal relationship any more, he's completely relaxed. He's good on texts and he emails quite a bit too. He's an absolute joy to work with and there's always a spark of humor in there, a bit of teasing because he's like that, so his personality comes through. He's great fun. Has a real twinkle in his eye all the time, particularly when he's with children. It comes up so clearly when he's with children; there's a little tease below those communications which is really nice to see."

HIV/AIDS is fiercely stigmatized in Lesotho—as is disability—and Sentebale had been running a program, named after Seeiso's mother, to support and teach children about it. Their ambition was to raise £2 million to build a permanent Mamohato Centre, to provide psychosocial care and friendship for children living with the disease and children with disabilities. King Letsie had donated a piece of land not far from Maseru, the capital, with stunning views towards the Thaba Bosiu mountain. And in February, after a few days visiting existing programs in Lesotho with Cathy, Seeiso and a posse of photographers and journalists, Harry spoke at a prestigious fundraising dinner in Johannesburg, their first in South Africa, where they hoped to tap into the huge wealth of that country.

"Our aim and hope is that we can influence a decline in the transmission of HIV and increase life expectancy, in a unique way for Lesotho: by addressing the psychological and social needs of the next generation, which is so important. Ultimately, this will strengthen family structures, instill hope in future generations of Basotho people, and enable them to realize their potential and achieve their ambitions. The impact of this program has the potential to change society."

It was only right, he said, that the center should be named after Queen Mamohato. "She was so loved as the Mother of the Nation. I hope she would be proud of what we are trying to achieve in her name. I hope that my mother will be proud, too. Maybe, just maybe, they are together somewhere up there, with blueprints and sketches already mapped out! I can only hope we put the swings in the right place."

Sitting at Harry's table that evening was Nacho Figueras, the professional Argentinian polo player and the face of Ralph Lauren. He had played in all the Sentebale matches with Harry; he is a friend and was set to become an ambassador for the charity. The auction wasn't going well and fabulous lots were being sold for peanuts, so when a pair of diamond earrings in the shape of forget-me-nots, specially designed and donated by Garrard's, came up and seemed in danger of going for less than they were worth, Nacho put his hand up. "Then the joke with Harry started," he says. "Hey, if I raise my hand will you promise that you will raise yours?" They were egging each other on, and everyone was laughing, until Nacho found himself the last one with his hand in the air. "That night when I went back to my room I thought, what have I done? I just spent $30,000 on something that I did not need. That was the way my brain was processing the information." The next day he and a small group (of which I was one) flew to Lesotho and spent three days visiting Sentebale projects and meeting the children, including herd boys up in the hills, who, before the charity took an interest in them, had been all but feral. "Right now," he said on the last day of our trip, "as we are coming down the road, I am looking at it from a whole different place. I have invested $30,000 in a thing that really makes me feel proud, and happy. I would do it again, even if I had to make an effort to [financially]. That's what happened to me."

Long before he ever met the children, it was Harry's sincerity that hooked Nacho. "I really felt that Harry meant what he was doing. You can see it in his eyes when you talk to him about this that he really means it and really wants it and really cares about it. Originally it was, 'Would you play this game, it's to raise money for this charity, Sentebale?' And you say, 'Of course, you're going to play polo, why not?' And then when you learn about it and see how much he cares about it, you say, 'Okay I want to do this,' I want to help him because it's important. He can do a lot, but if we help him, he can do more. It's not what he says, it's what you know comes from the inside, you can feel from his heart, he is telling you what he saw and what he feels about it. He's not just being a tape recorder and repeating something that he is supposed to say. He means it."

Despite Nacho's efforts, the total raised by the dinner was an underwhelming £275,000, but they were soon playing the Sentebale Polo Cup again, in Connecticut, which raised over $1 million in May 2013, as did another big fundraising dinner in Dubai in October of the same year, attended by Sheikh Ahmed Bin Saeed Al Maktoum. So, by the end of 2013, with a further injection of money from the Elton John Foundation, the Mamohato Centre was well on its way.

They were, as Harry had said, at "the end of the beginning. Unless we think big, unless we are ambitious, nothing will change." Sentebale's longer-term plan is to raise £20 million over the next five years, with the intention of replicating the programs into other southern African countries that are similarly affected by HIV/AIDS—possibly Mozambique, Botswana and Malawi.

"There is the potential to create a very significant global charity here with a very high brand awareness," says Philip Green: "a major charity. But for the short- to medium-term we will focus on Commonwealth countries and psychosocial support."

The brand awareness had a major leg-up at the RHS Chelsea Flower Show in 2013. "The one thing Harry is very good at is taking someone else's idea," says Philip, who had thought a garden around the forget-me-not flower might work. "He's not precious about the origin of an idea." In fact, he became so enthused about this one, that when Philip and Cathy told him, in passing, that their sponsor had dropped out at the eleventh hour, he was so upset that they had to find a new one. "He just said, 'That's such a pity, it's such a good idea, you can't let that go, it's too good to miss, we would get massive publicity for the charity and we could raise lots of funds, forget me-nots . . . it's such a good idea.'

"I went straight from St. James's Palace and called Ian Cheshire, who runs B&Q,' says Philip. "I said 'I've got a great opportunity for you. You're the leading garden retailer in the UK—how about doing something around forget-me-nots at the Flower Show?' He said, 'Give me twenty-four hours,' and he came back and said, 'We'll do it.' It was a lot of money [£350,000 before you can even apply to Chelsea], but the publicity we got from it and the awareness of the brand lifted us to another level in terms of awareness. We would have had to pay between £5 and £10 million to get that level of exposure. Media and press coverage is really important when you're a young charity because you can't afford to advertise. Hits on the website have gone up thousands of percents and that has translated into donations—but, to be honest, we were doing it for profile and awareness which is part of building a business for the long term."

Harry was fiercely proud of the garden. The designer, Jinny Blom, had cleverly created a real sense of the country and its culture, and Harry had been involved from the beginning, discussing it, looking at early sketches—some of which she emailed to him in Afghanistan—and he was always wanting more. And he was delighted when so many members of his family came to see it. "There was a really nice moment," says Cathy, "when Prince Charles and Camilla were on the garden. There was a beautiful inlaid stone with hearts and crowns and around the stone were 'babies' tears,' a tiny little plant that looks quite mossy, then interspersed with them were forget-me-nots. They were stood on it with Harry," says Cathy, "and were in mid-conversation with Jinny when Prince Philip approached and stood slightly back and didn't interrupt and then as they were coming off the garden, Harry was talking to Charles and he said, 'You do know your father's here? You two have met, haven't you?' And did a faux introduction between the two."

"Harry stumbled across the orphans in Lesotho quite by chance," says one of his team; "and because he is who he is, he turned it into a charity that is now absolutely staggering. It went through a difficult patch and it's come out of that patch much stronger, really clear, and that's because Prince Harry didn't give up on it. He could have gone, 'That was a good experiment for when I was young, let's fold it up and put it into another charity or do something clever with it'—they were all options available to him—but he was determined not to. He wanted it to go from strength to strength and—he wouldn't put it in these terms but—he sees it as an absolutely core part of what he can bring to the world."

BROTHERS IN ARMS

"Spending time on tour is the single greatest bonding experience anybody could ever have," says Martin Hewitt, the wounded ex-Para, who walked to the North Pole. "It's only when you're in a position where there's no easy way out that your true character comes out—and there's no easy way out of an operational tour. You've all got to pull through as a team to achieve what you need to achieve, whatever that may be—and our forces are now working in some of the most adverse environments in the world. I now work in the commercial sector and if you make a mistake there, if you're unlucky or someone gets something wrong, they might get a pay cut, or the sack or lose a client. You get things wrong out there, you're dead or, worse still, your men are dead. There's pressure and there's pressure, and there's bonding experiences."

Harry's passion for servicemen and -women and their families—especially, but not exclusively, the wounded ones—is almost certainly born out of that shared experience. One of the most moving speeches he has made so far was in May 2012, when he flew to Washington to receive a humanitarian award from the Atlantic Council for his work with veterans. He made it clear he was accepting it on behalf of his brother, their Foundation, all those who worked to support the wounded, and "particularly the guys. This is their award.

"It would be wrong of me to speak for these heroes, but not presumptuous of me to pay tribute to them: so many of our servicemen and -women have made the ultimate sacrifice; so many lives have been lost and so many changed forever by the wounds that they have suffered in the course of their duties. They have paid a terrible price to keep us safe and free.

"The very least we owe them is to make sure that they and their brave families have everything they need through the darkest days—and, in time, regain the hope and confidence to flourish again. For these selfless people, it is after the guns have fallen silent, the din of battle quietened, that the real fight begins—a fight that may last for the rest of their lives.

"We will all continue to support our Armed Forces in defense of freedom at home and abroad, but sooner or later the coverage of them in the media will diminish or cease as coalition forces withdraw from Afghanistan. They will no longer be at the forefront of our minds. But the injuries left from a 7.62 round, an IED, watching a fellow comrade injured or killed—these are experiences that remain with you for life, both physically and mentally.

"We must be there for our servicemen and -women, and their families, standing shoulder to shoulder with them. British and American forces train together, fight together and, tragically, some are wounded and some die together. It makes perfect sense to me, therefore, that we should—wherever possible and appropriate— work together, by pooling our expertise and experience, to heal and support the wounded veterans of both our Nations—truly, brothers- and sisters-in-arms.

"Last year, I struggled to keep up with the four British soldiers whom I joined for part of their expedition to walk to the North Pole. Each of these men had recently been gravely wounded on the battlefields of Afghanistan. Theirs was the fastest team to reach the Pole that season.

"At this very moment, another team of our wounded are returning from Mount Everest. Sadly, I understand that they have been frustrated from reaching the summit by the unusually warm weather, which brings particularly dangerous conditions. However, the mere fact that they are up there on that fearsome peak, I find totally amazing."

Harry was in Washington for no more than twenty-four hours,

but an important part of the trip for him was meeting a British team of disabled servicemen and -women who were in America to compete in a Paralympic-style event called the Warrior Games. The Games have been going every year since 2010 at the U.S. Olympic Training Center in Colorado, but this was the first year that a British team had been invited to take part—and Help for Heroes was funding them. Harry couldn't go to the Games himself, but Nick Booth from the Royal Foundation went instead, and found the experience incredibly moving. "It was really extraordinary to see quite severely injured servicemen and -women compete against each other in a very competitive but also extraordinarily supportive environment. Matt Webb, an English triple amputee, took off both his legs, one of his arms and swam two lengths of the pool that Michael Phelps trains in; one-armed, roared on by 250 other amputees and wounded servicemen. Even though he was going to be last by at least a length in a two-length race, it didn't matter. It was about him proving to himself and everybody else that he was still capable of doing it.

"And to see Private Pa Njie enter the 1,500 meters a few weeks after getting his prosthetic legs. He was really still learning to walk. There were two British guys in that race: Simon Maxwell, who's a great athlete, a single leg amputee, who got the gold medal. Pa Njie came last and, by the time everyone else had finished, he still had two laps to go and he was not going to be beaten. He kept going and kept going, roared on by a stadium full of people who all stood for two laps for him. I've worked in the child abuse field for twenty years, so you see some stuff you remember, but they remain two of the most extraordinary experiences I've ever had. I was like, 'I just need to step outside for a moment.'"

It was Nick's description that made Harry determined to see the Games for himself, and to bring them to a wider audience. So a six-day trip to America was duly organized in May 2013. He arrived in Washington, as always, killing several birds with one stone.

He started on Capitol Hill where he opened an exhibition for the HALO Trust (the mine clearance charity with which Princess

303

Diana was memorably associated), having become patron of its Twenty-fifth Anniversary Appeal. Then he attended a reception at the White House for the military and their families, standing on a receiving line alongside the First Lady, Michelle Obama. The room was full of children and, although he was only supposed to dip in for half an hour, he stayed for the whole event. Next he went to the Arlington National Cemetery, where more than 400,000 military casualties—dating back to the American Civil War—are buried. He laid a wreath in Section 60, which is for casualties since 2001, and laid a second wreath at the Tomb of the Unknown Soldier, which has been guarded continuously since 1937. And he visited the Walter Reed National Military Medical Center, America's equivalent of Headley Court, where he marveled at the advances in prosthetic technology and met wounded servicemen undergoing rehab.

But the most important part of the visit was to the Warrior Games in Colorado Springs, where he spent two days. He helped launch the competition by igniting a large symbolic flame, with Olympic swimmer Missy Franklin and blind U.S. Navy Lieutenant Brad Snyder. When the formalities were over, he was in his element, mixing with fellow servicemen and -women and playing sport—volleyball on his bottom—dressed in one of the British team's Union Jack T-shirts, emblazoned with the Help for Heroes logo. Afterwards there was a private reception where he met the competitors, including the American team with whom he would walk to the South Pole at the end of the year. "We had a room in a hotel where we just said to the guys, 'We'll keep out'—and we left them to it," says Help for Heroes co-founder Bryn Parry. "Harry went along and they had a few beers. They told him jokes, he told them jokes, they showed him photographs of their wounds etc, etc. He's a soldier—and he's a soldier who talks like a soldier and acts like a soldier and understands soldiers and they love him for it. And when Harry is sitting in that room with his beer in his hand, he is a young captain talking to other young captains and corporals. The only difference is, Nick has got no legs and Harry has."

The Games are surprisingly small; there are only two hundred or so competitors. They play seven sports—archery, cycling, shooting, sitting-volleyball, swimming, track and field and wheelchair basketball. And the spectators are mostly friends and family. They are run by the U.S. Olympic Committee on behalf of the U.S. government and had previously been very low key. Harry's presence changed all that, but for once he was pleased to see his media shadow. Before sounding a horn for the start of the ten-kilometer hand-cycle race, at the U.S. Air Force Training Academy in Colorado Springs, he said, "You've got the Olympics, you've got the Paralympics and you've got the Warrior Games; there's no reason why the Warrior Games shouldn't be recognized worldwide, with the same amount of attention as the Olympics and Paralympics." Then, gesturing to the bank of broadcasters, photographers and journalists, he added, "You've got all these guys here—it's not always great having them around—but today it's fantastic to get the message across to every other country that has eyes on here at the moment."

The day before, ahead of the opening, he had caught everyone off guard. Embellishing a speech that had been prepared for him by Nick Booth, he said, "I only hope in the future, the near future, we can bring the Warrior Games to Britain and continue to enlarge this fantastic cause."

Privately, and not so privately, he made it clear that the near future meant 2014. He wasn't the only one who wanted to see the Warrior Games replicated in London and opened up to the world. Bryn Parry and his colleagues at Help for Heroes had been thinking along the very same lines. They know only too well that when UK intervention in Afghanistan comes to an end, it will become less newsworthy, the support will start to dry up and the public will forget today's heroes. But it took Harry to make progress on the plans happen.

From the Games Prince Harry went to New Jersey, to see the damage done by Superstorm Sandy, which had destroyed the home of a U.S. soldier he had met in Afghanistan. Then on to New York, where he traveled on a red London double-decker bus with the Prime Minister, David Cameron, to Manhattan's trendy

Meatpacking District for an event with British entrepreneurs to promote the government's GREAT Britain campaign. And he launched the first charity outside the UK that the Royal Foundation has ever funded.

The Foundation already had an American offshoot called American Friends of the Royal Foundation, which was set up for William and Kate's visit to California in 2011. It was the beneficiary of one sunny afternoon of polo in Santa Barbara, which raised $1.6 million. This time, rather than asking American donors to raise money for British causes, they wanted it to stay in America, and looked for a project that sat comfortably within the remit of the Foundation. What they found was Harlem RBI (which stands for the baseball expression "Runs Batted In"—alternatively, Returning Baseball to the Inner Cities). It's a charity that takes young people from a challenging part of Spanish Harlem and uses baseball to engage them in health, fitness and education. The Foundation has a similar program called Coach Core, which William, Kate and Harry jointly launched in London the day before the Olympics. In a nutshell, Coach Core takes vulnerable adolescents off the streets and trains them to be sports coaches; and those coaches, in turn, become mentors to the next generation of vulnerable adolescents. It has been hugely successful, and a second scheme opened in Glasgow last year. This one in New York couldn't be called Coach Core for legal reasons, so it's known as Project Coach, but it is effectively the same and it is funded by the Foundation.

It was a given that if Harry was launching anything to do with a sport he would gamely pick up a bat, which is how he came to risk annihilation at the hands of New York's top baseball star, Mark Teixeira. "The Prince had been to visit the young people privately in their offices," says Nick, "but, of course, there was a huge media pack following the tour. So we set up the more public moment in the diamond, which is bang in the middle of New York, and there were a lot of media there. The kids were out doing their baseball drills and Harry threw some balls and did some ground fielding and then they wanted him to hit, partly for the press and partly for fun.

They got Mark Teixeira to pitch, and they got one of the kids to be the catcher, who was a small girl of about ten. You imagine being a small ten-year-old from East Harlem and you're about to stand, not only behind the Prince, but with the ball being chucked at you by baseball's equivalent of David Beckham and the world's press are looking at you. You could just tell in her face, it was like, this is not an everyday occurrence. And Prince Harry strolled out and the first thing he did was squat down and just check she was okay. They had this lovely interaction where he went, 'Are you all right in there? This is a big deal going on here.' She was like, 'Yeah, all right.' It was one of my favorite moments of the whole tour. Then he stood up, picked up the bat and smacked all three balls for a home run. Unbelievable."

A fundraising dinner followed at which celebrities were not the focus, but three of the young people from Coach Core in London and Glasgow. They spoke about what a difference the program had made to their lives. "Prince Harry spoke as well, so we raised quite a nice sum of money that night and it stayed behind in Harlem which was fabulous."

The next day Prince Harry swapped a baseball bat for a polo stick in Connecticut to raise over $1 million for Sentebale. "It was the most we've ever raised with one event like that," says Chief Executive Cathy Ferrier. "It was just fantastic. We got an incredible amount of support, lots of coverage for the charity. The U.S. is a big market for us; he is very, very popular there. and people genuinely seem to be interested in what the charity is doing. They warm to him, they like him. And in terms of sponsorship, people were literally beating a path to our door to try and get involved."

Nick agrees, "The American reaction to him was extraordinary. He's a very big star over there—he did a range of different activities and each one was really well received."

But he didn't please everyone. The headline in the *Washington Post* ran: "Prince Harry's 2013 U.S. tour: Painfully well-behaved this time . . . What have they done with our Harry?'?!? Sigh. Maybe he's just growing up.'"

ALL CHANGE

HRH Prince George Alexander Louis of Cambridge was born at 4:24 in the afternoon of 22 July 2013, in the middle of a heat wave. Harry was one of the first people William phoned with the news; Harry saw the baby the following day when the family was back at home. When asked about his nephew, Harry extended his hands and said, "He's about this long and this wide. It's fantastic to have an addition to the family. I only hope my brother knows how expensive my baby-sitting charges are."

Harry is clearly very taken by George, although not so taken that he's volunteered to change many nappies, but while his birth and William's marriage to Kate brought very real joy, they also marked the end of an era. The brothers are best friends and enormously close in every sense—their charitable work overlaps; they share an office and they live within the same complex at Kensington Palace; they shared the same childhood—and that bond will never diminish. But the relationship has inevitably changed as William's focus has changed. He is no longer in the military, no longer up for partying till dawn, or tripping over guy-ropes in the early hours at Glastonbury. He is more interested in getting an unbroken night of sleep and listening to George's growing vocabulary. It is what happens with most siblings when one of them starts a family of their own.

They have always been very different characters and, as they have matured and their choice of careers has exposed them to separate challenges and experiences, those differences have become distilled. William's instincts and enthusiasms are pure middle

England, cautious and conservative. He craves normality, and in another life would happily live as 90 percent of the population does. When Harry says he would like to be normal, Main Street is not at all what he has in mind. He is what someone who knows them both well describes as "an absolutely thorough-going, full-fat eighteenth-century aristocrat. He's a Rupert of the Rhine, a torrid figure, and I use the eighteenth century absolutely intentionally, where along with privilege went responsibility—which was lost in the Victorian era and certainly in the last century. Yes, absolutely, he lives life to the full and he has lots of money and he has friends, in the sort of Prince Hal way. He is much more altruistic and philanthropic than they were in the eighteenth century, but he does have that split which they had—this sort of hell-raising, Cavalry commander, using somebody as a mounting block type of thing; but with it, that real connectivity which they had, because the people were their power base. Harry is as English as English can be."

They still share the same passions, which are reflected in the three distinct causes that the Foundation supports (conservation, disadvantaged children and veterans), but they are no different from brothers working in any family firm; as they are becoming more experienced, more confident, more opinionated and engaged with the subjects, there are differences of opinion, clashes, tensions and jealousies between them. For example, Harry is every bit as passionate about conservation as William, but at the moment it is his brother who is seen to be its champion. It was his brother who led the launch of United for Wildlife, a major initiative that has brought together the seven largest wildlife charities to try and stop the illegal poaching of endangered species. And because of his expeditions to the Poles, it is Harry who is seen as the Prince of veterans; while the reality is that William is also very engaged in the welfare of veterans, but from a different aspect. And Harry's indisputable affinity to children doesn't mean that William is indifferent to their well-being—and each of them has a view about how best to tackle the problems.

"Thank heavens to date the strains have only been the natural thing between brothers," says one of their team, "and unlike quite a lot of brothers, they can then go and have a beer together and say, 'Okay, you do the conservation, I'll do the veterans.' That's literally how it sorted itself out. Jealousy is not a word in Prince Harry's lexicon: he doesn't get jealous, he's remarkable like that.

"I think they would still choose to spend an evening together, yes," says a friend. "It would be a different night from the one they would have spent three or four years ago, which would have been, 'Who can remain standing longest?' as it were. Harry loves going round and having supper with George and Kate and William. It's that sort of night they have now, because they're growing up. That's not to say Harry doesn't have an alternative night—he's probably got four or five alternative nights which he also enjoys, and William is probably not on those nights anymore and it would be a bit odd if he was. But they are very, very close and Harry loves the whole domestic bit which his brother's now doing—which is interesting because he's not longing to get married or anything but I think he sees what his brother's getting out of it, which is fantastic."

When, or who, Harry will marry is anyone's guess. For two years Cressida Bonas appeared to be a contender, until they broke up at the end of April 2014. Friends had said it seemed to be serious between them, but they had said much the same about Chelsy Davy. All that is certain is that, as both women know, being in love with Harry is the easy bit. Taking on everything else that it entails is a very different matter. Kate Middleton is an exceptional woman from a stable, loving family and she is rock solid. She might have been born for the job, and William was very lucky to have found her and got to know her in the privacy of St. Andrews. But she has made sacrifices for which no amount of red carpet, titles or tiaras can compensate.

Only Prince Harry and Chelsy know what brought their relationship to an end—although it must have been amicable because they are still friends. It may have been that she wasn't prepared to live with that level of media scrutiny and she valued her freedom too much. It may be she thought the whole royal set-up looked stultifying. Or it may be that the relationship had just run its course. But friends say that Cressida hates the media attention and she too is completely unmoved by the royal connection.

"Cressida, I do know, is about as interested in the whole royal thing as Chelsy was," says a friend, "which is to say not at all. Kate probably loved William very deeply very early, so she got it into her head this was what she was going to have to live with, and at least Kate will be Queen one day. That's a fairly substantial thing to do with your life; and if you conduct yourself well it will have an impact on a massive institution in British public life with this enormous history. If you're married to the spare-but-one, what kind of life is that? I think that's Harry's problem; to find anyone who will marry into that—because most substantial women wouldn't.

"I'm told he was very serious about Cressida but it's between the two of them what that really meant. Her family history isn't full of happy marriages, and neither is his, so I think there was a nervousness on both sides that if they went that way, would they really know what they're doing? I don't think anyone wants to second-guess that. She's a very, very nice woman. The impression I get is that, for her, the public-facing bit was a real issue. She really didn't want it, and was actively keen to avoid it—which in a way is quite encouraging. He was not going to find it easy to land that particular fish."

The truth is he is going to find it difficult to land any fish unless the media has a dramatic change of heart and gives him some privacy.

When George was born, William was still based in Anglesey, where he and Kate rented a farmhouse, but after much agonizing, and to many people's surprise, he decided to leave the military in September to concentrate on royal duties and charity work. It was announced at the time of their marriage that they would be taking over Apartment 1A, Princess Margaret's old house at Kensington Palace. It had been empty for years and needed complete refurbishment, so in the meantime they had the use of Nottingham Cottage, a dinky-looking two-bedroom building to the north of the Palace. When they finally moved into 1A in the autumn of 2012,

Harry took over Nottingham Cottage. So both brothers are now a stone's throw from each other's front door and a two-minute walk from their office, which is now also at Kensington Palace.

Harry's relationship with Kate is as good as it looks from the outside. It's relaxed, easy and he makes her laugh, but his relationship with the Middletons is less so. And the Middletons now play a prominent part in William's life. William adores them and they him. "They are incredibly nice," says a friend. "Carole is Carole, she is what she is; she's an alpha-male mother who's very open about who she is, but they are a terribly well brought up, polite family, very charming, nice people. The only downside of Harry is he can be a bit rough around the edges; in slightly unconventional way. The sort of guy who might start flicking food across a dinner table when you really wouldn't expect someone in polite society to do that. The Middletons would find that quite challenging. I am sure Kate has adjusted to it but there's an element of Harry that's quite...not laddish—unconventional. There are definitely people who have worked in Harry's orbit who have not enjoyed it, whereas the vast majority of people absolutely love him and would lay down their lives for him. If you were being really harsh you might say he was juvenile but I don't think that's fair."

There were major changes to the Household in 2013. Jamie Lowther-Pinkerton took a step back. Everyone who knows Jamie, without exception, says what a brilliant mentor he has been for William and Harry. He has steered them through some very difficult years and helped them build firm foundations for the future. "They are such cool guys, it's very difficult to go wrong with them. Prince Harry has his moments but even with old Harry and his wild moments, the guy's instincts are absolutely 100 percent brilliant. He just gets it; a very light finger on the tiller." Jamie's mission was to help them reach their personal goals. Now that's done, he felt they needed someone new for the next phase in their lives, when they would need a Private Secretary each. He is staying on in an advisory role but he has passed the baton on, believing that even the best people run out of ideas after seven or eight years.

Miguel Head, who was their Press Secretary, became William's Private Secretary. His place was taken by Ed Perkins, who used to look after Prince Andrew at the Buckingham Palace press office (and since all the royal press offices were amalgamated under the Prince of Wales's new Press Secretary, Sally Osman, at the beginning of 2014, he is now back at Buckingham Palace, where they are all based). Rebecca Deacon, who was at Sentebale, became Kate's Private Secretary. The only external appointment was Ed Lane Fox, who became Harry's Private Secretary in June 2013. He was a former captain in the Household Cavalry, who left the Army the year Harry joined and went off to work in PR. "He's not the opposite of Harry because he has the same sort of flair," says one of the team. "He's good and can spot the really good ideas and make them happen, but he's quite adjutant-ly, quite methodical, so you know with Ed when things aren't quite right. He's quite authoritative so he's rather a good match for Harry. He keeps his own counsel but what he says is pretty good. They're getting on really great; it's a fantastic teaming up and I think they'll be doing stuff for a long time to come, hopefully.

"Prince Harry's one of these people—you just dangle a carrot in front of him and he'll get excited. He always comes at things completely laterally, at an angle you're just not going to guess, and you'll talk to him and think, what are you on about? And then suddenly you'll go, 'Christ, I see what you're on about! Good idea.' I think lateral thinking helps being an Apache pilot, doing ten things at once and coming at things sideways. When I'm going through my lists with him, through ten different letters that people have written on ten different subjects; if I explain to him the rationale of why I'm making a recommendation, he'll go, 'Yeah yeah yeah, got that; but what about this? Couldn't we do that for them?' And I think, yes, of course. Christ, why didn't I think of that? He'll just come at it from an obtuse angle. I'm not sure he *can* come from a particularly straight angle, so he probably needs a Private Secretary who's dissimilar to him in that respect, who goes straight up the middle—so he can do the dancing round the edges. Ed will do really well with him."

POLES APART

Two members of the Everest team to whom Harry paid tribute in his speech in Washington, the night he collected the humanitarian award, were Martin Hewitt and Jaco van Gass, both of whom had also been to the North Pole. Ed Parker realized after that first expedition that WWTW had built up a momentum that couldn't be lost. He wanted to put together another challenge quickly. Because 2012 was the anniversary of Edmund Hillary and Tenzing Norgay's ascent of the world's highest mountain, he had settled on Everest as the target. It was again filmed by Alexis Girardet.

The resulting documentary, *Harry's Mountain Heroes*, was shown on ITV—and Prince Harry was patron of the expedition once more. He couldn't go this time because he was busy with pre-deployment training, but he did do press launches, interviews and some training with the team to give the expedition coverage a kick-start. He also went to see them off at Heathrow Airport and sent them an encouraging message when they were on the mountain. "We always knew he wasn't going to be a big part of it," says Alexis. "He said very clearly, 'If I'm going to do this I want to be part of the team that goes to the summit, not to just trek in and become the guy that does a little bit of these things. I want to do it properly with them.'"

It had been a great disappointment when the climb had to be called off. They had trained for seven months in the Alps and then they had climbed Manaslu in the Himalayas, which is the eighth highest mountain in the world—becoming the first disabled team ever to do so; but, as Ed says, "They got to Everest and the conditions were just too risky, so I pulled them down. The head guide and I talked every day and I smelt a rat. More people lost their lives on Everest that year than in the previous fifteen years. I didn't want to risk them."

Jaco and one other escaped two avalanches by a whisker. "Every day there were very high winds and someone was bivouacked out, having been hit by falling rock and avalanches. There wasn't much snow and it was too warm, hence the avalanches. We came back down and, sponsored by Glenfiddich, had quite a few bottles of whiskey. Next day, with very sore heads, the expedition leader said, 'I'm calling it, it's too dangerous.'

"You can get selfish about it; you or the team want to achieve your goal, but for us to reach the summit takes a team of fifty Sherpas. When we are lying in our tents in the mornings in base camp, those guys go through the Khumbu Icefall, they established Base One; they carry all the equipment, all the bottles, all the tents, they set up every camp. You walk from A to B and it's all done for you. They do ten times more than you have to. So it was too dangerous for us and for them. It was a bitter pill to swallow, but it was definitely the right call."

By then Ed had even more ambitious plans. "It was suggested to me in the middle of 2011, very much through Clarence House, that it would be a great idea to do something with the Americans," he says. "We fight alongside each other, we should draw on each other's expertise and experiences afterwards." He came up with the idea of a race to the South Pole, a British team against an American team but, at the suggestion of Clarence House, he added a Commonwealth team of Canadians and Australians as well. Alexis was again asked to make a documentary—*Harry's South Pole Heroes*—and Harry again agreed to be patron of the expedition. Ed desperately hoped he would walk with them, knowing it would make all the difference to the profile, and he did. In April 2013, seven months before the start date, he committed; immediately corporate doors started opening and Ed was able to raise the £1.8 million he needed.

Their headline sponsor was Virgin Money. "They put in a really properly grown-up sum of money," says Ed, "and the lead came through Prince Harry. The CEO is a lady called Jayne-Anne Gadhia who had been a trustee of Sentebale, and at the London Marathon [of which Harry is patron], he was standing at the finish and Jayne-Anne was there and Harry said, 'You should be talking with WWTW.' I then get a call from Clarence House saying, 'Quickly follow this up,' which I did, and to her eternal credit, she said, 'Right, let's have a proper look at this.' What I haven't told Clarence House is that we had already approached Virgin Money and they'd said 'No'! I went through different channels in a different way and I know they are approached by a million people, as every company is all the time, but this just came through with a little bit of sparkle and that's the difference.

"When we went to the North Pole, a rather unattractive individual asked how Harry had been paid for. I think I was nicely defensive but if anyone ever came this time, I would say, 'Well, I think his income rather outstripped his cost because he was there to introduce us to Virgin Money.' But he was also there to get the press interested. If he hadn't come, WWTW would be an eighth of the size we are." Not to mention that the Royal Foundation contributed "a nice six-figure sum" and the obvious endorsement implied by having its logo on all the publicity.

It is a happy by-product of these expeditions that the individuals come away with a sense of achievement, but the rationale behind them is not about the individuals at all—it is to inspire and demonstrate to other disabled people that injury does not have to be the end of their useful life.

"What becomes more complex," says Ed, "is those with no physical injury. They find it very difficult because they are not definable by you and me, so the psychological impact goes far deeper. We took three people with us who are physically pretty much right as rain but have mental injuries, and we took them so they could tell their story and engage a bit more with the public about who and what mental injury is about. It's important that employers understand that these conditions could lurk and how to deal with them if they manifest themselves. It's a bigger problem than the physical side."

For the first time there were women in the teams, which he says had a calming effect on the men. Each team had four wounded, plus a guide, a mentor from the charity (Ed Parker, Simon Daglish and Richard Eyre), as well as a celebrity. Harry was with the British team, Alexander Skarsgård, the Swedish star of *True Blood*, was with the Americans and Dominic West, Damian's brother and star of *The Wire*, was with the Commonwealth team. And among the wounded was a double leg amputee (the wounded in the British team had four legs between them), a Puerto Rican who is totally blind and hates the cold, an Australian who'd been shot through the neck, three people with mental injuries, a girl with 30 percent burns who was blown up by a suicide bomber, and a Canadian bomb-disposal expert who, after defusing a bomb, had stepped on an IED. For safety's sake, this time they took a medical team and two support vehicles.

"If things go wrong in the South Pole," says Alexis, "no one's coming to get you. If there's a storm they can't fly to you, they can't fly a helicopter. You're out of the range of helicopters. If your tent's gone, you're dead. There is nothing you can do. You're doing all the no-nos. You've got big fires going inside the tent because you can't do it outside to cook your water. You've got to melt snow for three hours every evening and two hours every morning, so you've got a stove roaring full blast inside the tent, probably two or three stoves, so it's easy for something to go wrong. You get a burn, yes, there's a doctor with us, and there are sat phones, but it might take five days to evacuate somebody off the continent."

The training was intense. Harry joined the teams in Iceland for a few days, but he was still based at Wattisham so did most of the training on his own. But walking about the countryside dragging tires to simulate sledges was as nothing compared to the twenty-four hours they were locked in a cold chamber in temperatures of up to -58°C with snow blizzards and winds of up to 75 km/h to give them a flavor of what was to come.

"Everyone assumes the North Pole and South Pole are alike," says Ed. "It could be as different as walking across grass and walking across sand. In the North Pole you're walking on broken ice, which is constantly moving, so there is constant danger of falling through the ice. When you go to Antarctica you are walking at over 9,000 feet, so there is an issue with altitude initially. It's flat; once you get up onto the plateau where you start, it is like a pancake, so there is nothing for the eye to look at apart from the man's back in front of you. So mentally, it's dull. You're on ice but on about four to six inches of soft snow, so pulling through that is bloody hard work. The chap at the front of your team is breaking a trail and the rest are just huddling behind him and following through, so if you're leading it's properly grown-up hard work and you do that for two hours and then rotate."

"They say it's 40 percent physical, 60 percent psychological," says Alexis. "You can train as much as you want physically but if it's not there mentally, you're in trouble. Round the edge of the continent it's lovely: there's mountains, sea, penguins, all that kind of stuff, then you get inland, on to the plateau, and it's a continent the size of Australia roughly and there is nothing. It's just flat for thousands of miles in every direction, literally nothing to look at. When we were there the first time we saw one bird in the first week and that was it in seven weeks. You can't talk to people because there's usually wind blowing, you're skiing along for ten, twelve, however many hours you go for during the day. And twenty-four-hour daylight, as there is in the North Pole as well, average temperature -35°C, it can easily get to -50°C, there's constant wind. Antarctica is the coldest, driest, highest, windiest continent on the planet."

Bad weather delayed their November start date, but they finally got going on 1 December 2013. On 7 December, however, Ed called off the race element. Conditions were very tricky, people were tiring rapidly (and some had to move to support vehicles for short periods on medical advice); this change in plan meant that the teams could travel together and support each other. On Friday 13 December, the three teams made it triumphantly to the geographic South Pole. It had taken them just thirteen days to cover 200 kilometers.

"It was harder than we had expected," says Ed, "and we played more jokers than I would have hoped to play, but that's the nature of the place. The biggest single factor was the size of the group that we took down there. It turned out we were the biggest expedition to have ever skied on the Pole—something I hadn't appreciated at the time—and there were so many different moving parts that needed to be aligned at the same time for everything to go smoothly. It wasn't just our own little world, but the terrain, the weather, the aircraft, the vehicles; everything needed to be aligned. We were scuppered by the weather, which put a lot of pressure on when we could start; then we were scuppered by the terrain. It was very broken and bumpy through the sastrugi, which are ice waves—it's the effect the wind has on the snow, it builds little ice ridges which become solid—so that caught us a little bit with our trousers down. We had two people who were exhausted. On top of that it was very cold, which might sound a little bit like, but surely you knew that? But we had this wind for two days where the temperature got down to around -45°C—we were expecting -25°C. When it gets that low, there is no margin for error, your face will get very badly frost nipped within minutes, your fingers will be en route to frostbite after two or three minutes."

Harry was not alone in suffering from the altitude, and had bad headaches for the first few days into the walk. "I remember saying to him, 'How are you doing?' says Ed, and he said, 'It's fine; I've still got the bloody headache, I wish it would go because I could enjoy it more.' It was just a bit debilitating, but he was great and immediately became part of the team, as you'd expect, and if you had been a stranger who had no idea who he was and you were dropped in from a high height and told one of those people over there is a member of the British Royal Family: guess. You would never have been able to guess it was him.

"The one thing I really noticed this time is that I think as a leader he's evolving. He spent time with the other teams, just talking to them, getting to know them, wanting to get a better idea of what their experience was and why they were there—we became a very close group—but then when things were tough, he would be one of the people who would say, 'You're doing brilliantly; come on,' or just try to engage with people when they were having a bad day. We all have bad days down there at some point and Harry...I noticed this time, I just felt he was becoming—it's an awful thing to say—responsible. It comes to him naturally, leadership. I think he was just part of our machine to encourage people and drive people and he spotted when someone was feeling a bit wobbly. I would think, I'd better go and see so and so and I'd look up and Harry would be there already. So he was an integral part of what we did.

"It's fascinating talking to the other teammates. Great friendship was developed; I think they consider him a friend. And, huge respect. I remember talking to one or two of them and saying, 'Do you find it extraordinary that he's Prince Harry?' And he's not to them. He's Harry, or H, or Spike or whatever it may be—and that's a hell of a gift to have because I think an awful lot of people in his position don't give off that warmth and that openness and acceptance and humility. So having him there was great. He's always good fun; I think he was very relaxed to be away from the eyes of the world."

Ivan Castro, the blind Puerto Rican, had been a particular worry. He was guided by two aluminum poles attached to the sledge in front of him, and Ed and his American teammates took it in turns to pull that sledge. He had never skied before, often fell over, and found the journey more difficult than anyone else; but repeatedly said, "It might be hard for me but think of the guys with no legs." He had said he would love to be guided by Duncan Slater from the RAF, who lost both his legs when an IED blew up his vehicle in Afghanistan. "I think Ivan was inspired by Duncan," says Ed. "No double amputee has ever skied to the South Pole." So, for the last mile, Duncan guided Ivan. "Symbolically it very much spoke about what we'd done and why we were there."

They all walked on to the Pole together. There is a symbolic one, a bit like a barber's pole flanked by a semi-circle of flags, then the geographical one about a hundred yards away, which moves about ten yards every year. "It was a very emotional time for a number of

people," says Ed. For him and Simon it was a huge relief that they'd
got there with everyone in one piece, "but I was watching some of
the team and for them it was a cathartic moment. There's an element
of survivors' guilt that these people feel and I think for some of them
it was a time when they could say goodbye to those people they had
lost. There were three or four of them who were very emotional.
Our psychologist had talked to them about this before we went. To
me that was very special because they stopped looking back and they
started looking forward. There was relief around everyone and a lot
of tears and a lot of laughter and a lot of happiness."

Antarctica is the last pristine wilderness in the world and they
left no trace of their journey. Every day when they camped they
would take it in turns to build a communal loo out of blocks of ice
carved with a wood saw. Harry was particularly good at the task
and decorated his with ramparts, but the following morning the
building would be flattened and everything solid taken away. "We
all had to do it," says Ed. "It freezes but it's still a bit unpleasant."
That said, they did leave one semi-permanent reminder of their
visit. They built an igloo at the side of the Pole, and blocked up the
door to make it last longer.

Disappointingly, the Pole itself is not pristine. "You've been in
this wilderness for three weeks, you don't see a sign of anyone and
then, on the penultimate day in the afternoon, we saw this tiny
black speck on the horizon; so very exciting, we're almost there.
We camped that night and the next day skied and this black speck
slowly became bigger and bigger. The South Pole is one of those
places that you would consider to be almost sacrosanct, yet there
suddenly is this American science base. It's a proper, proper mess—
it's hideous. They very kindly invited us in to be shown round
and we went there and were told a little bit about the science and
we walked past the canteen and we all thought, well, a cup of tea
might be nice, but we weren't offered so much as a glass of water."

As Alexis says, "They let you use a proper toilet, a flushing toilet,
that's like wow, then they take you into the canteen which has got
steaks, burgers, salads, lasagnas, all this stuff lined up; and all we've

been eating is this freeze-dried rubbish every day—breakfast, lunch and dinner—and they take you past all this and go, 'Right now, you've got to go, bye bye,' and lock the door. Actually, before that they take you into a shop and they've got bottles of Jack Daniel's, Pringles, Mars bars, crap food but stuff that we haven't had for a month and you go, 'Oooh...' but they won't let you buy any of that. You're allowed to buy souvenirs and to put a stamp in your passport, which is cool, but nothing off the shelves. They explain it by saying everything that is flown in is subsidized by the American taxpayer and if they catered to all the crews and explorers and tourists... It's just mean."

Ed was very unamused by their attitude, especially since they had four American wounded veterans with them. What's more, a couple of days later, a photograph of Harry, Alex Skarsgård and the doctor appeared in the *Mail Online*. It had been taken by a woman who'd shown them round. "They'd said can we take photos and we'd said, 'Yes but this is a private tour.' When the photo appeared I thought, you know what? You've got this wrong. You think down there you're away from the world.

"They were telling us about some quite interesting science they're doing there. Harry had a very good question. He said, 'Why have you built the base here? Why haven't you built it 20 kilometers away—you could still do the same research.' And the guy said, 'Because the runway's here,' and Harry said, 'Well, move the runway.'"

While the tired but triumphant teams waited for a plane to take them home, they celebrated with champagne, using Duncan Slater's upturned prosthetic leg as an ice bucket—and a couple of guys stripped off and danced naked in the snow. Then there were fond farewells. As Ed Parker gave Harry a big hug he said, "Thank you very much." Whereupon Harry said, as he had in the North Pole, "Well, thank you for having me."

"That's a very gentle, very ordinary thing to say, but actually it means a hell of a lot. It resonates; there's some humility there and I like that."

A FLURRY OF PHONE CALLS

"It was all a bit of a shock to the system," says Sir David Manning, of Harry's announcement at the Warrior Games with the implication that next year they would be coming to London. "But I can't say I was surprised. He was very fired up; his enthusiasm was enormous."

No one who knew or worked with Harry was surprised. The shock was in the timing—and it threw more than a few into a tailspin. "The Warrior Games suddenly became this enormous opportunity and challenge," says Nick Booth. "We returned from the U.S. trip to a flurry of phone calls from government and other people saying, 'Er, what did His Royal Highness say?' So we went quiet for a while and over the summer did a feasibility assessment, which I co-chaired with the Ministry of Defence on Prince Harry's behalf to say, 'Was it possible; if so, which countries, how big, how small?'

"One of Harry's observations, which was absolutely accurate, was that this could be brought to a much, much larger audience, and it's so powerful that as we approach the end of the Afghan conflict there is this sort of page-turning moment where we need to move the story on—this is really why he's interested in it—from being one of kinetic injuries, battlefield injuries, repatriation, very much a hard-edged conflict-based story to one that says, 'There are thousands of men and women with physical injuries who've been involved in the conflicts in numbers of countries who will now be with us as civilians for ten, twenty, thirty, forty, fifty years to come and they have, in some cases, very special needs, and in some cases they just need what everyone else needs which is a career that gives them the same stimulation, income, family security that they had when they were in the services."

Bryn Parry is only too conscious of this. "When you've got coffins coming back through Wootton Bassett and there are films and photographs in the media, people are inspired to do something. When the politicians say to us the war is over, for our guys the battle continues. The guys who have been physically injured are still going to be injured. It's not like they're going to get better, legs don't grow back and public support will wane. More people will be caught having fights in pubs or whatever and the soldier becomes Tommy this, an' Tommy that [after the Rudyard Kipling poem]. The young man who's twenty-two and glamorous and walks around in a Help for Heroes T-shirt and has prosthetic legs—someone buys him a pint in the pub at the moment. When he's fifty and he's got a shaven head and tattoos and a big stomach, is he still going to be as glamorous? So your boys walking to the South Pole—are they still going to be walking to the South Pole in ten years' time? What are those guys going to be doing? They can't spend their lives being wounded soldiers doing amazing things. That's not an endgame. So we will have the cohort of the wounded that we have at the moment, plus the ones who will start coming to us with the mental issues, plus, a third point is that the Armed Forces break people all the time, even if we're not fighting battles.

"Ninety percent of what we do is not glamorous. I think with the Paralympics, people went, 'Gosh, being disabled is no longer a disability, somehow it's almost heroic,' which it is, but that is the physical face of something; you're seeing someone being incredibly brave. What you don't see, is them at two o'clock in the morning when they can't sleep, or a girlfriend who's had to go and shut herself in the car because the guy is so angry he's beating up the house. And that's the reality and it will still be the reality and it will be even more of a reality when that boy is fifty."

As soon as the government gave the Games the final go-ahead in January 2014, Harry left his job with the Army Air Corps to devote himself to the Games. It was announced that he was moving to Horse Guards, to a Staff Officer job at HQ London District, which organizes ceremonial occasions like Trooping the Colour. Before he left Wattisham, he had qualified as an Apache Aircraft Commander—which was as high as he could go—and he had flown in an Apache display team at an air show at RAF Cosford in June 2013. He was indisputably at the top of his game—he had "achieved the pinnacle of flying excellence," as his commanding officer put it—but with British forces withdrawing from Afghanistan, he would not be going back to the desert. He had loved flying, but he had found a new passion, helping the wounded make new lives for themselves, and he knew that with his profile and title he could do something big. While he was sorry to leave his friends in the squadron, he was not sorry to leave Wattisham. It had been neither the most convenient nor congenial location—a giant, windswept wasteland, miles from Kensington Palace and the other strands of his life.

"Harry's focus has been on making the Games become a reality," says an aide, "and the most amazing team has come together—the whole of LOCOG [the London Organising Committee of the Olympic and Paralympic Games] under Sir Keith Mills. It's so exciting, and because it's Harry's vision, that needs to suffuse the whole organization and be in every message. Every department needs to know why this is happening, including the MoD, which partners with the Foundation. It's quite an interesting situation: the generals who are orchestrating the MoD input are taking vision from a captain in the Household Cavalry. But when he's in a coffee meeting with them, he's Prince Harry. So it's very convoluted; it's one of those ones that, if it works, you don't want to think too closely about lines of command and so on, otherwise you start to fry."

"This is Harry's big project for 2014," says Nick Booth "Really exciting but a crazy amount of work. The Olympics took eight years to organize and we've given ourselves less than one, so there's a little bit of 'Hold your nose.'"

"Sir Keith Mills said to me, 'About hotel accommodation, you know we booked the hotels for the Olympics eight years ahead?' And I'm like, 'No, I didn't know that.' Everywhere you look, security, diplomatic relations, sport management presentation, broadcast, litter, traffic—and there are twelve of us! So we're putting a dedicated project team together. Our job is to get it done, not to do it, that's the really important role of the Foundation. It will be great for Harry too, because in terms of his passion for the subject, this is a dial-moving exercise, this is saying to the world, 'These are very special people and they have talents to bring them together in a sporting context which is great—we fought together so we'll rehabilitate together.' This will be part of that process of moving on to the next stage of their lives as individuals, as well as in the team sense. The government are very excited about this one."

So, in March 2014, at the Copper Box arena at the former Olympic Park in London, Harry went public. The Invictus Games would take place right there in September 2014, and he made a passionate plea for Britain to come out and support them.

"It's not about supporting the conflict in Afghanistan, it's not about supporting war, it's not about supporting the Forces themselves, but come along and show your support, look at the journey these guys have been through.

"And also take the opportunity, if you haven't done so already, I'm sure there is a lot out there, come and sit in these iconic Olympic and Paralympic venues where we won a hell of a lot of medals back in 2012.

"It's not about winning or losing, the fact that the guys have got to this stage to be able to take part in these events, they've already won in my mind.

"The Games itself is an excuse to bring attention to the legacy part. We want to try and get as many of these servicemen and -women back into society—giving them jobs and making sure that all the core values that they've been taught in services to make them amazing, wonderful, strong, inspirational people—that they bring it back into the community for the younger generation, why wouldn't you do that?"

In explaining his original thought process, he said, "It was such a good idea by the Americans, that it had to be stolen; it's as simple as that."

Invictus is the Latin word for unbeaten or unconquered, evoking William Ernest Henley's 1875 poem of the same name. "I am the master of my fate. I am the captain of my soul." The logo cleverly picks out the letters "I AM." The Games are designed to showcase more than 300 people from thirteen nations in eight adaptive sports, including athletics, archery, wheelchair basketball, road cycling, indoor rowing, wheelchair rugby, swimming and sitting volleyball.

These Games are a perfect example of what the Royal Foundation is all about; what Nick Booth calls "catalytic philanthropy." "We can bring three things to any problem or opportunity: seed capital, awareness-raising, and the third one, which is probably underestimated, is bringing people together—convening and leverage and partnership building."

United For Wildlife, which William and Harry launched together in February 2014, is another example. The Princes, via the Foundation, have brought together and are collaborating with the seven largest wildlife and conservation charities, which have never previously spoken to one another, to use their combined clout to put a stop to the illegal killing of wildlife. "The poachers are now killing humans as well as killing animals," says Nick. "This is not just about an isolated guy shooting a rhino and selling it; they are coming in in helicopter gunships with rocket-propelled grenades. This is organized multinational crime on a global scale. The U.S. State Department is mobilizing, the UK government is mobilizing. People are getting very focused on this, not just because it's bad to kill those animals but because that money—$60,000 a kilo or whatever it is—is funding a whole bunch of activities that you really don't want it to fund. So it is a human as well as a wildlife issue. Going back to first principles, what can we uniquely do as a Royal Foundation? If we can play that kind of catalytic philanthropic role to bring together very big organizations—those seven have north of a billion-dollar annual revenue—so mobilize those resources with a bit of help from these few rooms here [at the Foundation], then the multiplier effect to the return on our investment could be quite significant."

"The convening power of Harry and the Invictus Games is quite extraordinary," says Sir David, "when you look at the sums of money, the numbers involved, and the venues that are going to be used. We are talking millions of pounds, the MoD coming in behind, certainly a dozen teams worldwide and we're going to use the Olympic facility. This is a huge thing and, of course, Harry hasn't done this single-handed, but he decided we were going to do it when we were in America last year and here we are. It's a pretty extraordinary example, I think, of the capacity these two have to ask people to come together behind a cause and get it done. Certainly when we came back [from America], we were all very skeptical about whether we could do it in the time—just over a year to put this thing together."

Ed Parker, who has co-chaired one of the Operations subcommittees, is very excited. "It's a brilliant thing and it's something Harry's passionate about, and he's really driven it. But it's a very ambitious project, and there are an awful lot of people running around at great speed at the moment. I think it illustrates how he's beginning to grab the nettle a bit more. It will be a fantastic celebration of our wounded; it will be a wonderful time for the families to be able to engage with their husband/daughter/son/wife, whoever it is that's competing. It won't all be about who comes first, it'll be who competes, who's actually there taking part. I can smell the politicians jockeying now; they think it's a good idea too so no doubt they will want to get their faces on the front of it all. I know that Harry is hoping we'll be able to progress a few people on to the Paralympics. That's not the reason for doing it but it would be a nice by-product if some of the wounded were able to compete in Rio.

"It's an important thing because it's not WWTW, it's not charity specific, and I very much hope no charity tries to hijack it. It shows the broader brief for Harry is inclusive, it's all the wounded, all countries, it's the way he's thinking."

The next WWTW expedition will be announced just after the Games. "It will be hot, it will be Africa, we'll cross something," says Ed, "and Harry has been involved in it from the start. I think he wants to start having a bit more ownership in what he does, and that's a definite change I've seen in the last four years. Four years ago he was keen to hear people's ideas, and if that idea was a good one he would support it. Now I think he wants to have much more influence on that idea and he's got his own. He'll say 'No,' which I think is really healthy. I love what we've just done [the South Pole] but this one won't take two weeks to get there and two weeks to get back and Africa would be significantly cheaper and it could tie in with other interests that Prince Harry and Prince William have. You can get on a scheduled flight and you're there, so we won't need so much of everyone's time. In the South Pole we collaborated with international military charities; next time we might look to collaborate with conservation."

WHAT NEXT?

William is the Duke of Cambridge; one day he will be Prince of Wales and one day, no matter how many years he has to wait, he will be King. Harry's future is not so clear-cut. He is now fourth in line to the throne and, if and when William and Kate have another child, he will be demoted further still.

When they were younger it seemed inconceivable that Harry would not be standing shoulder to shoulder with his brother, supporting him in the job. Jamie Lowther-Pinkerton used the analogy of John of Gaunt and the Black Prince, the fourteenth-century heir and spare. But Harry is no longer the spare—and William has a very loving, supportive and capable wife.

As a friend says, "He's a rich young man; he could decide to kiss goodbye to the whole thing. He could say, 'I waive my rights to the throne, I waive my rights to any money, I'm not going to live in palaces, I'm going to look after myself and do my own thing.' He would be relatively within his rights to do so, so long as he paid for his own protection and all the rest of it... Yes, they could work side by side, but William's not going to be King for a really long time. It could be twenty years at least. Meanwhile, there's two of them on the same territory. So if Harry decided for five years to disappear off to Africa to concentrate on Sentebale and being a helicopter pilot, if that's what he wants to do and flying anti-poaching patrols or whatever, he could still come back x times a year and do his royal duties.

"I think it's difficult to do that if you've got an apartment in Kensington Palace, but you could easily say, 'In return for having personal protection, which I don't particularly want but will have anyway, I will do my fair share of royal duties, but the rest of the time I'm going to look after myself financially and go and do this.' Would the public really care about that? Probably not. If what he's doing is stuff that's connected to his charitable interests and getting lost in Africa a little bit while he's there. He's not going to be living in Happy Valley in Kenya and having a high old time. His commitment to Sentebale seems pretty serious; I think he really means that to be his future, or a very large part of it; so if he combines a charity he cares a lot about and a continent he cares a lot about, maybe he never formally moves there but spends more and more time there . . .

"But I think there's a real danger that if they both settle down in five years' time, working side by side as young royals, cutting lots of ribbons, they will die of boredom shortly afterwards and I don't think that's in the public's interest either. Of course one can take a slightly pious view and say they have so many privileges they ought to pay them back. Sure, but I wouldn't want their life and neither would anyone else I know."

"Prince William's obviously got a very clear destiny," says Sir David Manning. "Prince Harry's destiny is much more open to discussion and much more open for him to decide and so I think although very close and in many ways passionate about the same things, like the military and wildlife and so on, Harry's got a field for maneuver that is much broader. William has always known he has to take on the lead role; he's got to be prepared or preparing—even if not consciously all the time—for a very clear end state. Harry's got freedom to choose; he can do all kinds of things. He can be very much a central part of the Royal Family, a great inspiration to his generation and others, or he could just ride off into the sunset and do whatever he wants, whereas that isn't really an option for William.

"They both have this extraordinary empathy with people. You see them with people who have been involved in earthquakes or floods or whatever and it's extraordinary, and maybe that's partly because if you lose your mother when you're very young you understand what it means to sit down with somebody and say, 'I know what it feels like.'

"I think it's unlikely that Harry will fade away. In theory he could be a royal who does a few royal engagements, but who basically is not involved in the day-to-day business of the Firm, but I think you'll find he's very passionate and engaged. But I may be wrong. He has options. He doesn't have to give the kind of leadership in the future that his brother absolutely has got to give, but my guess is that he will."

Jamie Lowther-Pinkerton is much less worried that Harry will disappear to Africa. "No, not anymore. Seven years ago my center of gravity was to dissolve that thought, but I think it's gone now. He's grown up a lot, he is grown in his thinking, he recognizes that that is not an option. What is an option is spending a fair amount of time on worthwhile proper causes, not just notional ones to get him to Africa. The great thing about Prince Harry is he's got an idea for every minute of the day. He's never, ever going to lack motivation—getting out there and doing stuff—and really the challenge for Ed [Lane Fox] is going to be to channel it, to focus it, to bring it to a tight point where we can go, 'That's what he's about and that's what he's doing.' It doesn't have to be forever, but that's what he's on at the moment. Clear message, really in the national interest or in the realm's interest. It doesn't have to be something totally beneficial, it has to be something the nation is proud of him doing, as well as just being of use.

"So if it's to do with children all over the world, that's great. It's a passion of his—his ability to communicate with kids is just phenomenal and he knows that too. It's an absolutely virtuous circle: because he's passionate about helping, particularly kids who have a real disadvantage in life. He gets a massive reward from it because he knows he can communicate with them, and they love him. So there's this wonderful self-generating thing. You need to swim with the current and if, hypothetically, that's what Harry is going to be game-changing at, then for the next ten years, that's what he focuses on. He becomes a world statesman, a globally recognized figure to do with lost children."

In March 2014, standing on stage at the Wembley Arena, in front of 12,000 young people, each of whom had done something to help others, Harry demonstrated all of that in spades. It was the first We Day—a youth empowerment event—to be held in the UK and he was the star speaker. Dressed in jeans and a casual shirt, he spoke articulately and passionately without a note for ten minutes, pausing like a pro for laughter to die down when he made a joke, and for the cheering to stop when he said something they liked.

"For those of you who were expecting Harry Styles here, I apologize and, no, I am not going to sing!

"Our society faces some very significant challenges. Each year approximately 100 million children are affected by disasters such as the Syrian crisis: one million children there have had to flee the country. Luckily, for most of us, it is unimaginable to picture leaving your home in the middle of the night, not knowing if you will ever return.

"But closer to home there are many communities in this country facing huge challenges, which will rarely, if ever, hit the news. Many young people in the UK live in households where domestic abuse, violence and addiction are part of everyday life. Others provide long-term care for a family member. These issues, and many others, can rob a child of their childhood. For these children, a little help could go so far.

"If young people at risk can be identified early; then supported and mentored by someone who has grown up in the same community, or had similar life experiences, then it is possible to avoid them going on a downward spiral. The mentors I am talking about are not super-human: they are people like you and I who are willing to spend a little time helping someone else.

"Some people don't think it's cool to help others; personally I think it's the coolest thing in the world!"

He had none of the awkwardness of the past, none of the hesitation, and despite confessing he was "incredibly nervous," he showed no trace of it. All he gave off was warmth and sincerity. It was an extraordinary performance and the audience loved him. The applause was thunderous, and Cressida, keeping a seat for him in the VIP box, gave him a congratulatory kiss on the cheek.

A month later, William, Kate and George were being similarly feted in New Zealand and Australia—retracing Charles and Diana's footsteps from 1983, when William was a baby. But whereas William had been kept out of sight for most of the trip, baby George was seen again and again, to the delight of the crowds. Both brothers are riding high and doing immeasurable good for Queen and country, but Jamie is not complacent about the future of either Prince. "One of the things it's important to look at right now is, if we believe in the monarchy and believe it is a good thing, and I think a lot of people agree with that, the threat to it can change very quickly in the modern age with modern communications. It doesn't take a reign or two to change things; it takes a couple of instants.

"Therefore, what are the threats to it? To a degree you've got to be very objective about this because if the threats to it are legitimate and it's not doing its job, then let's go back to 1648, let's do something else. It's got to be aligned with requirement, but the threats to it are not the republicans making a great play of how horrible the Royal Family are and how much money they spend. The threat to it is that it finds itself, almost by happenstance and bad luck, aligned with privilege and wealth and with this huge disparity which is now emerging and will continue to emerge; there are hard-working middle-class people who are now entering the bracket of just not being able to keep up.

"Now it's a fairly natural thing, particularly for our two, to occupy ground which will offset a lot of the threat. Their inclination is always to be with the little guy, which is what is so lovely about them. They want to be in Nottingham and thinking about knife crime and how to get young people in a position where they have some hope and this sort of stuff. Well that's what we've got to motor on. And a few less polo matches in California—even though the funds go to good causes—and a bit more time, which they both really relish, spent with the project in Nottingham. It's a shift in a way. Of course they've been full-time soldiers and there's been a requirement for the hard hit of fundraising. We're not going to be quite so pressured on the soldiering side in the future, so we can afford to be clever and look at how we avoid the pitfall of being brought down by association with privilege and wealth, which is going to become acute."

"Harry will do his duty, he's quite clear about that; he's going to support his father and his brother to the full, but he's going to do it in his own way. His view would be international. That's what he wants to do and, if the polls are to be believed, what the British public want of their Royal Family is to project Britain overseas as much as everything else, and I think that's where he'll find his metier. I have this vision of him being a global statesman—with a small 's'—in ten or twenty years' time, accepted in most places and really able to project soft power for our country but also doing a huge amount of good around the place. I think he's got the character and the talents for it.

"I'm not saying he's going to be winging around the world like some kind of superhero, trying to maintain the monarchy all over the place, but if you use that ability to influence some of the causes he feels really strongly about—and I would say foremost among those would be his passion to bring the spotlight onto the forgotten children around the world, the ones who really, really are up against it: Lesotho writ large, the favelas, the kids here, child sex slaves, all of those sorts of areas. He's got this thing about children and wanting to look after them and I think that will be something that features hugely in his life after he leaves the military and I think that will project him into all corners of the world. He's brilliant at not bringing neocolonial baggage. He leaves all that behind. White prince turning up in a black African country trying to tell them how to look after their children is a recipe for disaster with some. They expect him to turn up in white ermine and Harry arrives in his fleece and has them all bouncing off his knee.

He's right in the eye of the storm and in twenty years' time will be a hugely important figure in the monarchy and the projection of what's good about this place and what needs to happen."

"As they get older, the monarchy is about Prince William," says Sir David. "But Prince Harry has a very big ability to affect how we think about monarchy, but that's a different thing from saying he can bring it down. If he is successful in leading all sorts of causes and motivating people and mobilizing people—if he has this trick of staying in touch with his own generation—that is very powerful and is a huge asset to the monarchy, and I certainly think he can do them a power of good, there is no doubt about that, and probably worldwide.

"The monarchy's a global brand and Prince Harry's part of that. It's extraordinarily powerful because it isn't political and because anybody who wants to can associate with it without having necessarily to put their hands in their pockets and say 'I'm Labor, I'm Conservative, I'm Lib Dem.' The monarchy is a focus; we can project what we want onto it. If somebody like Harry is very successful and very courageous in doing various things, a lot of people can identify with that and it doesn't then start to seem like some remote, privileged organization; it starts to seem like a convener, an enabler, a champion of various things, and I think he can give the monarchy that. I think he can help. William can do this too, I really don't believe it's either/or, even though they do have different destinies."

What is less certain is how Harry's activities will be financed in the future. At the moment he has his military salary; and his staff, and his, royal and charitable work, like his brother's, are paid for by his father, with the income that comes from the Duchy of Cornwall. The only aspects of their lives that are paid for by the State are the cost of travel, when on official duties in support of the Queen as Head of State, and property services. These are paid for by the Sovereign Grant, which also pays for the Queen and Duke of Edinburgh's expenditure. This is a fixed sum that is reviewed every five years. It replaced the old system of a Civil List and Grants-in-Aid in 2012 and is the most transparent accounting that the monarchy has ever had but, just two years into it, in January 2014, a Commons committee warned that the Household's cash reserves were dangerously low. The problem is that the monarchy has never previously had three working generations. "They've never had this before," says an aide, "and my personal view is that they are not adjusted to that. So suddenly you have the Queen, who is still extremely active and very good; you have the Prince of Wales, and now you have the Prince of Wales's sons and one of the things they have to work out over the next two to five years is how are they going to manage the royal finances, particularly when the Princes are no longer in government service, or State service. This is a real issue and I don't know how it will be resolved. It seems to me they have not adjusted the finances and the administration to this. They have started to sort out the administration with the amalgamation of the press centers—but the powers-that-be at Buckingham Palace need to work it out."

The cost of the monarchy has always been a sore subject, like the amount of tax it pays, and every year when the royal accounts are published, the media gets into a feeding frenzy, but the reality is that the cost to every person in the UK is about 56 pence per year.

"I doubt whether you can ever get over the argument that this is a very expensive institution, because it's something that certain sectors of the media want to run, but I wonder how damaging it really is. I look at the polls of support and I think, if the Princes are unpopular because they're not seen to be doing stuff that matters, then that argument really matters to us. If they really are seen to be contributing and making a difference and mobilizing people to do things, and reaching areas government can't, then after we've had two days of people carping about, 'They cost £6 million,' which is the kind of money the Treasury loses on a wet afternoon, I think that goes away quite quickly. It's fine so long as they are seen to be valuable in their own right, and the moment they're not valuable in their own right, it doesn't matter what they cost, that will be just one more stick to beat them with."

The Princess Royal is one of the hardest-working members of the family, and for years she has sat at the helm of Save the Children, one of the most respected global charities of all time. She has towered over board meetings and driven strategy and no one who has worked with her will say a word against her. But she has never been famous for her charm, and her engagement with the children she so assiduously saves is minimal. Harry sprinkles fairy dust wherever he goes. He charms and delights and leaves the room a better place for his having been there. And, to children, he's like the Pied Piper.

He is only thirty, and I have barely scratched the surface of his achievements—or his disgraces. For someone who couldn't pass an exam to save his life, he has packed an extraordinary amount into his thirty years. He didn't find his childhood easy, and he has sometimes acted up, as many children of broken homes and difficult, unhappy childhoods do. And sometimes his father and others have despaired of his ever growing up. But Harry has always been a sweet and loving boy at heart, and that is the key to him. He is as brave as a lion, as honorable as a Prince of the Realm should be, and he is on a mission.

Whether his Las Vegas moments are over is yet to be seen. There is no doubt he has grown up and, with luck, those impulses are a thing of the past, but Harry will always be impulsive, unpredictable and dangerous. That is part of the genius.

Jamie Lowther-Pinkerton and others made sure that he wasn't thwarted in his ambition to serve on the front line. He saw there, in Afghanistan, the sort of reality that most of us only ever see on our television screens, and he didn't flinch. He flew his Apache into the teeth of enemy fire without a thought for his own safety, and his determination to champion the soldiers who weren't as lucky as he was, and who didn't come back in one piece, is unremitting.

He may say he's a child at heart, but he's a child with a very old soul.

ACKNOWLEDGMENTS

I am once again indebted to the Prince's team at Kensington Palace who have been incredibly generous with their time in so many ways over so many months—and to Prince Harry himself for allowing them and others to talk to me. He is surrounded by and associated with some exceptional and inspirational people. All of them have been incredibly generous with their time. Some were happy to be named, others preferred to remain anonymous; I would like to thank them all for their recollections, observations, and experiences; also their honesty and their trust. Huge thanks too to them all for checking the manuscript and weeding out inadvertent errors. I hope, as a result, that this is a fair, accurate, and enlightening portrait of the man.

Others who have been so important, and to whom I owe many, many thanks, are the wonderful team at Hodder & Stoughton. They are such a pleasure to work with: Rupert Lancaster, Kerry Hood, Jason Bartholomew, Maddy Price, and Camilla Dowse. I would also like to thank Penny Isaac, who is a terrific copyeditor; and my American editor, Gretchen Young, at Grand Central Publishing.

I also owe a special thank you to Martin Seager, consultant clinical psychologist and adult psychotherapist, for his guidance; and to clinical psychologist Linda Blair for her insights into birth order.

As always, Jane Turnbull, my agent, has been a true friend. She is so generous with her time, laughter, and support, it's easy to forget she has other clients.

And finally James Leith, my amazing husband, who makes everything possible.

Thank you all.

PICTURE ACKNOWLEDGMENTS

341

Tim Rooke, 15 (lower left). © Walking With The Wounded South Pole Challenge 2013: 15 (above left).

Every reasonable effort has been made to contact the copyright holders, but if there are any errors or omissions, Grand Central Publishing will be pleased to insert the appropriate acknowledgment in any subsequent printing of this publication.

INDEX

Beckham, David, 189, 235, 267
Belize, 264
Bertram, Willie, 31
Big Brothers Big Sisters, 226
Bignell, Geoffrey, 73
Birkhall, 105, 138–39
Blair, Cherie, 107
Blair, Tony, 86, 91, 107, 189
Blair Years, The (Campbell), 91
Blake, Robert ffrench, 34
Blom, Jinny, 299
Bolland, Mark, 82, 103–4, 105, 119, 140,
    141, 163
Bolt, Usain, 265, 266, 276
Bonas, Cressida, 264, 292–94, 295, 310,
    311, 334
Bonas, Jeffrey, 292, 293
Booth, Nick, 226, 227, 303, 304, 305, 306,
    307, 325, 327
Botsawa, South Africa, 230–31
Bovington Camp, Dorset, 179–80
Boyle, Danny, 274
Bradby, Tom, 149, 174, 244
Branson, Sir Richard, 294
Branson, Sam, 294
Brazil, 265, 267–68
Britannia (royal yacht), 26, 47, 79
British Army Air Corps, 212–18
    Harry as Apache helicopter co-pilot
        gunner, 2, 218–19, 224, 240,
        258–63, 282–91, 325
    helicopter pilot course, 213–14
    rules of engagement, 283–84
British Red Cross Lesotho Fund,
    195, 196
Broadfield Farm, Tetbury, 35–36, 153
Brooks, Rebekah Wade, 57, 105, 118
Brown, Des, 183
Brown, Harold, 54
Browne-Wilkinson, Hilary, 103
Browning, Sir Frederick "Boy," 223
Buckingham Palace, 11, 61, 87, 141,
    271, 313
    flag for Diana, 87
Bucklebury, England, 243, 245
bulimia, 11–12, 47, 69
Bupadhengo Primary, Uganda, 221

Burrell, Paul, 39, 54, 63, 134–35
    book by, 134
    Daily Mirror and, 133–34
    trial of, 132–33, 151–52
Business in the Community, 17, 54, 66

Calthorpe, Isabella, 294
Cameron, David, 305
Camilla, Duchess of Cornwall, 1, 40–41,
    65, 66, 190–91, 300
    Charles and, 40, 41, 42
    children of, 41
    Diana's threatening phone calls to, 62
    marriage to Charles, 140, 162–66
    public image of, 104
    Queen Elizabeth and, 163–64, 272
    staff of, 105
    as "third person" in Charles-Diana
        marriage, 7, 38, 66, 69–70
    title of, 165
    William and Harry and, 103–6, 162–66,
        179, 219
Camillagate, 56, 65, 177
Campbell, Alistair, 91
"Candle in the Wind," 189
Capello, Fabio, 234
Carling, Julia, 69
Carling, Will, 68–69
Carter-Ruck, Peter, 74
Castro, Ivan, 320
Cat and Custard Pot, Shipton Moyne,
    125
Catherine Elizabeth "Kate," Duchess of
    Cambridge, 12, 154, 189, 308
    Anmer Hall and, 101
    Australian trip (2014), 334
    birth of George, 6, 308
    charities of, 227, 228
    courtship and engagement, 242–44
    Diamond Jubilee and, 270–71, 272
    engagement ring, 244
    family of, 243
    media and, 243
    Olympic Games (2012), 275–76
    pregnancy of, 287
    Private Secretary for, 313
    Royal Foundation, 306

Charles and, 33, 35, 79, 247
childhood and early years, 14, 29,
    33–34, 43
confirmation in Church of England, 83
Diamond Jubilee celebrations and,
    270–72
Diana and, 43–44, 62, 63, 66, 70, 74,
    76, 78
Diana's boyfriends and, 39–40, 77
Diana's death and, 82–85, 87, 95–96
Diana's death, first anniversary and,
    106–7
Diana's funeral and, 91–94
Diana's *Panorama* interview and, 69–74
education, 33, 42, 51, 57, 68, 96, 110,
    111, 113, 120, 131
friends, 57, 171, 247, 248
funeral for the Queen Mother and, 130
gap year taken by, 120
girlfriends, 101
Harry and, 4, 7, 45, 68, 96, 120–21, 131,
    158, 170–72, 210–12, 215–16, 240,
    267, 308–10
as heir apparent, 1, 116, 121, 132, 330, 331
Help for Heroes and, 205–9, 224
Henry van Straubenzee Memorial
    Fund, 221–22
Highgrove and, 29–31, 32, 33
Household established, 222–24
Kate, courtship and engagement, 242–44
at KP, 33
Labrador Widgeon, 79
Mark Dyer and, 97, 99, 100
marriage, 12
media and, 55, 115–19, 142, 193, 211
media hacking phone of, 173–76
media scandals, effect of, 68, 70
mentor, Sir David Manning, 223–24
military service, 187, 215, 219, 224,
    240, 312

Morton book and, 48
nanny Barnes and, 23–24
national response to, 13
Olympic Games (2012), 275–76
partying by, 123–24
patronages of, 229–35
polo playing and, 34
PPOs and, 25–26
press photos and, 79–80, 116–17, 139
Princes' tour of South Africa (2010),
    229–30
reaction to Burrell book, 134–35
reaction to Dimbleby interview, 66
Royal Foundation, 226–27, 306, 309
Royal Wedding, 245–48
at St. Andrews, 120, 131, 243, 310
at Sandhurst, 170, 179
Sandy Henney and, 139–40
separation of parents and, 54, 55
staff of, 141, 159, 160, 211, 223–24,
    313
Tiggy and, 79
United for Wildlife, 309, 327–28
van Cutsem family and, 101
with the Vans at Polzeath, 58–59
William, Prince of Gloucester, 85
Wilson, David, 35, 36, 37
Windsor Castle, 26, 64, 110. *See also*
    Household Cavalry
fire at, 53, 55
marriage of Charles and Camilla at,
    162
Royal Lodge, 129
St. George's Chapel, 14, 83, 129

Young, Steve, 250

Zichy-Thyssen, Count Claudio, 153
Zimbabwe, 154–55
Zulu (film), 97, 98